Expressionist Book Illustration in Germany
1907–1927

Lothar Lang

EXPRESSIONIST
BOOK ILLUSTRATION
IN GERMANY

1907–1927

Translated by Janet Seligman

New York Graphic Society
Boston

Translated from the German
Expressionistische Buchillustration in Deutschland 1907-1927

International Standard Book Number: 0-8212-0617-6
Library of Congress Catalog Card Number: 74-21732

First published in 1976 in Great Britain by
Thames and Hudson Ltd., London
First published in 1976 in the United States by
New York Graphic Society Ltd., 11 Beacon Street,
Boston, Massachusetts 02108

Made in German Democratic Republic by
Druckerei Fortschritt, Erfurt

Contents

Foreword

This book is not a general study of Expressionism, its history, theory and criticism. On the contrary, its aim is to describe German Expressionist illustration, to define it more exactly than has been done before and to list the works that have come to light. Scholarly attention has not yet been directed to the nature of Expressionist illustration of literary works, its characteristic features and its achievements. The present book represents the first attempt in that direction.

I started work by searching in libraries and collections for books with Expressionist illustrations. The results of my inquiries are listed in the bibliography. As might be expected, there will be omissions. The reader is therefore earnestly invited to bring to my attention any material that I have missed and in this way to assist in making the second edition – should there be one – more complete.

Indeed, it is the bibliography that I hope will indicate the extent of Expressionist illustration. The text merely notes its essential character and offers an appreciation of such exceptional and enduring works as have become a part of the art of the book in Germany. If I include illustrations in periodicals and even occasional works with illustrations, which may appear to be marginal to my subject, it is not because German Expressionism as a group movement appears at its most powerful and effective in periodicals, but because the periodical press was often the trial ground for new typography and illustration and thus provided a not inconsiderable stimulus to the art of the book. The quantity of material that I am able to present will surprise those especially who have denied the existence of any Expressionist book illustration worthy of the name. Obviously I could not limit the search to the masters of Expressionism, and from the large number of illustrators who were influenced by Expressionism the reader will be astonished to learn how wide-ranging was the effect of this art: the bibliography names 157 artists and lists 380 works.

It may seem odd that there has been no detailed study and appreciation of Expressionist illustration of literary works before now. The argument that the prejudices of conservative book-designers and typographical fetishists have stubbornly endured for all these years and are the true explanation of current disregard is one that cannot be taken seriously. It is to say the least surprising to watch bourgeois art-historians extolling Expressionism and at the same time treating Expressionist illustration with shy reserve. Nor can the quality of the illustrations be held responsible for their timidity, for, in the case of the masters, they reach the same level as the rest of their work. But the distinction between paintings and free prints on the one hand and illustration on the other is comparable with that between the so-called 'fine' and applied arts. The 'fine' art of Expressionism was considered acceptable material for clever theorizing on art in general, though it often obscured the essentials of art and had little to do with the real work of the Expressionists. These theories were a useful means of devaluing other achievements in art – non-Expressionist, especially proletariat-revolutionary and therefore socialist ones. The 'applied' art of Expressionism was not susceptible to this sort of exploitation; it was seen from the first to be utilitarian, or at least practical, in intention, indeed, even in its most extreme manifestations, to be committed to a concrete purpose – in this case literature and the book. Its practical character was a thorn in the flesh of many theorists, just because it did not fit into their *clichés* about Expressionism. With a few exceptions (Kokoschka, Kirchner, Beckmann) most artists found it easiest to remain silent, especially as arguments for so doing were advanced by those conservative aesthetes of the book who held Expressionism and the art of the book to be incompatible.

The present book is an attempt to salvage the heritage that has come down to us from Expressionism in literary illustration from the flotsam of the history of the art of the twentieth century, to which it has been relegated unjustly and through no fault of its own. It will also be concerned to free these illustrations from the false judgments by which they have been submerged and to establish them within the tradition of the art to the German book – an art to which the Expressionists sincerely desired to bring new creative energy.

It is my agreeable duty to thank those who have in so cordial and unselfish a manner helped me in the preparation of this study. I should like to take this opportunity of thanking the publishers, Edition Leipzig, for their support and assistance on many occasions; without the publishers' enthusiastic backing, the realization of this project would not have been possible. I owe special thanks to Erich Schwanecke, Gert Klitzke and other colleagues at the Deutsches Buch- und Schriftmuseum of the Deutsche Bücherei Leipzig who so helpfully guided me through the collections in the library and in particular the collection of fine illustrated books. I have to thank the collectors Kurt Jung-Alsen and Professor Bruno Kaiser, both of Berlin,

7

who willingly allowed me the run of their libraries; Konrad Marwinski gave me access to the Dr Georg Haar Collection in the Thüringische Landesbibliothek, Weimar, Professor Leopold Reidemeister to the collections of the Brücke-Museum in West Berlin, and Dr Walter Huder to the archives of the Akademie der Künste in West Berlin. My grateful thanks are due to Friedrich Pfäfflin of Munich for innumerable kind acts of assistance. Finally I must thank the many artists who, during the preparation of this book, were ready with information and advice, among them Oskar Kokoschka, the late Erich Heckel, Richard Seewald, Conrad Felixmüller, and the late Otto Schubert and Magnus Zeller. I hope that this book may be regarded and accepted as a modest contribution to the history of the art of illustration in Germany in the twentieth century.

Erkner-Freienbrink,
August 1974   LOTHAR LANG

The dimensions of illustrations given in the captions (height precedes width) follow the system generally used in describing graphic works: relief and intaglio techniques – size of plate; lithographs – size of image; drawings – size of sheet. In the case of title-pages, text pages, bookbindings, covers and jackets, the format of the book or periodical is given. The number appearing in square brackets at the end of a caption refers to the entry in the Bibliography.

Introduction: Thoughts on Expressionism

German Expressionism was an art of protest and revolt against bourgeois reality; it was also an art that looked forward to a better age. The historical background to Expressionism is marked by events that shaped not only the decade 1910–1920 but the whole century: the universal crisis of the capitalist system with the First World War, the great Socialist Revolution of October 1917 and the November Revolution of 1918, which created the opportunity for a fundamental reorganization of social conditions in Germany.

This radical transformation of a whole historical epoch was bound to be reflected in art. One of the most passionate and dissentient of these reflections was German Expressionism. It was based on the then historically valid assumption that the end of the bourgeois world was inevitable and imminent. The prophecies proclaimed by the artists were of course sustained only by intuitions and visions and not by insight into the laws of historical processes. The crucial weakness of Expressionism – it is more obvious in literature than in the visual arts – lay therefore in the fact that most of its works subsisted on negation, on the rejection of bourgeois society; but its tragedy was that only a handful of its fellow campaigners in the struggle of the revolutionary proletariat to achieve a socialist order of society were able to see a way out of the crisis. Yet their sure presentiment of catastrophe is still remarkable. 'In their excited nerves, their overwrought emotions, the generation of twenty- and thirty-year-olds experienced the war before it came', wrote Thomas Mann in retrospect.[1]

The Expressionist revolt, directed as it was against propriety, stupidity, crushing restrictions, indeed, against trammels of every kind, was certainly a protest against bourgeois society, but it was aimed at superficial appearances and not against the socio-economic and political bedrock; consequently it remained itself imprisoned within the limits of the bourgeois view of life. The artists *thought* men free from all oppression and violation, and they saw the war which they had sensed in their 'excited nerves' as the Last Judgment, as the 'day of judgment and revenge, the turning-point in world history in the chaos of which all existing traditions of human history were tried and found wanting.'[2] This explains why many Expressionists welcomed the outbreak of war as a signal for the day of reckoning. Yet not one of them would have shared the chauvinism of Wilhelmian imperialism. On the contrary, the war increased their activism and even brought some of them to the

view that revolutionary action alone could destroy the old order. Consequently Expressionism became more radical – especially in lyric poetry.

The visions of destruction embodied in certain Expressionist verse and painting before 1914 made the mistake of equating the end of the ailing bourgeois Wilhelmian society with the end of the world itself. Jakob van Hoddis's poem 'Weltende' ('End of the World') is a notable example of this attitude:

Ernst Ludwig Kirchner: title-page to *Neben der Heerstraße* by Jakob Boßhart. Zürich/Leipzig: Verlag Grethlein & Co., 1923. The book contains twenty-four woodcuts. 192 × 127 mm. [174]

Dem Bürger fliegt vom spitzen Kopf der Hut,
in allen Lüften hallt es wie Geschrei,
Dachdecker stürzen ab und gehn entzwei
und an den Küsten – liest man – steigt die Flut.
Der Sturm ist da, die wilden Meere hupfen
An Land, um dicke Dämme zu zerdrücken.
Die meisten Menschen haben einen Schnupfen.
Die Eisenbahnen fallen von den Brücken.[3]

('His hat flies off the bourgeois' pointed head, everywhere the air rings like cries, slaters fall off roofs and break in two and on the coasts – one reads – the tide is rising. The storm has come, wild seas bound ashore to crush thick dams. Most people have a cold. Trains fall off bridges'.)

Behind the poet's grotesque images stands the recognition that it is no longer possible to live and write as before. Johannes R. Becher later described the profound effect of this poem: 'These two stanzas, these eight short lines, seemed to have changed us into different persons, to have lifted us out of a world of dull conventionality which we despised but did not know how to put behind us. These eight lines carried us away.... But these eight lines transformed, changed us, even more, it suddenly seemed that we could conquer, could master this world of apathy and repulsiveness.... We felt like new men, like men on the first recorded day of creation, a new world would begin with us and we vowed to bring about such tumult that bourgeois people would lose their sight and hearing and would almost deem it a mercy to be despatched by us to Hades.'[4] Freedom through poetry, through art. Art did not point a way out of social misery, and the plea for mankind to change was bound, for all the faith that was placed in it, to remain Utopian. The images of uncertainty that the Expressionists find in their motifs, for example in the metropolis and in figures of suicides (as in Werfel, Heym, Ehrenstein), madmen (in Heym, Stadler, Wegener), prostitutes (in Werfel, Stadler, Becher, Trakl), were never matched by the counter-image, the postulate of a historically viable new social force such as existed in the revolutionary working class. In declaring their solidarity with the outsiders and social outcasts they pronounced their rejection of bourgeois morality. And the motif of revolution (Heym, Lotz, Becher, Hasenclever, Meidner, Seewald) seldom produced more than a 'No!' flung out with gathered energy. When the counter-image of the rebirth and renewal of mankind did nevertheless emerge it remained general and blurred, despite Becher, Frank, Hasenclever, Unruh and Toller. The road from an anti-middle-class position to a proletarian awareness proved longer and harder than that which had led the artists to an anti-bourgeois attitude. This anti-middle-class attitude is a protest within the bourgeois consciousness. It is directed not against the capitalist régime of exploitation but against certain distortions of middle-class society. To exactly this extent the anti-middle-class attitude fails to break out of middle-class boundaries. For this reason the Expressionist counter-image of 'radical transformation' and of the 'new man' remained Utopian. The hopeless situation into which middle-class society had fallen with the universal crisis of the capitalist system, if not before, was thus mirrored in Expressionism; and Expressionism was therefore also a reflection of the state of decline which characterized the bourgeois system in its latter days.

Impotence in the face of social conditions was certainly one of the elements that caused the Expressionists to retreat into the domain of the individual ego. Cultivation of subjectivity, magnification of an individual psychical situation into a universal world problem, indeed an almost solipsistic philosophy were early[5] recognized as distinguishing features of the artistic attitude of the Expressionists; the influence of reactionary ideas drawn from the philosophies of Bergson and Nietzsche is not difficult to identify. We have since grown accustomed to sharing Ludwig Justi's view of Expressionism as an art which conveyed the 'artist's inner vision or inner experience'.[6] The 'unlearnt' and the 'unwilled' were suddenly declared to be the crucial 'source of artistic power'.[7] Some art-historians therefore go as far as to assert that at its deepest level Expressionism stands for 'mysticism, self-examination, contemplation of the other-worldly, and speculation on the infinite'.[8] Though the correctness of such judgments – which occur frequently in art-historical writing – is not in question, it must be said that subjectivity and irrationality as the theoretical impulses behind Expressionism cannot be regarded simply as a philosophical negative; they are equally a sign of flight from that capitalist reality which these artists no longer accepted. A 'flight inwards' as a romantic escape from unmanageable reality. The dangers of such a reaction are well known: they can mean the 'dehumanization of the subject-matter of an image', as Richard Hamann observed in 1922.[9] We can now understand why the work of Dostoyevsky became so far-reaching an influence on countless German Expressionists. The mysticism in the writing of the great Russian was an important factor. The Expressionist's longing for a better world is so often tinged with fatalism or mysticism. The concept of a classless, abstract humanity and a naive belief in the brotherhood of all men were bound to lead to idealistic notions of how the world should be improved. The architect Bruno Taut's plan for a stellar city and his grand design for transforming the Alps (*Alpine Architektur*, 1919) were as characteristic as the poets' extravagant dreams of renewing society in the future simply through the refinement of human inwardness – all 'sounds from Utopia', as Becher called one of his poems ('Klänge aus Utopia'). Thus bold dreams, tumult, haste, conviction are present in Expressionism, as well as anxiety and distress. They were incompatible with an idyllic idiom. So landscape in painting, for example, cannot be quiet and reticent; instead, nature becomes dynamic, becomes a field of daemonic tensions, a tumult lashed by furies exists side by side with its diametric opposite, an icy, suffocating emptiness. The classic site for these contrasts in the Expressionist view was the metropolis. Here is the fascination of life, the intoxication of speed, the rule of technology and here too is the world of the masses in which the lone individual may be destroyed. Atrocities and scandals occur in the metropolis, transports of love and sex murders, pleasure and frenzy, vice and blameless purity, ruin and misery side by side with glamour and riches – the metropolis for the Expressionists was life itself. Expressionist art is predominantly an art of the metropolis. On the one hand the metropolis cast its spell upon the artists, on the other it rejected them: the curse of capitalist civilization weighs upon it. Thus the motif of the metropolis contains both Messianic and nihilistic principles, the *civitas urbana* is redemption and torment:

Die Menschen stehen vorwärts in den Straßen
und sehen auf die großen Himmelszeichen,
Wo die Kometen mit den Feuernasen
Um die gezackten Türme drohend schleichen.[10]

('People stop in their tracks in the streets and gaze upon the great portents in the sky, where comets with fiery noses steal menacingly round the jagged towers'.)

Thus wrote Georg Heym, and the works of Becher, Benn, Zech and of Meidner (*Ich und die Stadt*; *I and the City*, 1913) contain comparable accounts of doom-laden catastrophes occurring in cities. Certainty has fled, the sense of security belongs to the past. The Expressionist, alarmed and menaced by the bourgeois world in its late phase, breaks radically with his society; although he does not know where he is going he breaks with the past, too. The same repudiation characterizes the artistic image. The ecstatic gesture, the 'expression of a vision',[11] in the visual arts engulf the optical image, forms – 'form is lust'[12] – are shattered, the poet undermines 'traditional academic sentence structure, the architecture of middle-class speech; rhythm,

melody, metaphor all reel ...'[13] The 'emotive and mystical distortions'[14] of Expressionism, often interpreted[15] as an expression of disillusionment and impotence, set the painters' images free from identity with nature, produced pure, liberated colour, the 'autonomous' work. The rejection of all harmony produces that lack of moderation which is characteristic of Expressionism;[16] emotions and visions, intuition as the sole creative principle, repulse the rational desire of the artist for order. Expressionism differs from Fauvism, the parallel movement in France, in precisely this passionate tumult, in this unbridled power of colour; in contrast to the Fauves, the Expressionists fail to find equilibrium between all the expressional factors in a work

Conrad Felixmüller: woodcut 'Kranker Pierrot' ('Sick Pierrot') from *Lieder des Pierrot Lunaire* by Arnold Schönberg to words by Albert Giraud, 1913. Suite of ten woodcuts (no edition in book form). 245 × 170 mm. [53]

of art. They are prevented by their implacable desire for a logical requital and a liberating renewal. Years later Becher wrote them a fine memorial: 'Ignorant of social laws, under the delusion that we ourselves need acknowledge no social limitations, assuming that in us and with us the world was for the first time truly genuine and we ourselves the real creators of the world and its first poets – so we set forth, so we went astray, and some fell by the wayside and some were destroyed. But one thing was certain: something monstrous drove us on, a passion without equal motivated us in our inspired turbulence and we were ever ready to sacrifice ourselves for our "mission"; and for this, although perhaps for this alone, we can call to succeeding generations: "Follow in our footsteps!"'[17]

Taken as a whole, German Expressionism was an extremely self-contradictory movement. The unifying factor lay in its break with tradition,[18] in intuitive vision, in a magnification of the ego that expressed overweening high spirits and greed for life and in a rejection of bourgeois society which did not yet extend to its economic and political reality. Its artistic image and its social activity, contradictorily enough, did not remain constant: their nature underwent a change during the First World War, and another change followed after 1917/18. Expressionism is as unsuitable as a model for contemporary artistic activity: artists of today must follow other paths because our time poses other problems and calls for solutions that cannot be crystallized in the visual maxims offered by an inherited art.

The term Expressionism itself derives from painting; it is reputed to have been used for the first time in 1901 to describe the paintings of one Julien-Auguste Hervé. Kahnweiler remarked, however, that the term was exclusively German, that French critics had never used it.[19] Recent publications show that it was used for the first time in 1911 by Kurt Hiller and Wilhelm Worringer.[20]

It is in itself no easy matter to compile the register of Expressionist artists. Besides the fact that many did not regard themselves as Expressionists, there is the disadvantage that general criteria which would make classification possible either do not exist or are imprecise. In his book *Graphik des deutschen Expressionismus* (Feldafing, 1959), Buchheim lists some eighty names, including Käthe Kollwitz, Otto Dix and George Grosz. The concept of Expressionism in the visual arts is generally associated with the artists of Die Brücke and Der Blaue Reiter, that is, with Ernst Ludwig Kirchner, Erich Heckel, Karl Schmidt-Rottluff, Max Pechstein and Otto Mueller, with Wassily Kandinsky, Franz Marc, August Macke, Paul Klee, and with Oskar Kokoschka, Emil Nolde, Ludwig Meidner

Conrad Felixmüller: title-page and 'Abel' for *Hebräische Balladen* by Else Lasker-Schüler, 1914. Suite of eight woodcuts (no edition in book form). 120 × 110 mm., and 307 × 110 mm. [54]

and Max Beckmann. The list of names in itself reveals the differences and contrasts that combine within Expressionism. The case of the musicians (Alban Berg, Béla Bartók, Paul Hindemith, Arthur Honegger, Igor Stravinsky) is similar. Likewise that of the writers, among whom Becher, Benn, Däubler, Goll, Heym, Lasker-Schüler, Lichtenstein, Lotz, Stadler, Stramm, Trakl and Werfel are usually regarded as the poets of Expressionism; its prose writers were Edschmid, Ehrenstein, Döblin, Klabund, Mynona, Schickele, Werfel and Zech; Reinhard Johannes Sorge, Walter Hasenclever, Georg Kaiser, Ernst Toller, Ludwig Rubiner and Paul Kornfeld were its dramatists. Yet each name is a programme in itself! It is when we try to enumerate the artists and to establish the personal boundaries of the Expressionist movement that we become acutely aware of the lack of any precise basic research. Dating is less difficult. Expressionism in painting begins in *c*. 1905/6

(Emil Nolde and Die Brücke), poetry follows in 1911 (Heym, Werfel), music in 1912 (Stravinsky) and drama in 1912–14 (Sorge, Hasenclever). By 1914 early Expressionism had become outmoded; during the war, and particularly towards its end, the artists reached important decisions, mostly of a political nature. By 1918 the phase described as late Expressionism had begun. At this period Expressionism became fashionable everywhere. By *c.* 1920/21 the first articles to mention the end of Expressionism were already appearing. In 1923 Paul Fechter in *Das Kunstblatt* examined the 'post-Expressionist situation'.[21] In 1925 G.F. Hartlaub organized in the Kunsthalle, Mannheim, the first comprehensive exhibition of a new art under the title 'Neue Sachlichkeit' (the 'New Objectivity'), and in the same year Franz Roh wrote a book about it called *Nach-Expressionismus. Magischer Realismus. Probleme der neuesten europäischen Malerei* (*Post-Expressionism. Magical Realism. Problems of the most recent European painting*). The time is ripe for the art of Otto Dix, Karl Hubbuch, Alexander Kanoldt, Heinz Maria Davringhausen, Carlo Mense, Georg Schrimpf ... The 'Expressionist decade' is over. That 'decade' was also the period of Expressionist book illustration, which evolved between 1907 and 1927.

1 Thomas Mann, 'Deutsche Literatur um 1920', in *Essays*, vol. 2, Berlin, 1956, p. 71.

2 Klaus Ziegler, 'Dichtung und Gesellschaft im deutschen Expressionismus', in *Imprimatur. Jahrbuch für Bücherfreunde*, new series, vol. III, Frankfurt am Main, 1962, p. 99.

3 Jakob von Hoddis, 'Weltende', *Gesammelte Dichtungen*, Zürich, 1958, p. 28.

4 Johannes R. Becher, *Das poetische Prinzip*, Berlin, 1957, p. 103f.

5 See O. Grautoff, *Formzertrümmerung und Formaufbau in der bildenden Kunst*, Berlin, 1919, p. 49; O. Flake, *Die neue Rundschau*, 1915, p. 1284.

6 Ludwig Justi, *Neue Kunst*, Berlin, 1921, p. 7.

7 E. Heckel in *Kunst und Künstler*, XII, no. 12, 1914, p. 30.

8 B. S. Myers, *Expressionism, a Generation in Revolt*, London, 1957, p. 38, and New York, 1963 (*The German Expressionists* ...).

9 R. Hamann, *Kunst und Künstler der Gegenwart*, Marburg 1922, p. 19.

10 G. Heym, 'Umbra vitae', in *Nachgelassene Gedichte*, Munich, 1924, p. 1.

11 H. Walden, *Einblick in Kunst. Expressionismus, Futurismus, Kubismus*, Berlin, 1917, p. 19. Cf. also K. Edschmid, *Über den Expressionismus in der Literatur und die neue Dichtung*, Berlin, 1920, p. 54.

12 Ernst Stadler, *Dichtungen*, Hamburg, 1954, vol. I, p. 127.

13 J. R. Becher in *Die Literatur*, 26, 1923/24, p. 91.

14 B. S. Myers, op. cit. (note 8), p. 11.

15 Erich Fromm, *Escape from Freedom*, New York, 1941.

16 Cf. K. Edschmid, op. cit. (note 11), p. 52.

17 J. R. Becher, *Das poetische Prinzip*, op. cit., p. 49.

18 To lose no time in pointing out the contradictions within the movement: Kirchner was aware of tradition in book-making and was committed to classical principles; Schmidt-Rottluff was not.

19 Kahnweiler in *Das Kunstblatt*, 1919, no. 11, p. 351.

20 K. L. Schneider, *Zerbrochene Formen*, Hamburg, 1967, p. 9.

21 Vol. VII, 1923, p. 321.

I. Expressionist illustration: characteristics, major works, chronology

The dawn of the twentieth century saw a renaissance in the art of the book. It began in England and soon spread across the Continent. The artists responsible were men of a practical turn of mind, who saw the book as a total artistic unity of type, decoration, illustration and binding. Their names – William Morris and Walter Crane – are associated less with the history of graphic art than with the development of the art of the book. In Germany Melchior Lechter's design for the volumes of Stefan George's poems (beginning 1897) and Henry van de Velde's edition of *Also sprach Zarathustra* for the Insel-Verlag (1908) quickly created model precedents in the art of the book.

Thus, when the Expressionists produced their first illustrations, between 1907 and 1910, they found the arts of illustration and book design at a high level of quality and sophistication: of that there can be no question. Most of the works belonged to the Jugendstil or were by Impressionist artists. In some respects the Jugendstil as a whole had prepared the ground for Expressionism, for it opposed the academic historicism and empty illusionism of the Gründerjahre (1871–73) and to that extent it lent urgency to the discontent with society felt by many artists since the turn of the century. The goal of the Jugendstil – after its own day often dismissed with contempt but of recent years reinstated on a pinnacle of esteem – was to encourage art to permeate every sphere of life. In the graphic field it liberated art from the dominion of illusionism; line and surface were raised to the status of weighty, symbolic bearers of the pictorial idea and the psychological effect of pure colour was rediscovered. It drew inspiration and influence from the highly evolved art of the Japanese woodcut, from the stylized line of Beardsley and Jan Toorop and from the plane surfaces of Gauguin, Vallotton and the artists of the *Revue blanche*, the French organ of the new movements in art. Stylized ornament, the most brilliant feature of the decorated book, was now admired: in the hands of Otto Eckmann ornament was floral, in those of Henry van de Velde abstract. We have to remember that a year after Erich Heckel created his woodcuts to Oscar Wilde's *Ballade vom Zuchthaus zu Reading* (*Ballad of Reading Gaol*), which mark the beginning of Expressionist book illustration, Hebbel's *Judith* appeared with Thomas Theodor Heine's elegant and arabesque-like illustrations (Munich, Hans von Weber, 1908) and that these are a major achievement of Jugendstil

illustration. Furthermore, from 1907 onwards Germany had seen the emergence of private presses from which came books, most of them printed by hand, that were looked to as models. The first were the Janus-Presse and the Ernst-Ludwig-Presse (1907), Melchior Lechter's Einhorn-Presse followed in 1909, the Bremer Presse in 1911, the Offizina Serpentis in 1913, the Rupprecht-Presse in 1914 and the Cranach-Presse in 1915. Not one of these presses commissioned an Expressionist master to illustrate a single book. Important though they were in the history of the handsomely printed and bound book in Germany, they were, like the societies of bibliophiles, conservative in matters of art. No one would wish to belittle the achievements of Harry Graf Kessler and his Cranach-Presse, yet the fact remains that between 1910 and 1920 he gave no place in his press to contemporary German art.

In addition to the Jugendstil and to the presses the Expressionists also found important Impressionist illustrators. 1908 saw the publication of Max Slevogt's lithographs to *Sindbad, der Seefahrer* (*Sindbad the Sailor*), published in that year by Bruno Cassirer in Berlin, and to *Lederstrumpf* (J. Fenimore Cooper's *Leatherstocking Tales*), the first publication of Paul Cassirer's artistically adventurous Pan-Presse. Bruno Cassirer had published *Ali Baba und die vierzig Räuber* (*Ali Baba and the Forty Thieves*) as early as 1903. In 1910 Lovis Corinth's twenty-two coloured lithographs, *Das Buch Judith* (*The Book of Judith*), appeared as the second publication of the Pan-Presse. The domain of the Impressionists was the lithograph and the drawing.

Impressionist illustration is entirely committed to description, to the specific, it seeks closeness to the word and paints the events narrated by the author, usually with great imagination. It is often sketchy, it loves movement and the fleeting moment in its scenes, it seizes every opportunity to strike a whole gamut of finely graded tones between black and white. Its character is therefore painterly: much use is made of light – in particular the use of light and shade on the lithographer's stone; contours are soft and rounded the line, now swelling, now attenuating, produces the floating, velvety, free effect that is peculiar to all Impressionist illustration. It is a gay art, a drawing of the moment, a feast for the eyes and a gem in the book – so long as draughtsmen like Slevogt and Corinth did not overstep the limitations of the typographic image, which, of course, they often did.

Into this flourishing and varied field of German illustration, represented by such talented artists as Hugo Steiner-Prag, Paul Scheurich and Karl Walser, the Expressionists irrupted *c.* 1910 with a savagery that was almost barbaric. The linear violence of Oskar Kokoschka's drawings to his drama *Mörder, Hoffnung der Frauen* (*Murderer, the Hope of Women*), shattered the sublime refinement of the illustrative style as it had been known up to that moment. Standards broke down in the face of this new art; nor were they looked for, let alone redefined, for the presses and most of the publishing houses considered such crudity, barbarity and violence to be unsuited to the serious urbanity of the book. Most historians and bibliophiles also disdained Expressionist illustration. Curt Glaser wrote in 1919 that the Expressionists had destroyed the unity of the page.[1] Hans Loubier, listing only Oskar Kokoschka, Max Kaus, Charlotte Christine Engelhorn, Richard Seewald and Otto Nückel as Expressionist illustrators, remarked in 1921 that 'the technique of Expressionist drawing does not accord with a printed text, can never, never combine with it to produce an integrated whole',[2] and that 'the Expressionist style of illustration will not make the book an artistic unity'.[3] Emil Preetorius also disapproved.[4] And in 1939, decades later, Arthur Rümann, widely known and respected for his writings on the history of book illustration, was still declaring that Expressionism was at odds with book illustration. He does, however, see in the renaissance of the woodcut a power that is capable of development, yet he believes that the reckless individuality of the Expressionists had destroyed the unity of the book.[5] In so saying Rümann does in fact draw attention to the difficult and conflicting problems of Expressionist illustration to be described a little later on, but one cannot escape the impression that he (like other publishers and historians of the book) feels the intrusion of Expressionism into the art of the book as an attack on traditional bourgeois taste, which the German illustrators of the Jugendstil and Impressionism never for one moment, of course, abandoned. The same underestimation of Expressionist illustration had also been apparent in the international exhibition of the art of the book in Leipzig in 1927, the first exhibition since the celebrated BUGRA (Internationale Ausstellung für Buchgewerbe und Graphik, Leipzig) of 1914. Apart from Barlach and Kubin, the only artists from Expressionist circles to be represented were Willi Geiger, Ludwig Meidner, Hans Orlowski, Karl Schmidt-Rottluff, Otto Schubert, Richard Seewald and Max Unold, and some of these showed works that had

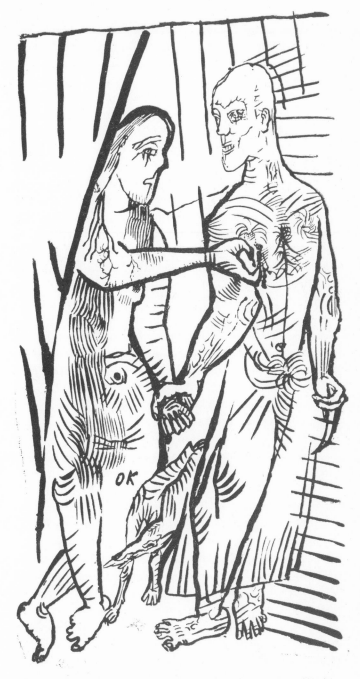

Oskar Kokoschka: Drawing on title-page of his drama *Mörder, Hoffnung der Frauen*, published in the weekly *Der Sturm* (No. 20), 14 July 1910. Also appeared in book form in an edition limited to 100 copies (Berlin: Der Sturm, 1916). 240 × 135 mm. [186]

ceased to have any connection with Expressionist ideas. The Expressionist element in the new book illustration had simply not been recognized. Even after 1945, despite the high regard in which Expressionism was generally held, opinion had changed little. In his *Deutsche Buchkunst 1890–1960*, Georg Kurt Schauer reproaches the Expressionists with having only made 'isolated attempts to develop a typeface'.[6] Ernst Ludwig Kirchner had, however, shown that a perfect book could be made by using existing typefaces. The experiments of Ludwig Tügel at the artists' colony at Worpswede (1920–24), Christian Heinrich Kleukens's Judith type (1923), the gothicizing type of Georg Mendelssohn (1923) and Rudolf Koch's various typefaces, which were designed to create for the Expressionist woodcut and drawing a face exclusively suited to it, were bound to fail because the rational form of the type itself was in fact irreconcilable with Expressionist sentiment. This does not mean, however, that Expressionist illustration – the only practitioners of which to be mentioned by Schauer are Paul Klee, Richard Janthur, Ernst Barlach, Oskar Kokoschka, Frans Masereel and Alfred Kubin – could not have been reconciled with strict use of type. It is wrong to assume that a new style of illustration must also create a new typeface for itself. The fact that there are but few successful books with Expressionist illustrations proves not that Expressionism was unsuited to book design, but simply that circumstances were against it. Kandinsky, Klee and Kirchner, in complete contrast to the Expressionist hatred of tradition in other spheres, wished to make well-designed 'classical' books.

German book illustration has lost much from the fact that, because conditions were unfavourable, the illustrators had little opportunity to realize their intentions with regard to book design. Many Expressionists had all the makings of illustrators. Again, friendships between writers and painters and the many individuals who were gifted in both arts offered a rare foundation for an illustrative art that would match the writing well, because it was born of the same spirit. The much commended community of ideas that existed between the writers and artists – and was reflected in the leading periodicals – and the congenial spirit that resulted formed a unique basis for the ideal illustration of contemporary literature. Moreover, certain works – by, for example, Ernst Barlach, Wassily Kandinsky, Oskar Kokoschka, Alfred Kubin, Else Lasker-Schüler and Ludwig Meidner – illustrated by the writers themselves represented the ideal case of perfect harmony: these illustrations are a direct continuation of the text using different means. They are not a mere accompaniment, a trans-

position and visual interpretation; they are instead an autonomous 'second creation' out of the same spirit. In these illustrations by the writers themselves we have drawings of which the inner structure is firmly tied to the poet's word. They are witness to a struggle for the ultimate, unsurpassable form. These artists' ideas are heightened by being stated twice over.

We can now see that an odd situation has arisen. During the decade following 1945 Expressionism was rediscovered and classed as what might be called one of Germany's 'sacred relics'; and it was quickly declared – sometimes not without concealed ideological intent – to be the only, or at least the main, artistic tradition of modern Germany. Yet the democratic tendencies in this art simply went unrecognized – as they still are. Among the democratic tendencies in Expressionism I would include the ambitions of book-designers, although, contrarily enough, when they did manage to get into print they appeared in ludicrously small editions. The exclusiveness that thus became a feature of this art was not at all what the artists intended. More probably it suited certain publishers, who, in later years when Expressionism had become fashionable, decided to put books containing original prints on to the market, since there was at the time a boom in prints and therefore no lack of speculative opportunity. Certain present-day journalists and collectors suggest that there was no Expressionist book illustration at all, that the Expressionists were uninterested in book-making. Kästner is almost totally given over to the French illustrated book,[7] including some in which the painter-illustrator has destroyed the unity of the book. His love of these noble volumes, worthy collectors' pieces that they are, is one thing, his underestimation of German illustrative art in the twentieth century is another. Not only does he dismiss the Expressionists in a few words, but also Slevogt, Liebermann, Corinth, Marcks and others seem not to exist for him. Kästner's view characterizes an extreme élitist attitude to the problem, and my own view differs from Kästner in just this: I am seeking to preserve those precious examples of the art of the book bequeathed to us by Expressionism from oblivion and from faulty judgments. One such erroneous assessment of the state of affairs occurs in an article by Abraham Horodisch, who represents his own experience as a general truth. He writes[8] that during the 1920s he elicited from Otto Mueller,

Richard Janthur: page from *Gilgamesch*. Berlin: Fritz Gurlitt, 1919. The book, which contains eleven etchings, appeared in an edition limited to 125 copies. Layout by Georg E. Burkhardt; printed by Otto von Holten. Page: 353 × 270 mm. [145]

VIERTE TAFEL

Und Schamasch· der Sonnengott· sprach zu GILGAMESCH:
›Mache dich auf mit dem Freunde· zu streiten gegen Chum-
baba! Er ist zum Hüter des Zedernwaldes bestellt; durch den
Zedernwald geht es zum Götterberge hinauf. Gegen mich hat
Chumbaba gefrevelt· darum geht und erschlaget ihn!‹
GILGAMESCH hörte das Wort des Herrn und rief zusammen die
Edlen des Volkes. Mit Enkidu trat er hinein in die Halle. Und GILGAMESCH tat seinen
Mund auf und sprach:

›Uns hat Schamasch geheissen· zu streiten gegen Chumbaba. Friede sei mit euch
und mit allem Volke!‹

Der Älteste unter den Edlen der Stadt erhob sich und sprach:

›Immer beschirmte Schamasch seinen Freund· den herrlichen GILGAMESCH. Seine
schützende Hand sei nicht ferne von dir! Furchtbar ist der grimmige Hüter des
Zedernwaldes. Schamasch· der des Kampfes Beginn dir verkündete· gab den
Freund dir zurück· möge er heil den Gefährten erhalten! Er stehe dir hilfreich zur
Seite und hüte dein Leben· o König! Du· unser Hirte· du wirst vor dem Feind
uns beschirmen.‹

Sie verlassen den Ort der Versammlung· und GILGAMESCH sagt zu Enkidu:
›Freund· nun wollen wir gehen zum Tempel Egalmach und zu der heiligen Priesterin.
Lass uns hingehn zu Rischat· der Mutter und Herrin! Hell sieht sie· zukünftigen
Schicksals kundig. Sie gebe den Segen zu unsern Schritten· in des Sonnengotts
starke Hand lege sie unser Geschick.‹

Sie gehen zum Tempel Egalmach und treffen die heilige Priesterin· die Mutter des
Königs. Sie vernahm alle Worte des Sohnes und sprach:

›Möge Schamasch dir gnädig sein!‹

Dann trat sie hinein in die Kammer der Feierkleider. In heiligem Schmuck kehrte
sie wieder zurück· gehüllt in ein weisses Gewand· auf der Brust die goldnen
Schilder· auf dem Haupte ihre Tiara· in der Hand die Schale mit Wasser. Sie sprengte
den Boden· dann stieg sie den Turm des Tempels hinauf. Oben hoch unter freiem
Himmel stieg der duftende Weihrauch empor. Opferkörner streute sie hin und hob
zum erhabenen Schamasch ihre Hand:

›Warum hast du GILGAMESCH· meinem Sohne· ein Herz gegeben· dessen Ungestüm
die Ruhe nicht findet? Wieder hast du ihn angerührt· denn er will gehen den fernen

Lyonel Feininger and Emil Nolde in personal conversations the admission that they were uninterested in book illustration. This is certainly true. What is also true – and here we need only recall Franz Marc, Max Beckmann and E. L. Kirchner – is that many other Expressionists yearned passionately to illustrate books; Kirchner's letters and diaries contain a quantity of material on the subject. I have no wish to insinuate that in the case of Horodisch the bad conscience of the erstwhile publisher (Euphorion-Verlag) may be stirring and that he has yielded to the temptation to conceal the omissions of earlier days with the story that Expressionist illustration did not exist or that the Expressionists eschewed book-design. It is not as simple as that. There is also the fact, as this book demonstrates, that the concept of 'Expressionist illustration' can be reduced neither to the masters of Expressionism nor to the woodcut book, which is what Horodisch does. The creative will of Expressionism was wider in scope and its practitioners were not only those artists who are celebrated today; nor did it express itself in the woodcut alone but by the use of every graphic technique of that time.

The books containing German Expressionist illustrations discussed here and listed in the bibliography make up a varied and sharply differentiated picture. Examined from the point of view of the authors whose works are illustrated, it shows that contemporaries are very fully represented, although they are not always the really first-class writers. Among earlier writings, editions of works by Goethe and E. T. A. Hoffmann appear more often than do those of other poets, but they in turn are surpassed by Dostoyevsky, with whose work the Expressionists felt an intellectual affinity.

German Expressionist illustration does not occur outside the two decades between 1907 and 1927. Its appearances in commercial editions before 1917 were few, although important from the first. By 1918 the number of books with Expressionist illustrations had risen by leaps and bounds and by 1922 it had doubled in relation to 1918. This increase was sustained until 1924. Expressionism had now become fashionable. A host of mediocre artists working at the level of commercial art exploited the creative principles discovered by the masters.

Expressionist illustration begins with Erich Heckel's woodcuts to Wilde's *Die Ballade vom Zuchthaus zu Reading* (*The Ballad of Reading Gaol*), executed in 1907 but first published in book form by Ernest Rathenau in New York only in 1963. Heckel was followed in 1910 by Oskar Kokoschka with drawings to his drama *Mörder, Hoffnung der Frauen*, the first Expressionist illustrations to be published.

A year later Paul Klee illustrated Voltaire's *Kandide* (*Candide*), although this did not appear until 1920. In 1912 Kokoschka produced his illustrations to Albert Ehrenstein's *Tubutsch*, and the book designer and typographer F. H. E. Schneidler made his remarkable illustrations to Heine's *Atta Troll*. Wassily Kandinsky and Ernst Ludwig Kirchner illustrated their first books in 1913, and Ludwig Meidner, Else Lasker-Schüler and Conrad Felixmüller were already at work. Max Beckmann's first contribution dates from 1918. A climax was reached in 1924 with the publication of Beckmann's *Fanferlieschen*, Kirchner's *Umbra vitae* and Pechstein's *Yali und sein weißes Weib* (*Yali and his White Woman*).

The following books, listed chronologically, stand out from the mass of material as the major works of Expressionist illustration. (The works of Barlach, Kubin and Masereel are omitted here because of their their special position; see chapter V.)

1907 Erich Heckel: illustrations to Oscar Wilde's *Die Ballade vom Zuchthaus zu Reading* (first published in book form in 1963 by Ernest Rathenau in New York).

1910 Oskar Kokoschka: illustrations to his own drama *Mörder, Hoffnung der Frauen* (published in Herwarth Walden's *Der Sturm*).

1912 Oskar Kokoschka: illustrations to Albert Ehrenstein's *Tubutsch* (Vienna and Leipzig, Jahoda & Siegel).

1913 Ernst Ludwig Kirchner: illustrations to Alfred Döblin's *Das Stiftsfräulein und der Tod* (*The Canoness and Death*), published by Alfred Richard Meyer in the series 'Lyrische Flugblätter'. Wassily Kandinsky: illustrations to his own poems in the volume *Klänge* (*Sounds*), published by Reinhard Piper, Munich.

1914 Oskar Kokoschka: illustrations to Karl Kraus's *Die chinesische Mauer* (*The Great Wall of China*), published by Kurt Wolff, Leipzig; and to the words of Bach's cantata *O Ewigkeit – Du Donnerwort*, published by Fritz Gurlitt, Berlin.

1916 Oskar Kokoschka: illustration to his dramatic poem *Der gefesselte Kolumbus* (*Columbus Bound*), published by Fritz Gurlitt, Berlin.

1917 Oskar Kokoschka: illustrations to his drama *Hiob* (*Job*), published in Berlin by Paul Cassirer; and to Victor Dirsztay's *Lob des hohen Verstandes*, published by Kurt Wolff, Leipzig.

1918 Max Beckmann: illustrations to Kasimir Edschmid's *Die Fürstin* (*The Princess*), published by Gustav Kiepenheuer, Weimar.

Karl Schmidt-Rottluff: illustrations to Alfred Brust's *Das Spiel Christa vom Schmerz der Schönheit des Weibes* (*The Play Christa of the Pain of the Beauty of Woman*), published by Franz Pfemfert in the series 'Der rote Hahn', Berlin.

Conrad Felixmüller: illustrations to Walter Rheiner's *Kokain* (*Cocaine*), published by the Dresdner Verlag von 1917.

Ludwig Meidner: illustrations to his book *Im Nakken das Sternemeer* (*Behind one, the Sea of Stars*), published by Kurt Wolff, Leipzig.

1919 Richard Janthur: illustrations to *Gilgamesch*, published by Fritz Gurlitt, Berlin.

1920 Willi Geiger: illustrations to Prosper Mérimée's *Carmen*, published by Fritz Gurlitt, Berlin.

Walter Gramatté: illustrations to Gogol's *Der Mantel* (*The Overcoat*), published by Gustav Kiepenheuer, Potsdam.

Paul Klee: illustrations to Voltaire's *Kandide* (*Candide*), published by Kurt Wolff, Munich; and to Curt Corrinth's *Potsdamer Platz oder Die Nächte des Neuen Messias* (*Potsdamer Platz, or The Nights of the New Messiah*), published by Georg Müller, Munich.

Ludwig Meidner; illustrations to his *Septemberschrei* (*September Cry*), published by Paul Cassirer, Berlin.

Carl Rabus: illustrations to Wieland's *Oberon*, published by the Hesperos-Verlag, Munich.

Richard Seewald: illustrations to Gellert's *Fabeln* (*Fables*), published by Fritz Gurlitt, Berlin.

1921 Max Beckmann: illustrations to the volume of poems by Lili von Braunbehrens *Stadtnacht* (*City Night*), published by Reinhard Piper, Munich.

1922 Carl Hofer: illustrations to *Liebesgedichte* (*Love Poems*) by Alfred von Hatzfeld, published by Alfred Flechtheim, Berlin.

Richard Janthur: illustrations to Daniel Defoe's *Robinson Crusoe*, published by the Insel-Verlag, Leipzig.

1923 Oskar Kokoschka: illustrations to Victor Dirsztay's *Der Unentrinnbare* (*The one from whom you cannot escape*), published by Kurt Wolff, Munich.

Else Lasker-Schüler: illustrations to her volume of poems *Theben* (*Thebes*), published as no. 24 in the series 'Flechtheim-Drucke', by the Querschnitt-Verlag, Frankfurt am Main and Berlin.

Hans Orlowski: illustrations to Heinrich Heine's *Die Cholera in Paris*, published by August Kuhn-Foelix, Berlin.

Ernst Ludwig Kirchner: illustrations to Jakob Boß-

hart's *Neben der Heerstraße* (*Near the Heerstraße*), published by Grethlein, Zürich and Leipzig.

1924 Ernst Ludwig Kirchner: illustrations to Georg Heym's *Umbra vitae*, published by Kurt Wolff, Munich.

Max Pechstein: illustrations to Willy Seidel's *Yali und sein weißes Weib* (*Yali and his White Woman*), published by Fritz Gurlitt, Berlin.

The foregoing list includes books only. In addition, at least two suites of prints deserve mention because they clearly demonstrate the illustrative ambition of the Expressionists: Ernst Ludwig Kirchner's colour woodcuts to Chamisso's *Peter Schlemihl* (1915) and Max Beckmann's etchings to Brentano's *Fanferlieschen* (1924).

Ernst Ludwig Kirchner: woodcut title to *Das Stiftsfräulein und der Tod* by Alfred Döblin. Berlin: Alfred Richard Meyer, 1913. The novella, published as one of the series of 'Lyrische Flugblätter', contained five woodcuts by Kirchner. 227 × 177 mm. [171]

Specific characteristics emerge from the illustrated works we have mentioned, and from others, which justify us in using the term Expressionist illustration. Where, notwithstanding all individual differences, do we find the characteristic features of this style of illustration?

Expressionist illustration in the years between 1907 and 1927 is a graphic art related to a text, an art which is subjectively exaggerated, simplified in form, in which the psychic excitements and the outlook of the illustrator alter the object of his illustrations. These illustrations express a fantastic vision – immoderate, often grotesquely formulated – in which the element of draughtsmanship is subor-

dinated to a metaphorical process. Basically a metamorphosis takes place in accordance with the intentions of the artist, whose egocentric outlook deals freely with the literary subject. It is true that important differences gradually emerge, as for example between Schmidt-Rottluff, Meidner and Hofer, but generally the forms create a spectacle which differs from the optical appearance of things and is usually ecstatically and emphatically heightened. For these artists the literary subject usually provides a welcome opportunity to display their own view of the world. The narrative element in the image, – beloved of the Impressionists – does not, therefore, interest them. They seek in their images to texts something deeper, something mysterious, some element of primordial man. They are therefore concerned less with the events recounted by the writers than with their meaning. The principle is not representation but interpretation, not a loving delineation of isolated incidents but the compression of many descriptive elements in the text into a symbol. This is one of the reasons, and a not unimportant one, why Expressionist illustration is usually also free graphic art, which means that the illustrative context does not exhaust the sense of the forms: they are meaningful as independent graphic images. It also explains the Expressionists' desire for full-page illustrations and for the graphic design to be carried over to bindings and dust-jackets. A loading of the optical impression with psychic excitement and a subjective, usually missionary and idealistic, outlook is characteristic of Expressionist illustration – and it is carried so far that sometimes the desire for expression exceeds an artist's formal ability. For the rest, the whole formal vocabulary of Expressionist art is found in Expressionist illustration: the abbreviating drawing (Kirchner's 'hieroglyph'), unbroken colour, rejection of classical perspective, the aggressively cubic quality of the folded and criss-crossed picture area, the collisions between pointed forms and hard surfaces, the clash of different formal thrusts, the dazzling contrasts of dark and light, the over-heated rhythm and the passionate dynamics, the false proportions of the figures and the disturbance of natural dimensional and spatial relationships. The terseness of the woodcut lent itself naturally to such a language. The woodcut technique had long ceased to have any importance except as a method of reproduction, but William Nicholson, Félix Vallotton, Paul Gauguin and Edvard Munch had already re-established it as a means of artistic expression. The artists of Die Brücke did the same for the woodcut in Germany. All the other techniques of drawing and printmaking also occur in Expressionist illustration but it is in the woodcut that the intention of these artists is always

Ernst Ludwig Kirchner: woodcut title (impression in black and white) to *Peter Schlemihls wundersame Geschichte* by Adelbert von Chamisso, 1915/16. 285 × 220 mm. [172]

most impressively displayed. Moreover, the plane-surface art of the woodcut permits the greatest possible aesthetic alliance between the typography and the image, because text and woodcut can be printed together in one process. Certain Expressionists, Kirchner among them, had studied the combination of pictorial motif and (cut) type in the early broadsheets and block-books.

Despite its essential consistency, Expressionist illustration is extraordinarily varied, intellectually, formally, technically and in its relationship with the book; Pechstein favoured etching and limited himself to creating an optical equivalent of the literary description; Kirchner expressed himself mainly by means of the woodcut; he retained the illustrative form and its closeness to the text, though he heightened the expression and interpreted in conformity with his own outlook; his cuts are at once illustration and independent image; Kokoschka and Klee gave free rein to their emotions and visions, using for preference a linear idiom, to which Kokoschka, after his earliest efforts, added tone and rich light values; Beckmann took the properties and characters offered by the text and built up a crushing panorama of life; Schmidt-Rottluff ruthlessly subordinated the text to his own vision; Kandinsky became lost among the giddy heights of abstract decoration; Meidner's drawings transformed every text into so many lines of rhetorical emotion . . .

1 In *Die neue Bücherschau* (Munich), vol. for 1919, no. 2, p. 10.
2 H. Loubier, *Die neue deutsche Buchkunst*, Stuttgart, 1921, p. 113.
3 Ibid., p. 114.
4 E. Preetorius, 'Gedanken zum illustrierten Buch', in *Ganymed. Jahrbuch für die Kunst*, vol. 5, Munich, 1925, p. 154.
5 Arthur Rümann, 'Die deutsche Buchillustration. Anmerkungen zu ihrer Geschichte von 1880–1925', in *Imprimatur. Jahrbuch für Bücherfreunde*, vol. IX, Weimar and Berlin, 1939, p. 143.
6 Hamburg, 1963, vol. I, p. 217.
7 Cf. E. Kästner, 'Das Malerbuch unserer Zeit', in *Philobiblon*, vol. VI (1962), no. 1.
8 Cf. A. Horodisch, 'Zum Problem expressionistischer Buchillustration', in *Antiquariat* (Stammheim/Calw), 1968, no. 5, p. 115 ff.

Ernst Ludwig Kirchner: 'Triumph der Liebe' ('Triumph of Love'), for a suite of woodcut illustrations to Petrarch, 1909 (the suite remained unpublished). 245 × 230 mm.

II. Trends in Expressionist illustration

German Expressionism emerges as a movement of immense variety. Its stylistic intentions extend from the masters of Die Brücke through Beckmann and Kokoschka; that is, from the artists who first redefined theme, figure and form, to those who worked not from an inner striving after a new, 'as yet non-existent' pattern, but established themselves as followers of fashion, some more gifted than others. We must remember in this connection that the so-called second wave of Expressionism had set in by *c*. 1913 –

Oskar Kokoschka: Jacket design for *Nicht da nicht dort* by Albert Ehrenstein. Leipzig: Kurt Wolff Verlag, 1916. (Used for part of the edition only.) 204 × 122 mm. [194]

with the emergence of Felixmüller, say – and that after 1919, when Expressionism was enjoying wide recognition, is was regarded as 'modern' to accept Expressionist principles of style. By this time Expressionist art was 'in'; it was accepted by the art market, then booming, and came to be regarded as respectable by the establishment.

Any attempt to make the differences and fragmentation intelligible is dogged by the danger of over-simplification. I have accepted this risk simply in order to demonstrate the complexity of the movement at large. The definitions of terms and classifications of artists in this book must therefore be used with great care and caution – as indeed they are employed here, having been formulated gradually and used as provisional guides in working through the mass of material. It will be obvious that Beckmann and Kokoschka are difficult to align with any specific trend. These artists and the masters of Die Brücke might be described as the classics of Expressionism. As regards Kokoschka and Beckmann, Meidner and Felixmüller, certain of their works give ground for identifying a REALISTIC trend within the Expressionist movement; certainly this trend is characteristic of the work of Barlach and Masereel, distant relations of Expressionism, and of less important but still considerable artists, such as Edwin Scharff, Renée Sintenis, Hans Orlowski, Franz Maria Jansen and Willi Geiger. But to describe a painter, graphic artist and illustrator such as WILLI GEIGER as an Expressionist leads us into immediate difficulties. Geiger formulated his response to the movement after the First World War. Around 1920 a will-o'-the wisp Expressionism begins to dart through his illustrations, his 'spiritualized' and elongated forms reflecting his encounter with Velásquez. His adoption of Expressionist formative principles is most clearly apparent in his lithographs to Frank Wedekind's *Frühlingserwachen* (*Spring Awakening*; Munich, Georg Müller, 1920), his etchings to Prosper Mérimée's *Carmen* (Berlin, Fritz Gurlitt, 1920) and to Dostoyevsky's *Das junge Weib* (Leipzig, E. A. Seemann, 1924). Yet by 1923/24 Geiger had already left the movement behind him; it is true that works still influenced by Expressionism are to be found in various illustrated books, yet his handwriting had long been developing along its own lines. Geiger was no more than tangential to Expressionism. The same may be said of HANS ORLOWSKI, whose work as a woodcut artist begins in *c*. 1923, the period of late Expressionism. The firmly organized plates to *Das jüngste Gericht* (*The Last Judgment*; Berlin, Wendekreis Verlag, 1923), to *Amiran* (Berlin, Wendekreis Verlag, 1924), a Georgian variant of the Prometheus legend, and to Heinrich Heine's *Die Cholera in Paris* (Berlin, August Kuhn-Foelix, 1923) are related, in the vigorous gathered forms and the figures that look as though they had been rammed into the ground, to the style of Barlach as it first appeared in 1916/17.

The realistic element in Geiger and Orlowski is apparent in the primacy of a naturalistic, figurative character that is stylized only to the extent that is necessary for the dynamics of the statement: form does not become autono-

mous but remains subservient to an assessable theme. A realistic trend in this sense of the word, the concern of which, in illustration, is to elucidate a written truth, occurs as an undercurrent in the work of many Expressionists. I would not hesitate to call it realistic – and that quite independently of the degree of Expressionistic stylization – but only when it concerns the depiction of socially relevant truths; yet it would appear desirable to use the term 'realistic' in relation to Expressionism with due reserve, especially since book illustration does not provide the most suitable material for it. This applies particularly to the successors of Die Brücke and to the folkloric, naturalistic

Das tat Amiran ohne jede Anstrengung. Dann sagte ihm die Mutter des Toten: „Du bist die Ursache des Todes meines Sohnes. Wäre ich nicht in der Lage, in der ich bin, würde ich dir zeigen, was Recken= kraft heißt.“ Immer weiter ging Amiran und vernichtete überall seine Feinde, so daß bald kein einziger Recke mehr übrig blieb, nicht nur in Filich sondern auch in den umgebenden Ländern. Danach fing Amiran an, seine Kraft an gewöhnlichen Leuten zu erproben, es fielen ihm auch eine Menge Christen zum Opfer. Aber Jesus Christus machte dem bald ein Ende. Er stieg einst in der Gestalt eines gewöhn= lichen Menschen auf die Erde nieder und forderte Amiran zu einem Zweikampfe

Hans Orlowski: woodcut and text page to *Amiran. Eine georgische Sage*. Berlin: Wendekreis-Verlag, 1924. Type: Maximilian-Gotisch, 28 pt. The book (containing four woodcuts) appeared in an edition limited to 50 copies. 195×155 mm; page 318×245 mm. [260]

trend in Expressionist illustration – and to a certain extent even to the 'pathetic-ecstatic' and the 'fantastic-daemonic' trends. If we regard the style of DIE BRÜCKE in its various phases as one of the trends in illustration, we cannot forget those artists who sought to become their successors. Since we shall examine the most important illustrations by the artists of Die Brücke in detail in the next chapter, we will at this point merely name a few graphic artists who were glad to adopt and carry on the ideas of the Dresden group. Mention must be made of MAX KAUS, who worked under the influence of Heckel and Kirchner, of OTTO SCHUBERT, who in his lithographs indeed also made use of Impressionist stimuli derived from Slevogt, and of the imposing galaxy of late Expressionists in Dresden. CONRAD FELIXMÜLLER is particularly important, although he did also receive inspiration from Ludwig Meidner. The politically activist trend in Expressionism was strongly apparent in his art. Felixmüller came to illustration in 1912 through the first performance in Dresden of Arnold Schönberg's *Lieder des Pierrot Lunaire*. The characteristics of the approaching second wave of Expressionism are already present in their ultimate form in the ten woodcuts (1912/13) to the *Lieder*: clear-cut contrasts between black and white, which betray a knowledge both of the art of Die Brücke and of the plane-surface principle of Vallotton. The eight woodcuts of Else Lasker-Schüler's *Hebräische Balladen* (*Hebrew Ballads*) of 1914 also owe much to the Expressionist *Sturm und Drang*; they are some of the most convincing illustrations to have come out of Expressionism up to 1914. Felixmüller's close association with literature was due to his friendship with many writers, among them Theodor Däubler, Walter Rheiner, Carl Sternheim, Raoul Hausmann, Ludwig Meidner and Franz Pfemfert. The experience of the war made his attitude more radical: he became aware of the world about him and was from now on a deliberate revolutionary agitator, as his illustrations to Pfemfert's literary journal *Die Aktion* show. His illustrations of 1917 to works by Walter Rheiner are more concrete, their gesture is social, they are full of rhetorical feeling, presumably stimulated by his meeting with Meidner. During these years Felixmüller enlarged his creative vocabulary, stimulus came from Kokoschka as well as from Meidner, he even responded to Cubism and tested its relevance to his own work. This man's art became an ethical creed, in its early days developing affinities with Dix but rapidly moving away again and then at the beginning of the 1920s combining an expressive use of line with a faithful rendering of objective themes. Felixmüller began in Expressionism, examined its possibilities, and through political partisanship for the struggling workers discovered an expressive realistic style which was capable of sustaining further development. His illustrative works reflect this change, show how he sought and found a realistic position. This artist's illustrative plates of the year 1917 could, indeed, equally well find a place in the 'PATHETIC-ECSTATIC' category of Expressionist illustration, the master of which was Ludwig Meidner. This trend is not, however, identical with the triple constellation of the 'Pathetiker' ('Pathetic Ones') – Meidner, Steinhardt and Janthur, – or the 'Neopathetiker' – the poets who worked on the journal *Das neue Pathos*. Meidner and Steinhardt were no doubt also 'Pathetiker' in illustration, but Janthur was not; his art was much more concerned with the concepts of folklore and nature.

Title-page of the first number of *Das neue Pathos*, Berlin, June 1913, with a drawing by Ludwig Meidner. 245 × 181 mm.

The group of 'pathetic-ecstatic' illustrators would be incomplete without a word about Carl Rabus – as regards a part of his *œuvre* – also Willy Jaeckel, who included visionary and sometimes mystical elements. In the case of each of these artists the depth of feeling is accounted for by quite different motives: Meidner longed fanatically to bring about a change in human nature, Jakob Steinhardt drew his formulations from his religious awareness as a Jew, and Jaeckel was prompted by metaphysical visions of human existence. JAKOB STEINHARDT's illustrations have an Expressionist character which appears most notably in the woodcuts to Yvan Goll's *Naomi* (Berlin, Soncino Verlag, 1924) and to Alfred Wolfenstein's *Der Flügelmann* (Dessau, Karl Rauch, 1924). His illustrations to Wolfenstein's little dramatic poem give a picture of this artist's ethos, of his social responsibility. This is also the point of contact with WILLY JAECKEL who had condemned the war with great severity in his series *Memento mori* of 1914/15. Jaeckel was early felt to be an antipole of Expressionism, indeed he was almost defined as the diametric opposite to Meidner. The truth was that Jaeckel's romantically effulgent introspectiveness was merely the other face of the revolutionary ecstasy of Meidner. Ecstasy and introspectiveness went hand in hand in so far as they wore the guise of feeling. But of course a greater difference than that between Meidner and Jaeckel could hardly be imagined: the one desired to found a new humanity through a radical rejection of the sated bourgeoisie and he appealed for a change in existing conditions, although his demands and aims were Utopian dreams, divorced from the actual functioning of the law and therefore far removed from class warfare in society; the other, although his first work was certainly a brilliant criticism of the Moloch of war, owing everything to Goya, devised a fanciful system of metaphysics, naive, blunt, irradiated by mysticism, preoccupied with the cosmos, with becoming and passing, with the human vocation and mission, which he often saw in a transcendental light. Jaeckel's outlook figures in his five-part *Menschgott – Gott – Gottmensch* (*Man-God – God – God-man*; 234 etchings in portfolio, 1922) as a metaphysical eclecticism compounded of Biblical texts, cosmogony and mysticism.

During the period 1917–1924 the artist's work in illustration was influenced by Expressionism. It is clear from the very fact that an Expressionist attitude is only occasionally discernible in his various works and then only in an odd plate, not in the complete set of illustrations, that Jaeckel's position is an intermediate one. His lithograph to Walt Whitman's poem from *Children of Adam*, 'One hour to madness and joy' (Eine Stunde der Raserei und Freude), is undoubtedly an Expressionist illustration. Man and woman hurl themselves into an embrace of tumultuous energy. Whitman writes:

> O something unprov'd! something in a trance!
> To escape utterly from others' anchors and holds!
> To drive free! to love free! to dash reckless and dangerous!
> To court destruction with taunts, with invitations!
> To ascend, to leap to the heavens of the love indicated to me!
> To rise thither with my inebriate soul!
> To be lost if it must be so!
> To feed the remainder of life with one hour of fulness and freedom!
> With one brief hour of madness and joy.

And Jaeckel draws the 'madness and joy' as an emotion that is not esoterically morbid but almost brutal and instinctual: the two bodies cry out in a wild fervour of love.

Compared with the ecstatic approach, the trend in Expressionist illustration that is concerned with FOLKLORE and NATURE strikes an almost idyllic note. Here again within simple, yet formally strict, contemplativeness and lyrical meditation there exists the greatest artistic variety imaginable: there are more disparities than resemblances between Seewald, Caspar, Marcks, Hofer, Janthur and Unold. And yet characterizing them all is a narrative, decorative simplicity, an ornamental language, sometimes echoing that of the pictorial broadsheet, an ingenious use even of decorative elements, together with a strict though stylized commitment to the appearances of reality; it is folkloric in the sense that it is a popular visual epic and in the sense that it uses popular conventions. There is little in the work of these artists of the passionate outcry, the wild desire to attack tradition and convention by overturning and fragmenting all optically perceptible forms. Yet Expressionism as a stylistic trend does exist in their works. The case of Hofer, the painter, is as characteristic as that of Marcks the sculptor.

CARL HOFER's style has nothing in common with the defiant immediacy of the Expressionists; it is built up like pictorial architecture, rather similar to that of Hans von Marées or Paul Cézanne. After 1919, however, when his style had matured, Expressionist values began to show themselves in his mask-like characterization and in the language of his gestures, appearing as simplified forms in both movements and features. Hofer only once used book illustrations as the channel for his Expressionist sentiments.

The illustrations are his ten lithographs to Adolf von Hatzfeld's *Liebesgedichte* (*Love Poems*); Berlin, Galerie Flechtheim, 1922). Hofer's lyrical Expressionism is apparent in the flat, disk-like faces that are as de-individualized as it is possible to be. The delicate linear idiom of the lithographs reflects the writer's intentions, usually in a very concrete way.

Wenn der Mond die Waldgebirge überhängt,
mein Gefühl zum Atem der Natur sich drängt,
denk ich dein, Geliebte, auf der nächt'gen Flur
dein gedenk ich, Tochter der Natur.

Gerhard Marcks: 'Lachend erhob sich in die Luft Wölundr' ('Laughing, Wölundr rose into the air'), woodcut to *Wielandslied der älteren Edda*, Munich and Weimar: Bauhaus-Verlag, 1923. Ten woodcuts in portfolio (110 copies) bound by Otto Dorfner. 198×145 mm. [220]

('When the moon hangs above the hills, my emotion surges to the breath of nature, I think of thee, beloved, in the nocturnal meadow, I think of thee, daughter of nature'.)

These lines from the poem 'An die Geliebte' are faithfully reproduced in the image: among fir-trees against a background of hills a girl lies resting on her elbow; above her, slightly to the left of the central axis, hangs the great disk of the full moon. It is a drawing in which the artist has managed to express his feeling for nature and his sense of style with equal harmony.

The woodcuts made by GERHARD MARCKS during his Bauhaus period are also simple and economical. Outwardly, however, they bear rather more resemblance to Expressionist formal concepts than do Hofer's lithographs. This may be due in part to the woodcut technique, but it also reflects direct Expressionist influence, to which Marcks was for a time exposed, until his trip to Greece in 1928 finally enabled him to conquer it. The finest record of this artist's encounter with Expressionism is the portfolio bound by Otto Dorfner containing ten woodcuts to *Das Wielandslied der älteren Edda* (Weimar, Bauhaus-Verlag 1923) that appeared in an edition limited to 110 copies printed in 1923 on the hand press at the Staatliches Bauhaus in Weimar. The style recalls the naive illustrations of old fairy tales.

MAX UNOLD was another woodcut artist of the folkloric-naturalistic trend. In contrast to Marcks and Hofer he illustrated many books, but not all reveal his contact with Expressionism. His encounter with the movement dates from 1918. This was a somewhat fleeting contact, but we owe to it an extremely fine book and the artist's most mature work to that date, Gustave Flaubert's *Die Legende von Sankt Julian dem Gastfreien* (*La Légende de Saint-Julien l'Hospitalier*). It was published by Piper in Munich in 1918 as the seventh publication of the Marées-Gesellschaft and contained woodcuts, borders and initials. Wilhelm Hausenstein spoke of the 'Gothic taste'[1] of the Swabian artist and the plates to Flaubert's text gave it scope for expression. A concise, linear style reminiscent of early book illustration harmonizes most happily with the type, a Gothic face designed by William Morris. Unold achieves a similar unity of type and image on the binding of Heinrich Lautensack's *Altbayrische Bilderbogen* (*Old Bavarian Picture-book*; Berlin, Fritz Gurlitt, 1920). Where Unold, because of his chosen technique, was harsh and austere, Caspar and Seewald dwell on the lyrical aspects.

The painter KARL CASPAR illustrated a single book, *Die Cumäische Sibylle* (*The Cumaean Sibyl*) by his friend Konrad Weiß; this was published in 1921 in Munich by Georg

Müller. Expressionist and Baroque elements merge in the eight lithographs in a way that reminds one of Kokoschka. RICHARD SEEWALD did work that is close to Caspar's illustrations, as for example his lithographs to *Die Argonauten* (*The Argonauts*; Berlin, Propyläen-Verlag, 1923). There is a Baroque energy in the work of this artist too and ideas may have come besides from Campendonk and Marc. Of the illustrators of the folkloric-naturalistic trend Seewald had the most marked taste for the fairy-tale element. His talent for decoration served him well without leading to flatness; Seewald sought a classical lucidity of form. The finest manifestation of the folkloric trend in Expressionist illustration occurs in his woodcuts to Virgil's *Bucolics* (Berlin, Euphorion Verlag, 1923) and outstandingly in his woodcuts (some coloured) to Gellert's *Fabeln* (*Fables*; Berlin, Fritz Gurlitt, 1920). Seewald too touched Expressionism only in its late phase. Many of this artist's illustrations, including the lithographs to the widely admired *Hasenroman* (*Le Roman du lièvre*) by Francis Jammes (Leipzig, Kurt Wolff, 1916), are far removed from the Expressionist idea. RICHARD JANTHUR, the most important of the illustrators of the folkloric-naturalistic trend, is far more deeply rooted in Expressionism, although he differs considerably from the other artists discussed here. From 1919 onwards he produced a rapid succession of illustrations to literary texts. Janthur is concerned with the destiny of man, with the conflict between life and death, with a primitive and naive, de-socialized relationship with nature. The state of social arousal that appeared in the artists of Die Brücke, the desire to challenge the world that is apparent among the 'Pathetiker' is absent; in short, Janthur is unmoved by social conscience. This latecomer to the Expressionist movement creates a human image that is optically perceptible but is metaphysical and abstract and, detached from all social commitment, serves a belated and historically anachronistic pantheism. This cast of mind is clearly expressed in *Gilgamesch* (Berlin, Fritz Gurlitt, 1919), Janthur's first important set of illustrations: man himself has to prove his mettle, he is a creature of biological instincts, even a mythical creature, but not a social individual involved in the reality of class struggles. The same is true of his illustrations to other works: Defoe's *Robinson Crusoe* (Leipzig, Insel-Verlag, 1922), or *Der goldene Esel* (*The Golden Ass*) by Apuleius (Berlin, Franz Schneider, 1924). Janthur's coloured lithographs to *Robinson Crusoe* – unimaginable without Kokoschka's influence – are powerfully impressive. His etchings to *Der goldene Esel* are more agitated in style. The artist illustrated numerous books in his naturalistic, decorative style compounded of many elements used by the Expres-

Richard Janthur: initial D to *Tamango* by Prosper Mérimée. Berlin: Franz Schneider Verlag, 1922. The book appeared, as vol. 1 of the series 'Luxusgraphik Schneider', in an edition limited to 200 copies. 59 × 56 mm. [153]

sionists (including Franz Marc) that had by now become almost popular, were readily intelligible and were rather the external elements of the style. He worked with taste and a marked feeling for opulence.

Janthur, unquestionably still an artist of notable stature, stands at the point at which Expressionist art lapses into pure modishness, in which forms, emptied of the spirit that generated them, lead an independent and self-regarding life. The artist was unable to withstand the temptations to which this position exposed him, yet his work contains a spontaneous creative power. However, the realistic undercurrent in Expressionist illustration that is still present in the work of a Seewald, a Hofer, or an Unold, to say nothing of Meidner or Felixmüller, has disappeared from that of Janthur. And it occurs at most intermittently in the illustrations of the FANTASTIC-DAEMONIC type, more pronouncedly in the work of Kubin than in that of Klee, more obviously in the work of Gramatté than in that of Burchartz and Segall, more vigorously in the work of Zeller than in that of Rabus and Gleichmann. These are the most important among the names that were in one way or another involved in this trend. The outstanding master of the fantastic-daemonic was Paul Klee, whose illustrations will be considered later in this book. The others were Burchartz, Segall, Gramatté, Gleichmann, Rabus and Zeller.

MAX BURCHARTZ was a member of a circle of artists in Hanover centred on Paul Erich Küppers, the first artistic director of the Kestner-Gesellschaft, and on the Paul Steegemann Verlag. Burchartz's eight drawings on the stone to Dostoyevsky's novel *Die Dämonen* (*The Possessed*) appeared in 1919 in the series 'Die Silbergäule' (no. 43/44), and in the same year the ten lithographs to the Russian writer's *Raskolnikoff* (*Crime and Punishment*) formed the second publication in the series 'Ausgaben der Galerie Alfred Flechtheim'. The lithographs, with their overheated, ecstatic drawing, could scarcely have come into existence without Burchartz's experience of the work of the Futurists: backgrounds slide together, forms overlap one another, elements from behind press forward, space develops vertically instead of in depth. These are some of the most chaotic among Expressionist illustrations. They too stand at a turning-point: as with Klee, the fantastic-daemonic pattern combines with a formal intention that is moving towards abstraction. In his illustrations Burchartz's style does not reach abstraction, although he too forms a bridge by which the road leads away from Expressionism – to Dadaism. In fact the lithographs to *Die Dämonen*, executed at the same time, are close to Kurt Schwitters's work in illustration. The same applies to Otto Gleichmann who also lived in Hanover and whose house was a meeting-place not only for Küppers, Adolf von Hatzfeld and Burchartz, but also for such masters of bourgeois art as Kandinsky, Schwitters, Lissitzky and Arp. Influences did not fail to make themselves felt. Gleichmann's art, it is true, was closer to that of Klee than to Schwitters and the others who enjoyed his hospitality. He came to the fore with the portfolio *Chimären* (*Chimeras*; Düsseldorf, Galerie Flechtheim, 1921); his lithographs to *Judas Makkabäus* and *Antiochus* (Berlin, Paul Cassirer, 1919) had appeared a little earlier; there are also a few single sheets to Edgar Allan Poe, Gogol, Proust and Dostoyevsky. This Dostoyevsky lithograph (1919) illustrates the scene in which Raskolnikov meets Sonya in the street for the first time and protects her from Svidrigayelov. The fine-nerved, sensitive, brittle stroke creates a restless network on the page voicing a fantasy that appears almost surrealist but is in fact a sovereign achievement of this late phase of Expressionism. In marked contrast to Gleichmann, the work of WALTER GRAMATTÉ, who felt an intellectual kinship with the artists of Die Brücke, expresses a feeling of pessimism. It is apparent less in the nervously flickering style than in the emotionally hounded and hunted figures in the drawings, unquiet creatures like the artist himself. Gramatté's illustrations are remarkable enough as personal confessions. This late Expressionist artist was another introvert who used his illustrative drawings to rid himself of his oppression. Gramatté's earliest illustrations, four etchings illustrating the text of a story by Manfred Georg, *Der Rebell* (*The Rebel*), appeared in *Marsyas*. The

MARSYAS

EINE ZWEIMONATSSCHRIFT

HERAUSGEGEBEN VON

THEODOR TAGGER

VERLAG HEINRICH HOCHSTIM · BERLIN

MAI 1917

Title-page with vignette by Erich Thum to the bi-monthly *Marsyas*. Berlin, May 1917. 400 × 295 mm.

most important of this artist's Expressionist illustrations are the twelve crayon lithographs to the story *Der Mantel* (*The Overcoat*) by Nikolai Gogol (Potsdam, Kiepenheuer, 1919) and his drawings to Victor Hadwiger's *Il Pantegan* (Berlin, Axel Juncker, 1919). The plates depict human existence menaced and in peril. The same goes for the lithographs executed by LASAR SEGALL to Dostoyevsky's *Die Sanfte* (*The Meek One*; Dresden, Dresdner Verlag von 1917, 1922), except that in this artist the urge for abstraction was stronger: his illustrations are like signs, his line resembles geometric hieroglyphs. In contrast to Segall, CARL RABUS produced many illustrations. His chief works are his etchings to Wieland's *Oberon* and E. T. A. Hoffmann's *Das öde Haus* (*The Empty House*) – (both Munich, Hesperos-Verlag,

1920) – and his lithographs to Alfred Döblin's *Blaubart und Miß Ilsebill* (*Bluebeard and Miss Ilsebill*; Berlin, Hans Heinrich Tillgner Verlag, 1923). Fantastic elements play an important part, combined with symbolist features drawn from the Jugendstil and an Expressionist manner; and a similar emotional content suggests a parallel between those illustrations and Ludwig Meidner. Rabus's skill in adapting his illustrations to a literary text is most apparent in his etchings to E. T. A. Hoffmann, in which there is a romantic feeling that harmonizes well with the Expressionist distortion. Rabus was undoubtedly the most gifted book illustrator among those of the fantastic-daemonic trend. His plates are well suited to the book, for which typefaces were carefully chosen. The fact that no less an artist than Emil Preetorius was responsible for the *mise en page* of the E. T. A. Hoffmann book in itself speaks in Rabus's favour. Rabus later abandoned the Expressionist style; his adoption of alternative artistic approaches was unfortunately severely prejudiced by fashionable compromises.

The social critic among the draughtsmen of the fantastic-daemonic trend was MAGNUS ZELLER. Figures of an almost disembodied slenderness, combined with a secret love of the grotesque, early pervaded the drawings and paintings of this pupil of Corinth. Zeller's style of cubically interlocked groups and flowing, ecstatic figure drawings is already present in twelve lithographs executed in 1917 but not published until 1920 when they appeared under the title *Entrückung und Aufruhr* (*Rapture and Tumult*) in an edition of 105 copies as a portfolio accompanying poems by Arnold Zweig. They were run off at mortal risk on the printing press of the press section of the Commander-in-Chief (East), where Zeller had met Karl Schmidt-Rottluff, Richard Dehmel, Herbert Eulenberg and Arnold Zweig. They are not, indeed, illustrations in the strict sense since Arnold Zweig's poems were written for the lithographs, thus reversing the relationship between writer and artist. The message is clear: the plates promise the downfall of the Wilhelmian empire. Zeller's activist convictions led him into direct political partisanship; with Bernhard Kellermann he belonged to a revolutionary soldiers' council and on 10 November 1918 he was present at the plenary meeting of the Berlin Workers' and Soldiers' Council in the Zirkus Busch. The jewel-like pointed manner, the gothicizing elongated and angular forms which Zeller used with a virtuoso's command, occur in many paintings and drawings of these years. Zeller's style of illustration, influenced as it was by Expressionism, is seen to its purest advantage in his lithographs to Arthur Holitscher's *Ekstatische Geschichten* (*Ecstatic Stories*; Berlin, Hans Heinrich

Tillgner Verlag, 1923) and his etchings to Leonid Andreyev's *Das rote Lachen* (*The Red Laughter*; Berlin, Euphorion-Verlag, 1922).

Zeller's politically committed art, together with that of Felixmüller, which resembles it in also having an ideological bent, stand in direct contrast to the ABSTRACT trend in Expressionist illustration. It is true that it is difficult to imagine contrasts greater than those between Kirchner and Arp or between Kokoschka and Kandinsky, but these differences are primarily artistic and formal. The gulf be-

KANDINSKY

KLEINE WELTEN

ZWÖLF BLATT ORIGINALGRAPHIK

IM PROPYLÄEN·VERLAG ZU BERLIN

Wassily Kandinsky: title-page for his 12-page *Kleine Welten*. Berlin: Propyläen-Verlag, 1922. 450 × 339 mm.

Hans Arp: initial J from the almanac *Der Blaue Reiter*.
Munich: Kurt Wolff Verlag, 1912. 40 × 35 mm.

tween the social critics and the abstract illustrators is widened still further by the political, ideological dimension. These very oppositions demonstrate the contrasts that characterized Expressionism. The abstract trend in illustration proves, of course, to have been one of the ancestors of non-figurative (abstract) art, which has nothing to do with Expressionism. Dadaism was an offshoot of this development and was another movement marked by inconsistencies – suffice it to note in passing that the Dada of Berlin differed from that of other Dadaist centres.

The initiator of the abstract trend in Expressionist illustration was Kandinsky, whose work we shall examine in greater detail in the next chapter. We must at this point mention CURT STOERMER who, with his woodcuts to Baudelaire's *Der Verworfene* (Hanover, Der Zweemann Verlag, 1920), occupies an intermediate position between abstract art and Dadaism, and especially HANS ARP, who of course also played a not unimportant part in Dadaism. In fact, only his first known woodcut, a self-portrait dating from 1912, and some early dry-point etchings dating from *c.* 1924 are Expressionist in the narrower sense. The abstract trend in Arp's work begins with his woodcuts to Huelsenbeck's *Phantastische Gebete* (*Phantastic Prayers*; Zürich, collection dada, 1916), continues in his illustrations to Tristan Tzara's *25 poèmes …* (Zürich, collection dada 1918) and appears in numerous other works, including a volume of his own poems, *der vogel selbdritt* (Berlin, privately printed by Otto von Holten, 1920). The woodcuts are comparable in many ways with Kandinsky's abstract illustrations to *Klänge*. They have lost all concrete point of reference to the text and are pure form. In a certain sense, since the uncontrolled and uncontrollable ego has now finally become absolute – always a possible consequence of Expressionism – they have ceased to be Expressionist and belong elsewhere in the history of art.

It is interesting and odd that it was an outsider not normally concerned with illustration who produced a book, the unusual style of which places it on the dividing line between the Jugendstil and Abstract Expressionism. This was the book-designer, typographer and type-designer F. H. ERNST SCHNEIDLER, whose version of *Atta Troll* by Heine was published by Morawe & Scheffelt in Berlin in 1912 with his own decorations (a cover design, frontispiece, initials, vignettes, full-page and smaller woodcuts, some of them coloured). Some of these designs recall the abstract features of the Vienna Jugendstil, some reflect tendencies that are better described as symbolist and some of the pages are reminiscent of Kandinsky (there is even a 'Blauer Reiter' facing page 104). Schneidler's illustrations probably belong rather to the threshold of Expressionism, yet they are clear proof that from the first many trends, most of them already adumbrated in the Jugendstil, worked together within Expressionist illustration.

The present attempt to make the innumerable currents of Expressionist illustration a little more intelligible, to find the common ground between divisive elements, calls, as I have already said, for understanding and patience: creative powers easily elude the marshalling hand of the historian, and every art-historical system or classification contains within itself the danger of levelling down the original, the true personality to the uniformity of a line of development. This has not been my intention. I have endeavoured, rather, to show that Expressionist illustration was an amalgam of widely differing styles.

Such an attempt would be incomplete without a mention, however brief, of those artists who merely adopted the Expressionist formal vocabulary in a more or less epigonal and eclectic way; and those who exploited Expressionism commercially, treating it as a fashion; and finally there were artists who, with no mind to initiate new forms, experimented briefly with those of Expressionism. A flickering reflection of Expressionism can be observed in certain works by Ottomar Starke, Hugo Steiner-Prag, Ernst Stern, Karl Rössing, Georg Walter Rößner and many others, even in some of Lovis Corinth's illustrations.

Among the artists who followed the Expressionist illustrators temporarily as their less distinguished heirs were Rudolf Schlichter, Bruno Krauskopf, Will Wanzer, Josef Weisz, Wilhelm Plünnecke, Carl Gunschmann, Georg Alexander Mathey and Felix Meseck. One of the most active was JOSEF EBERZ, who was greatly impressed by Grünewald and by Macke and Marc. From 1918 onwards he decorated numerous books and was partly responsible for the fact that Expressionism in illustration – admittedly much watered down – began to enjoy general favour. By 1920 at the latest Expressionism had gained public recognition and even the less venturesome museums now introduced Expressionist works into their sacrosanct galleries. By this time any artist who was still working in the Expressionist manner in fact no longer needed to fear that he was running a risk. So, as Paul Westheim wrote in *Das Kunstblatt* in 1922, things had to put up with being 'dislocated, made angular and hard-edged. Colours cry shrilly to one another. Surfaces are obscured by emotion.'[2] The number of artists who were drawn in this way into the wake of an Expressionism that had long passed its peak, or rather who plunged in so as to share, if only belatedly, in the bonanza is extraordinarily large. The bibliography will undoubtedly omit some of these, and I prefer not to list names here. Basically their 'Expressionism' derived not from any inner creative compulsion but from a time-serving desire for solidarity.

1 W. Hausenstein, 'Max Unold', in *Junge Kunst*, vol. 23, Leipzig, 1921, p. 8.
2 Vol. VI, 1922, p. 445.

III. The masters of Expressionism as illustrators

Kokoschka – Artists of Die Brücke: Heckel, Kirchner, Pechstein, Schmidt-Rottluff – Kandinsky – Klee – Beckmann – Meidner – Occasional works with illustrations.

The masters of German Expressionism were closely bound up with literature and with writers, just as the writers were on friendly terms with the artists. They met one another in studios, at readings, in the homes of patrons, in famous cafés, and they appeared in the same avant-garde journals.

Oskar Kokoschka: drawing for his drama *Mörder, Hoffnung der Frauen*, published in the weekly *Der Sturm* (No. 24), 11 August 1910. 250×190 mm. [186]

There were shared experiences and ideas, as well as a uniting sense of impending doom. It was natural for the writers to be stimulated by the images of their painter friends and for the painters to draw inspiration from the writings. Not all of these inspirations were expressed as illustrations to literary texts, yet some of the works of Expressionist writers of such importance as Alfred Döblin, Kasimir Edschmid, Albert Ehrenstein and Georg Heym (in 1924) were indeed illustrated.

The leading masters of Expressionist painting and graphic art contributed in greatly differing degrees to the art of illustration. No books exist with illustrations by Emil Nolde, Otto Mueller,[1] Franz Marc or August Macke, although, as I shall show, Marc was very much interested in illustration. Oskar Kokoschka and Ernst Ludwig Kirchner were the only ones who took seriously and at all regularly to literary illustration, the others grasped at the opportunities that came their way or at whatever happened to coincide with their own artistic urges. Kokoschka illustrated the largest number of books; then came Max Beckmann and Ludwig Meidner, Kirchner and Pechstein, Klee, Schmidt-Rottluff, Heckel and Kandinsky. Kokoschka can also claim the distinction of having published the first Expressionist illustration, though the credit for having produced the first book to have been designed as a whole must go to Kandinsky. The most complete and compelling achievement of Expressionist art in the sphere of the book was, however, the work of Ernst Ludwig Kirchner.

Kokoschka

Oskar Kokoschka was never over-sensitive in his approach to his themes: he seized them with both hands. He used them as a means of expressing his own, often sombre, thoughts and feelings, feelings that were impossible or difficult to put into words. He faced his text in an independent spirit. He rarely submitted subserviently to the writer's word; the books and portfolios are usually pieces of pure Kokoschka, even when the texts are from the pens of authors as eminent as Karl Kraus or Albert Ehrenstein. It is unwise, therefore, to insist upon the term illustration in connection with Kokoschka and other Expressionist artists. He neither explained the text nor decorated it with images: this painter presented his own vision of the world. Kokoschka stemmed from the Vienna Jugendstil, in particular from Gustav Klimt, to whom he respectfully dedicated his first book, *Die träumenden Knaben* (*The Dreaming Youths*; Vienna, 1908).

Most, however, of Oskar Kokoschka's illustrations – eleven out of seventeen – belong to the various stages of his Expressionist phase. His Expressionist drawings to literary texts begin in 1910 with the plates to *Mörder, Hoffnung der Frauen* (*Murderer, the Hope of Women*) and continue through to the illustrations to Victor Dirsztay's novel *Der Unentrinnbare* (*The one from whom you cannot escape*; 1923). Even in the two etchings to scenes from his brother Bohuslav's *Geh, mach die Tür zu, es zieht* (*Go and shut the Door, there's a Draught*; 1926) there remains a reflection of an Expressionist stylistic intent.

Kokoschka wrote his drama *Mörder, Hoffnung der Frauen* in 1907 when he was twenty-three years old and under the influence of the psychoanalytical discoveries of Sigmund Freud, which, rephrased in easy catchwords about the science of dreams and day-dreams, was occupying the minds of the Viennese intelligentsia; to this was added his experience of Van Gogh and probably also emotional strain at that time. The drama was the first in a series of literary works which continued until 1918 and which are generally held to place Kokoschka among the creators of Expressionist drama. In his *Mörder, Hoffnung der Frauen, Der brennende Dornbusch* (*The Burning Bush*), *Der gefesselte Kolumbus* (*Columbus bound*) and *Orpheus und Eurydike* the logical causality of language has been shattered; everywhere is the mystical ecstasy of cries and stammerings, passions, presentiments and hopes burst from the scourged soul of a man who sees his relationship with woman magnified to the proportions of a cosmic problem. This transposition of the most private emotions into a problem involving mankind is itself typically Expressionist: the individual destiny, the uncharted country of the most intimate psychic states are made public. Kokoschka's self-portraits and the appearance of his own features in many of his drawings show clearly enough that his concern was with his own ego. In this respect, too, Kokoschka's drawings to his own writings are extremely revealing. As early as 1917 Paul Kornfeld wrote in the programme notes to the performance of the dramas *Mörder, Hoffnung der Frauen, Hiob* (*Job*) and *Der brennende Dornbusch*, produced by Kokoschka himself in the Albert-Theater, Dresden (3 June 1917): 'A drama by Kokoschka is but a variation on his paintings, and conversely. The tone and melody, rhythm and gesture of his words are parallel to those of his

paintings.' *Mörder, Hoffnung der Frauen* was first performed in Vienna in 1908, the year that saw the publication – probably prior to the production – of the drawings to the piece.

The illustrations that were published with the drama in 1910 in Walden's *Der Sturm* – 'upon which half the subscribers cancelled their order for the journal'[2] – are some of the most important and earliest formulations of Expressionist draughtsmanship; they express a man-and-woman problem that has become a terror. 'Mein Auge sammelt der Männer Frohlocken / Ihre stammelnde Lust kriecht wie eine Bestie um mich' (My eye treasures up the exultation of men. / Their stammering lust creeps like a beast round me) and 'Ich will dich nicht leben lassen. Du! / Du schwächst mich – / Ich töte dich – du fesselst mich! Dich fing ich ein – und du hältst mich!' ('I will not let thee live. Thou! / Thou enfeeblest me – / I kill thee – thou fetterest me! / I captured thee – and thou holdest me!'). These are the wild, anguished emotions of the young Kokoschka and they became both word and image. They were in Hans Kaufmann's opinion 'not viable as a symbiosis of painting and drama',[3] yet as a combination of the printed word and the draughtsman's image they are an early and important document of the Expressionist art of illustration. The power of the fragmented type area, the bunches of crying words, are matched by the broken, sharply contoured, angular linear script, the character of which, in its almost chaotic dissonance, undermined the old tradition of drawing and helped to lay the foundations of a new linear style. The passion of the artist's emotions, moods and experiences is felt in every line. A further progression of these drawings occurs in Kokoschka's portraits of intellectuals of the year 1910 published in *Der Sturm*. The style is the same, disciplined and mature now, but now, as before, expressive of inner excitement and, though these drawings never cease to be portraits, they seek to expose the soul of the artist's own ego in the features of others.

All Kokoschka's later illustrations are softer in appearance than the drawings to *Mörder, Hoffnung der Frauen*, although similar structures and principles of composition continue to appear for a few more years. The gentler language of the later illustrations stems from the means: the plates to *Mörder, Hoffnung der Frauen* were drawn in ink with pen and brush, whereas most of the later ones were done with chalk on transfer paper. The different material produces a painterly tone which is outside the scope of ink drawings. Even the plates to Ehrenstein's *Tubutsch* (executed 1911, published 1912) are softer, for the artist used broader brushes and tinted a few of the drawings with watercolour. A new phase in Kokoschka's painting began

Oskar Kokoschka: *O Ewigkeit – Du Donnerwort*, title-page of a book containing text of the cantata by Johann Sebastian Bach and eleven lithographs. Berlin: Fritz Gurlitt, 1918. (The lithographs first appeared in portfolio in 1914; both editions were limited to 125 copies.) 546 × 420 mm. [189]

in 1911 and appears in these drawings too: in the paintings the contour evaporates, colour takes on an iridescent effect, and prismatic structures form the picture space. Indeed, in the drawings to *Tubutsch* the contour also recedes and there are prismatic structures in the linear framework. *Tubutsch*, by Albert Ehrenstein, is not a great work; it is by a writer whose main importance is as a lyric poet and is a story of endless reflections, in which the hero, Karl Tubutsch, meditates on his life, watching it pass by in solitude, empty and isolated; weakness of will alone prevents

him from making an end of such an existence. Kokoschka takes up Tubutsch's meditations and these sheets become his own questions about the meaning of life.

Kokoschka's eight lithographs to Karl Kraus's essay *Die chinesische Mauer* (*The Great Wall of China*) drawn in 1913 – the year of his great journey with Alma Mahler to Italy, where the work of Tintoretto affected him profoundly – are concerned with the same problems. These plates, that gave the 1914 edition in book form its distinctive appearance, proclaim as before the power of Eros, of Eros in peril; but the threat is no longer the uncertainty of the conflict between man and woman, it is now the chaos of war, terrifying to the imagination for it means an end and death. The eavesdropper is Death; holding in his right hand a flaming weapon, he attacks the lovers in their secret place. The end is prophesied in the first sheet, 'Ein Mord ist geschehen' ('A Murder has been Committed'). The message of these works is inherent in their structure: concentrated, prismatically beamed and cubically fractured, these drawings proclaim the destruction of bourgeois philosophy.

Another important series of illustrations appeared in 1914, before the outbreak of war. These were the eleven lithographs to the words of one of Johann Sebastian Bach's cantatas *O Ewigkeit – Du Donnerwort, so spanne meine Glieder aus* (*Eternity, thou fearful word . . .*). They were published by Fritz Gurlitt in 1914 in portfolio, and by the same press in 1918 in the series 'Die Neuen Bilderbücher'. The musicologist Paul Bekker pointed out as early as 1917 in Westheim's *Das Kunstblatt* that the lithographs 'had little more than the title in common with Bach's cantata.'[4] Although Kokoschka had become acquainted with this cantata through a piano recital by his friend Leo Kestenberg, his intention from the first was to draw images to the text, not to interpret the music. And here again Kokoschka allowed himself to be guided more by the underlying states of mind – despair, fear, hope – than by individual passages in the text. 'O heavy path to the final struggle and conflict' – such was Kokoschka's theme in a double sense: the bewildering, disconcerting and deeply affecting experience of womankind in the person of Alma Mahler and – again – the presentiment of a danger, erotic as well as social. So it is small wonder that the figure of the man continually assumes Kokoschka's features while that of the woman often calls Alma Mahler's appearance to mind.

There is a certain Faust-like element in the apocalyptic character of Kokoschka's lithographs to Bach's cantata: the ego is interrogated and another ego, a 'counter-ego', replies.[5] The Faust principle can be seen in other series of illustrations, but it is most prominent in the Bach cantata: the artist, reflecting his own spiritual situation, searches unremittingly for an intelligible and valid answer. However, his 'awareness of the vision is no condition in which to recognize or understand things, it is a state of that awareness by which it experiences itself'.[6] Kokoschka's Expressionist position ist once more apparent in *Von der Natur der Gesichte* (*Of the Nature of Visions*), although in the meanwhile his style had moved far away from that of the drawings to *Mörder, Hoffnung der Frauen*. Certainly the angular tectonics of many of the drawings remain as an external mark of his Expressionist style, and the clusters of lines, sometimes laid criss-cross one above the other, suggest an impression of menace, but the tone is ultimately softer, its character painterly. More importantly, in the lithographs vital and powerful curves thrust forward and bring to mind that Baroque tendency in Kokoschka that is so often referred to in the literature of art. It was the artist's powerful, life-loving 'Austrian' allegiance that gradually calmed his Expressionist turbulence and enabled him to find a way out of Expressionism. This trend in Kokoschka's drawing had been foreshadowed as early as 1913 in the lithographs to *Der gefesselte Kolumbus*, published, also by Gurlitt, in 1916. From the point of view of the history of Kokoschka's development these lithographs occupy a position midway between the Expressionist exaltation of the plates to Kraus's *Die chinesische Mauer* and the more disciplined expression of the Bach cantata. They foreshadow the transition, although the text, as we know, follows immediately upon *Die träumenden Knaben* and was, indeed, conceived as its sequel. In these works again we find Kokoschka's love of self-portraiture in his drawings of the man, and Alma Mahler's face appears as before. An Expressionist turmoil – revealed in emotive clusters of lines: ('Mann und Skelett' 'Man and Skeleton'), 'Der Weg ins Grab' ('The Way to the Grave') – alternates with lyrical, almost Impressionist moods – 'Das Paar im Kerzenlicht' ('Couple by Candlelight'); and in a few sheets – 'Der Apfel des Paradieses' ('The Apple of Paradise'), 'Das Gesicht des Weibes' ('The Face of Woman') and 'Die reine Gestalt' ('The Pure Form') – a more balanced and more harmonious linear script emerges. This product of a radical stylistic change helped to prepare the way for the controlled style that within a few years was to become an increasingly frequent characteristic of the artist's work as a draughtsman. This refined language continued in *Hiob* (1917) in a way that explains Carl Georg Heise's belief that 'later on we shall be able to situate Kokoschka much more securely in the final phase of Impressionism'.[7]

Erich Heckel: woodcut title-page to *Die Ballade vom Zuchthaus zu Reading* (*The Ballad of Reading Gaol*) by Oscar Wilde, 1907 (published 1963 in book form in an edition of 600 copies by Ernest Rathenau, New York). 294 × 210 mm. [113]

In Dirsztay's *Der Unentrinnbare*, a late salute from Kokoschka to his Expressionist phase, which appeared in 1923, the illustrations again combine enormous vitality with intensity, and the expansive manner, though moderated, is still there. The drawings depend upon linear contours, are toneless and have no inner lines. With these drawings Kokoschka bids his final farewell to Expressionism, although the passion that brought him into the movement persists.

Heckel

Erich Heckel was one of the leading artists of Die Brücke.

Few of his works have a literary theme; among those that have are a woodcut of 1905 to Psalm 90, and *Roquairol*, a romantic portrait dating from 1917 that exists both as a woodcut and as a painting in tempera and is based on Jean Paul's novel *Der Titan*. His illustrations to Dostoyevsky's *Der Idiot* (*The Idiot*; 1912) and *Die Brüder Karamasoff* (*The Brothers Karamasov*; 1913) enjoyed a wider circulation and are more familiar to the public; of these, a woodcut and a lithograph appeared, together with sheets by Vlatislav Hofmann, Otto Gleichmann, Carl Hofer, Paul Holz, Richard Janthur, Walther Lomnitz, Fritz Schaefler and Alfred Kubin in an issue of the periodical *Die Schaffenden* (vol. 2, portfolio 2, 1919/20) devoted to Dostoyevsky. Both pieces are executed in the gothicizing, angular and jagged style that had been Heckel's characteristic manner since 1910. A typical example is the woodcut inspired by the final scene of *The Idiot*, for which the artist had been seeking a pictorial image since 1912. Forms collide and interpenetrate prismatically to produce an impression of anguish and menace.

The only work complete with text and plates with which Erich Heckel enriched the field of literary illustration was, however, executed much earlier, in the year 1907. This was the woodcut title and eleven woodcut plates to Oscar Wilde's *Ballade vom Zuchthaus zu Reading* (*Ballad of Reading Gaol*). These plates are the incunabulae of Expressionist woodcut illustration; they stand at the very threshold of Expressionist book illustration. No Expressionist illustration dating from before Heckel's woodcuts is known. However, the woodcuts were not published in book form with Wilde's text during the Expressionist period. Heckel did, of course, expect them to be published, but he himself never offered them to a publisher. Karl Schmidt-Rottluff showed them to Harry Graf Kessler, but Kessler declined to publish them.[8] So the blocks lay unused until 1944, when they were destroyed in an air-raid on Berlin. It is both tragic and curious that these, of all the woodcuts, were first published in the last Expressionist illustrated book. This was issued in an edition limited to six hundred numbered copies in New York in 1963 by Ernest Rathenau (formerly of the Euphorion Verlag, Berlin) as a mark of homage to the artist and in memory of the age of German Expressionism.

In a letter to Robert Ross of the 8 October 1897 Oscar Wilde drew his friend's attention to the stylistic problems of his poem: it 'suffers under the difficulty of a divided aim in style. Some is realistic, some is romantic ...'[9] Using as his point of departure his own shattering experiences in prison, the poet describes the last hours of a man condemned to death. Heckel was himself inclined to introspective romanticism: his woodcuts intensify the romantic feeling of the writing and create a sombre atmosphere.

The only concrete portrait is in fact that of the imaginary prisoner, who had been found with a dead woman:

Er schlug die Frau, die er geliebt,
In ihrem Bette tot.

('The poor dead woman whom he loved / And murdered in her bed.')

Heckel's woodcut portrays the murderer's cold, hard features and the 'cricket cap on his head' as described by the poet. Except for the two other portraits, the remaining plates suggest a melancholy atmosphere that mounts to frenzy; they do not illustrate specific passages of text. The underlying note struck by the woodcuts is that of fear.

Fear appears in many guises: in the terrifying emptiness that surrounds the prisoner, in his horrified fantasies of death, in oppressive dream-images that visit him by day and night, until at last the end brings appeasement and fear is transfigured by the crucified Christ: the prisoner is comforted and his agony and martyrdom are over. Thus Heckel's images illustrate the emotions and moods and the oppressive tone of the ballad, and all incidentals are omitted.

The language of these woodcuts is impressive. We may assume that Heckel was influenced by Edvard Munch; certainly his inspiration is apparent in some of the plates. Munch's new graphic style had made its first appearance between 1898 and 1903: he used the wood grain as a compositional means in addition to the hollows made by the gouge, the marks of which slightly soften the contrast between black and white. Earlier, in Paris, Munch had seen woodcuts by Paul Gauguin who, following Millet, had revived the plane-surface technique as a means of independent artistic expression. Thus ideas sprang from Gauguin and Munch, were borrowed and worked up in the woodcuts of the artists of Die Brücke and a graphic idiom was created such as had never before existed in the history of art. Heckel's part in this development was an influential one.

His woodcuts to Wilde's poem do not yet have the sharp-edged lines and crystal-clear surfaces that set whites within angular compartments against deep black surfaces. The black-and-white structure of these plates is tattered and stringy in appearance. The 'outlines flutter in uncertain fringes and spikes', remarked Gustav Schiefler, who also wrote of the 'painterly style of the woodcut'[10] in Heckel's hands. The artist did not use the style again. Stylistically and as illustrations his woodcuts to Wilde's *Ballad of Reading Gaol* remained unique.

Kirchner

Recognition came late to Ernst Ludwig Kirchner. Today he is considered the most important of the artists of Die Brücke; he was also more closely concerned than any of them with literature and the art of the book. He continued to make plans for illustrations right to the end of his life – he committed suicide in 1938. In 1933 he produced sheets to *Tausendundeine Nacht* (*The Arabian Nights*), in 1935 he began to make drawings for Goethe's *Wilhelm Meister*, in 1937 he thought of illustrating *Faust*, *Part II*, and Whitman's *Leaves of Grass* excited his interest as a draughtsman.

Ernst Ludwig Kirchner: colour woodcuts to *Peter Schlemihls wundersame Geschichte*, 1915/16. Reproduced from the rare prints from the woodcut illustrations in the Print Room of the Öffentliche Kunstsammlungen, Basle. [172]

39

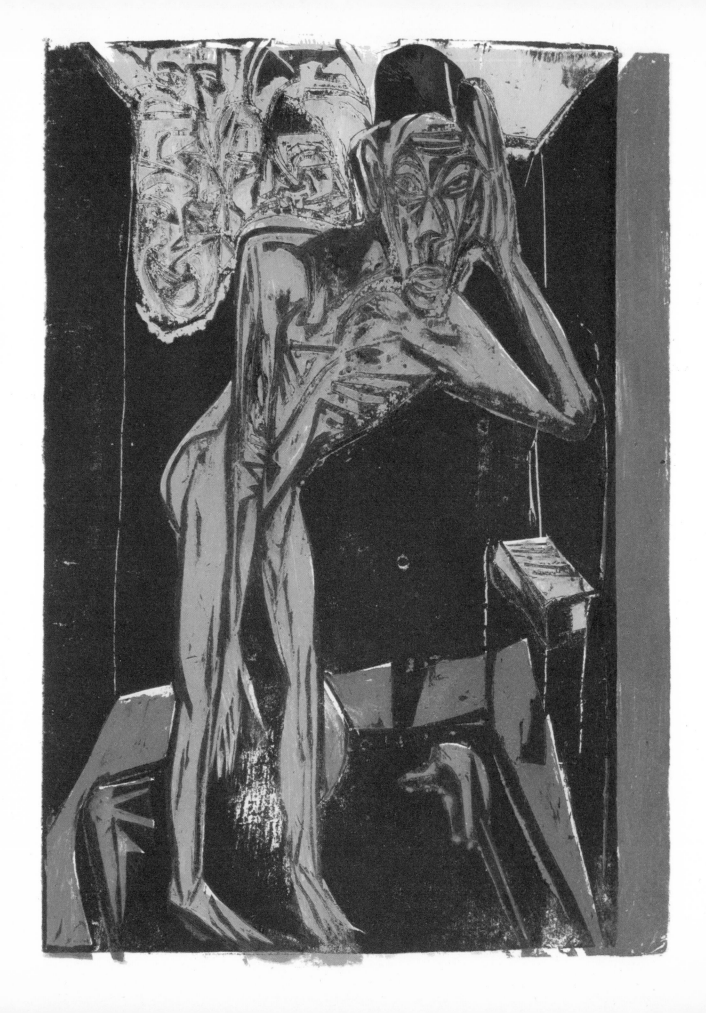

We find ten graphic works dating from Kirchner's Expressionist period, most of them suites of prints that relate to literary themes. They include works by Petrarch, Chamisso, Boßhart, Heym, Döblin and Zola. But only three sets of illustrations were published in book form. The five plates to *Sakuntala*, an oriental fairy-tale, are among Kirchner's earliest lithographs and his earliest illustrations. The lithographs are composed in a painterly brush writing. Separate linear elements combine with self-contained surfaces coloured in extremely finely graduated tones of grey. Kirchner was already employing his technique of etching on the stone to give slacker edges to his lines. He followed this innovation with the practice of colour printing from one stone. His colour lithographs to Zola's *La Bête humaine* (1913/14), however, were still printed from two stones.

Kirchner's first illustrated opuscule appeared in November 1913; it was one of the series of 'Lyrische Flugblätter' published by Alfred Richard Meyer, and contained Alfred Döblin's novella *Das Stiftsfräulein und der Tod* (*The Canoness and Death*). Kirchner cut a title and four full-page plates. The illustrations are pictorial repetitions of characteristic incidents in the story. Kirchner adds nothing. Yet already the relationship of these woodcuts to the text has ceased to be one of simple subservience, for they could well exist as free prints: they are conceived in visual terms. The woodcut title is of particular interest since the image and the woodcut lettering together form that unity which distinguishes Kirchner's work. It is a model for future work. Kirchner referred repeatedly to the unity of image and letterpress. The woodcut, 'the most graphic of all graphic techniques', is still fairly austere in his illustrations to Döblin's novella, cutting of surface and of contour meet without the wealth of interior cutting which becomes typical in Kirchner's later work. This appears subsequently, and at once in great profusion, in the seven colour woodcuts to Adelbert von Chamisso's fantastic novella *Peter Schlemihl* (1915), which appeared only as a free suite. Kirchner wrote in a letter of 27 July 1919 to Gustav Schiefler: 'The story of Schlemihl, when stripped of all romantic embellishment, is in fact the life history of the persecution-maniac, that is, of the man who is jolted by some event into an awareness of his measureless insignificance, but at the same time recognizes the ways in which the world in general blinds itself to this knowledge.'[11] Explanations of the individual plates follow. It is obvious that Kirchner has used the Schlemihl material as a means of purging himself of the 'shattering experience of his military service'.[12] To this extent the colour woodcuts are primarily a representation of his own

fate and only secondarily illustrations of the literary text. The plates, which illustrate pivotal points in the text, are entitled: 'Der Verkauf des Schattens' ('The Sale of the Shadow'); 'Die Geliebte' ('The Beloved'); 'Kämpfe' ('Conflicts'); 'Schlemihl in der Einsamkeit des Zimmers' ('Schlemihl in the Solitude of his Room'); 'Begegnung Schlemihls mit dem grauen Männlein auf der Landstraße' ('Schlemihl's Encounter with the Little Grey Man on the Highway'); and 'Schlemihls Begegnung mit dem Schatten' ('Schlemihl's Encounter with the Shadow'). In these colour woodcuts Kirchner develops a method that he had seen in Edvard Munch's work: leaving aside the primary concrete pictorial idea, the woodcut emerges as a pure composition of forms and colours. The effect was achieved by printing several colour blocks one on top of the other without using a key block. These woodcuts are therefore not coloured prints. The colours are applied as colour shapes, as elements of construction: they are not used to tint pre-existing forms. The distinction is crucial: colour is not added to a block that prints black and white, but is itself conceived as a cut shape and is printed with other colour shapes one on top of the other. Technically, too, with *Schlemihl* Kirchner has discovered the specifically Expressionist colour woodcut, a development that added much to the history of print-making in general. The process made it possible to take into account the optically sovereign effect of different forms, independently of the object represented.

Kirchner's woodcuts to *Peter Schlemihl* would have been almost unthinkable in their existing form – their hounded and hunted character expressing a sense of fear – without his experience in Berlin. They are an expression in graphic terms of the fusion of an optically perceptible object with the freest invention. Thus, in the plate 'Schlemihl's Encounter with the Shadow', Schlemihl hurries along with his cloak streaming behind him and is abruptly confronted by the cold black of the shadow – a truly fantastic situation. Kirchner printed in five colours: black, blue, green, yellow and red. The black block provides the dramatic element in spikes, splinters and clusters of lines that penetrate into the yellow or green. The colours too suggest excitation: man is splintered apart in fragmented form. But form does not break up or disintegrate: under the master's hand it becomes as firm as a rock, with each single element dovetailed into the surface. With Kirchner's illustrations to *Peter Schlemihl* the art of the colour woodcut reached a peak of excellence never before achieved.

Two more suites of prints and an illustrated book separated this major work of Expressionist woodcut art from Kirchner's most brilliant piece of book design, Heym's

Umbra vitae. The prints illustrate *Der Triumph der Liebe* (*The Triumph of Love*), after Petrarch, and *Absalom*, based on the story in the Old Testament; the illustrated book is Jakob Boßhart's volume of stories *Neben der Heerstraße* (*Near the Heerstraße*).

Both suites date from 1918 and Kirchner is again concerned with his own experience. The Petrarch suite deals with relations between the sexes: seeking, finding, flowering, renunciation. In *Absalom* the artist grapples with the problem of the generations, the rift between youth and age,

Ernst Ludwig Kirchner:
one of forty-seven woodcuts to *Umbra vitae* by Georg Heym.
Leipzig: Kurt Wolff Verlag, 1924. Edition limited to 510 copies.
147 × 91 mm. [175]

situating it within the descriptive context of the story of David and his son Absalom. Kirchner's woodcuts to Boßhart's impressions of Swiss village life may simply have sprung from his friendship with the writer from 1922 onwards. They belong to a style in which horizontals and verticals in the surface plane are stressed, thus bringing a more static repose to his graphic art.

Kirchner's major work in the realm of book design is *Umbra vitae*, a collection of poems by Georg Heym published with forty-seven woodcuts by Kurt Wolff in 1924. The first plates were not part of the commission; but Kirchner did them, some as early as 1919, and most at the beginning of 1922,[13] in idle moments for his own enjoyment. The idea for the book itself reached the publisher from another source. In January 1922 Hans Mardersteig, advisor to the publisher in visual art and a bibliophile, wrote to his friend Kurt Wolff about a book which Kirchner had illustrated. He told him that Kirchner had been illustrating Heym's *Umbra vitae* for years, 'taking the old edition and inserting a little woodcut below each of the poems, none of which fills the page, so that the part of the type area that was blank is now filled, up to the page-number. K. would visualize a new edition as appearing in the same format, printed in the same type, the only difference being that the little woodcuts would be placed between the title and the opening stanza of each poem. Each poem would then fill the whole type area. I would most strongly advise you to bring out a new edition of the little volume with the woodcuts.'[14] Kurt Wolff agreed immediately. In a letter of 2 March 1922 he was already considering how to put the plan into practice, despite the fact that 'in the purely bookselling sense' the choice of this text was not particularly happy: '*Umbra vitae* is a very difficult book with a small readership; during the 10 years since Heym's death we have sold – believe it or not – 1,000 copies ...'[15] Furthermore, Heym's collected works had just appeared in an edition of 3,000 copies. Nevertheless Wolff accepted the project. But as a businessman he calculated that sales would be small, 'the buyers of this book will be the devotees of Kirchner's graphic art'. He decided in the first instance to print an edition of 550 copies.[16] On 8 January 1923 Kirchner received the final form of the contract from the press.[17]

To Kirchner the poems seemed to hold the 'substance of life'. In a letter to Curt Valentin he imagines Heym as a sort of follower of Walt Whitman: 'Georg Heym ..., a Whitman transposed into the German psyche who saw and wrote prophetically about the recent decades of our era'.[18] Kirchner came to Heym's poetry because he found ideas and images in it that echoed his own imaginings. He made forty-seven woodcuts to the poems; forming a unity with the text, most are complete illustrations though some are only pictorial borders. The illustrations follow the text exactly. Such fidelity to the text naturally brings its problems: Heym's poetical idiom is itself strong in imagery and dominated by symbols. An illustrator, by repeating them in visual form, runs the risk of merely weakening the poet's sequences of images. Kirchner avoided this danger by transposing the atmospheric quality of the text into a suitable visual equivalent. In this way poet and artist met on the same level. Kirchner referred to passages in the text, seeking a point in the subject-matter of the poem out of which he could evoke the atmosphere. The poem 'Im Garten der Irren' ('In the garden of the insane') opens with the verse:

Am roten Teiche stehen viele Schatten
Bei dünner Bäume schwächlichen Gesichten,
In Stille fort. Nur selten daß sich einer
Herunter zu dem trüben Wasser bücket.

('At the red pond many shadows stand by the weakly faces of thin trees, in continuing silence. Only rarely does one stoop down to the muddy water'.)

Kirchner shows the shadows on the right, figures with long staffs in their hands; the foremost figure stoops down to the water. Later in the poem comes the verse:

Der Strom ist weit hinab im blanken Scheine
Bei Erlen und den krumm gebornen Weiden.
Und wer mit leichtem Kahn ihn überbrücket,
Er wird im Licht die gelben Blumen pflücken.

('The stream is far down in the white gleam by alders and the crookedly grown willows. And whoever bridges it in a light skiff will pick the yellow flowers in the light.')

So the artist in his woodcut shows the stream as a diagonal separating the shadow-figures from the trees and the yellow flowers. It is a landscape plate of great density showing the lines and rings of force round the sun, the many-spiked, splintered forms of the plants and the jagged, angular shadow-figures. This woodcut could pass at any time for an autonomous work, independent of a text, yet its importance as an illustration lies in the very fact that it takes up the subject and mood intended by the poet and translates them into the woodcut's own idiom. Thus the merit of the illustration is twofold: it is committed and closely follows the text, and it is visually autonomous. The artist, therefore, is in no way subservient to the poet, instead he joins forces with him to assert their singleness of purpose. This approach becomes typical of Kirchner.

In these illustrations the artist sometimes returns to earlier, indeed abandoned, stylistic traits – for example in the woodcut to the poem 'Die Städte' ('Cities') where the figures of women bear a certain resemblance to the types in his Berlin paintings and prints. The woodcut to the poem 'Der Krieg' ('War'), the culmination of Heym's visions of cata-

DER GARTEN DER IRREN

Am roten Teiche stehen viele Schatten
Bei dünner Bäume schwächlichen Gesichten,
In Stille fort. Nur selten daß sich einer
Herunter zu dem trüben Wasser bücket.

Und manche gehn in die entleerten Hecken
In kühlen Gängen, die schon voller Lichter,
Und schleifen mit den Füßen in dem Laube
Und sitzen wieder sanft in den Verstecken.

Der Strom ist weit hinab im blanken Scheine
Bei Erlen und den krumm gebornen Weiden.
Und wer mit leichtem Kahn ihn überbrücket,
Er wird im Licht die gelben Blumen pflücken.

Ernst Ludwig Kirchner:
page from *Umbra vitae* by Georg Heym.
The book was designed entirely by Kirchner. Type-face:
Grotesque bold. 230 × 157 mm. [175]

strophe, is also most compelling. The poet, who was accidentally drowned in 1912 while skating on the Havel, missed the horrors of the First World War, but his illustrator, working in 1924, had lived through them. He respected Heym's symbolic language and avoided the representation of concrete scenes. War for him is a frightful head with shrieking jaws agape; everything whirls furiously round it, figures break away as though touched by an invisible, deadly breath. For Kirchner war is clearly the most terrible, the most incomprehensible disaster that can befall mankind. War is total chaos. These illustrations again are self-confessions. Ernst Ludwig Kirchner's hatred of war and of the metropolis is there for all to see.

Kirchner was uniquely fortunate in being able to design the whole book. Not only did he produce the illustrations, he also chose the paper and specified the Grotesque bold sans serif typeface 'in which the small letters are more than half the height of the large ones'[19] and thus emphasize the vertical aspect of the type matter; he indicated how the type matter should be arranged, designed the frontispiece, the endpapers and the binding. He also contributed hand-lettering, in relation to which the woodcuts have none of the quality of marginal decoration; instead, lettering and image are cut together, the page of the book is an integrated composition of image and lettering, entirely in the spirit – though not in the style or technique – of the early illuminated book. Here is an example of the acute awareness of tradition that marks Kirchner's Expressionist book design.

One of Kirchner's wishes as a book designer was that the pictorial blocks should be printed simultaneously with the type matter. He wrote to his publisher: 'The blocks must be *inserted into the type matter* and printed *simultaneously* with it. This is *very important* as it is the *only way* of integrating type matter and illustration.'[20] This particular requirement, however, caused technical difficulties in printing, though these were overcome in the end. Kirchner did the basic typographic design for the book: he designed the type area, in which each line of text was to be centred because this would produce 'a direct graphic image of the verse rhythm'[21] and illustration and type panel would be firmly integrated. By comparison with the typographical experiments of the Futurists and Dadaists, long familiar by 1923, Kirchner's arrangement of the type panel appears almost conservative. In fact as a book designer the Expressionist Kirchner adheres to classical values. The modernity lies in the undoubted overall perfection with which the artistic idea was expressed. Finally Kirchner was anxious that there should be a precise interval between the image

and the text; and he was concerned about the colour of the ink, which he imagined not as pure black but as a 'dark tone of sepia, shading into black'.[22] He later instructed the printer not to print too heavily or too darkly.[23]

As his correspondence with Kurt Wolff shows, Kirchner was anything but an easy-going book-designer. He demanded the highest standards and was inflexible in his artistic principles.

On 4 June 1924 Kurt Wolff sent Hans Mardersteig the first copy of the book, writing that he had not believed that it would ever be finished.[24] As the letter shows, the publisher had at that time no idea how fine the book was. The edition as finally printed consisted of 510 copies. Production costs were extremely high and sales were small. A year and a half after publication, on 13 December 1926, Wolff wrote to Mardersteig that the firm would not make money on the book 'buk I would like at least to see the possibility of recovering the capital that has been invested – but so far there is no prospect of doing so'.[25] One must conclude from the small sales of the book that neither Kirchner's stature nor the achievement of Expressionist art in the field of book had been recognized by the beginning of the 1920s. Curt Glaser's words sounded like a voice in the wilderness; he wrote that Kirchner's work was 'the first piece of book design ... to reflect the spirit of our time'.[26] This is undoubtedly an exaggeration: the book certainly does not express the spirit of a whole period. It is nevertheless clear that there were some contemporaries who thought highly of this book.

The importance of *Umbra vitae* in the history of book design and book illustration is so widely recognized today that it is discussed in the simplest manuals on the art of the book.

Pechstein

The popularization of the Die Brücke style began with Max Pechstein. Until 1920 Pechstein was looked upon as the most important of the Expressionist artists and in 1912 was the subject of the first monograph,[27] but criticism of his work increased during the following decades. The robust, exuberant vitality[28] that had united him with the artists of Die Brücke had for some time been spending itself in mere decoration. This decorative character, described by Paul Ferdinand Schmidt as the 'academicizing of the original Brücke style',[29] was in itself a crucial aid to the immediate intelligibility of his art, but unfortunately it entered his work at the expense of its substance, causing a loss of artistic density. The suite of woodcuts *Vater Unser* (*Our Father*) issued in 1921 by the Propyläen-Verlag in Berlin, demonstrates this conflict between Expressionist principles of style and decorative superficiality. The twelve plates are straightforward illustrations of the Lord's Prayer and the artist has added Expressionist formal elements for their decorative effect alone. The Expressionist style does not arise out of an inner urge for creative analysis but is laid on, superimposed on the material. It is a process that innumerable nominal members of the Expressionist movement – most of them pseudo-Expressionists – worked to death.

Pechstein produced his first graphic works in 1906; these were woodcuts. He did little work for books. A few of his designs were used as cover decorations. He was a leading member of the November Group[30] and as such produced effective decorations for the jackets of the important political pamphlets (both 1919) *An alle Künstler!* (*To all Artists*) and *Aufruf zum Sozialismus* (*Call for Socialism*).

Pechstein illustrated four literary texts, two in the journal *Marsyas*: Sternheim's *Heidenstam* and Stehr's *Schatten* (*Shadows*). As graphic sheets they are more austere and more stylized than his two book illustrations, and fortunately the decorative element is absent. The book illustrations

Max Pechstein: title-page and woodcut to *Das Vaterunser* ('The Lord's Prayer'). Berlin: Propyläen-Verlag, 1921. Twelve woodcuts in portfolio, edition limited to 250 copies, 50 coloured by hand. 580 × 410 mm. [267]

Max Pechstein: coloured design for jacket of the pamphlet *An alle Künstler!*
Berlin, 1919. 200 × 140 mm. [265]

were his lithographs to Lautensack's *Samländische Ode* (*Samland Ode*, 1918) and his etchings to Willy Seidel's *Yali und sein weißes Weib* (*Yali and his White Woman*, 1924). Both books were part of the series 'Die Neuen Bilderbücher', well produced books published by Fritz Gurlitt, a generous benefactor to Pechstein. Both sets of illustrations are based on the artist's experiences in the South Seas dating from his stay in the Palau Islands in the south-western Pacific at Gurlitt's expense.

Pechstein's decorative lithographs to Heinrich Lautensack's ode carry the atmosphere of Samland, on the eastern Baltic coast, to the South Seas. The poet writes of the women's hair, that it seems to have been '... aus dem Samland-Boden gezogen. Scheint so der Erd' entwunden ... Scheint so reifgelb, als hätt's in Euerer Wiege gegrünt! Wie süß'te Frucht vom Baum scheint's aus dem Boden gezogen.' ('Nurtured in the ground of Samland. Seems to have been tugged from the earth ... seems so golden ripe, as if it had blossomed in your cradle. Like the sweetest fruit from the tree it seems to have been nurtured in the ground'.) In Pechstein's lithographs, however, these women come not from Samland but from the Palau Islands. The bodies, the landscape, the branches of the trees, all unite to create a harmonious decorative rhythm.

Pechstein's etchings to Seidel's exotic and fantastic tale *Yali und sein weißes Weib* suffer from such incongruities as the almost naturalistic drawing of certain details (birds and trees), the expressively simplified rendering of the natives and the idealistic, over-beautiful drawing of the figure of the woman. These disparities are disturbing throughout the book; even the letterpress, printed in a gothic type, is out of harmony with the illustrations.

The fact is that Max Pechstein's most successful illustrations were published not in books but in *Marsyas*, an exclusive journal for collectors. These will be discussed in a later chapter.

Schmidt-Rottluff

Karl Schmidt-Rottluff was the most powerful and the most spontaneous of the artists of Die Brücke. Though he taught lithographic techniques to his brother artists, he himself found in the woodcut the proper medium for his passionately excited statements.

Until 1923 his favourite graphic method was to cut and gouge wood. His earliest pieces show traces of Edvard Munch, but by 1910/11 Schmidt-Rottluff's style had acquired an individual accent.

Karl Schmidt-Rottluff: one of nine woodcuts to *Das Spiel Christa vom Schmerz der Schönheit des Weibes* by Alfred Brust. Berlin: Verlag der Wochenschrift 'Die Aktion', 1918. The little book formed part of the series 'Der rote Hahn', edited by Franz Pfemfert. 140 × 110 mm. [300]

His woodcuts include a few decorative pieces for books. His work on the journal *Kündung* is important. Schmidt-Rottluff gave the title its distinctive appearance and cut many initials. At other times he did several printed broadsheets and leaflets, for he spurned no sort of occasional work in graphics. Schmidt-Rottluff was responsible, for example, for the title line of the programme sheet of the eighth and ninth evenings (1911/12) of the Neuer Club (p. 62) in Berlin by Kurt Hiller, Erich Unger, Jakob van Hoddis and Erwin Loewensohn.

Schmidt-Rottluff illustrated only one book. This was Alfred Brust's *Das Spiel Christa vom Schmerz der Schönheit des Weibes* (*The Play Christa of the Pain of the Beauty of Woman*), a small, slim volume of forty-five pages which appeared in the year 1918 as volume 29/30 in the series 'Der rote Hahn' which was printed on the press of the weekly *Die Aktion*. In the same year Kurt Wolff published *Kristus*, a portfolio which contained nine woodcuts. These are considered to be the most successful of Karl Schmidt-Rottluff's woodcuts.

Karl Schmidt-Rottluff: 'Der Gang nach Emmaus' ('The Road to Emmaus') from *Kristus*, a suite of nine woodcuts in portfolio. Munich: Kurt Wolff Verlag, 1918. 395 × 500 mm.

The theme of the little book by the Expressionist writer Alfred Brust is compulsive, daemonic, heavily carnal lust and spiritualized, disembodied ecstasy. Schmidt-Rottluff illustrated the text with nine woodcuts that flout all the conventions of typography. The only way in which an integrated whole might have been achieved would have been for the artist to cut the text in wood also. As things are, however, a greater incongruity between letterpress and woodcut would be difficult to imagine. Schmidt-Rottluff's woodcuts overstrain the modest dimensions of a book. They require a wall or at least a large portfolio. These plates are not illustrations, for they are only loosely related to the text, although based upon it. The artist's knife has ripped the surface open, forming ridges, trenches and peaks. The wood-grain is visible in the rough black fields forming a natural interior element which is not cut into or incised; the surfaces and hollows confront one another in black and white, austerely, with a power that puts one in mind of the Old Testament. The block-like weight of the woodcuts is horribly expressive, they are loaded with inner drama. The heads are chipped and squared as though the wood had been worked with an axe. Impersonal daemonic faces stare fixedly at the spectator. It is not hard to see that Schmidt-Rottluff was acquainted with Negro sculpture. The *Kristus* suite is dependent upon this style, although the plates, simply because they are many-figured compositions, are more complex. The war hovers in the background as the experience of a generation that feels itself forsaken yet is seeking a way. These woodcuts reach their culmination in the plate 'Gang nach Emmaus' ('The Road to Emmaus'). The sun, the trees, the landscape, the road and the three travellers – all the forms are plastically simplified and forged into a single unit. The trees are like stakes that have been rammed into the earth and the mask-like staring faces remind one of totem poles. Graphic fields clash violently against one another, angular, pointed forms evoke a sense of drama. Yet the plate breathes a devoutness and repose that arise from the long-drawn, unbroken contours, a stylistic device that appears often in the work of Schmidt-Rottluff.

Kandinsky

To mention Wassily Kandinsky in connection with Expressionist book illustration is to invite disagreement, for the artist is after all the protagonist of abstract art. He certainly decorated several of his works, mostly theoretical writings, with graphic designs, yet these pictorial embel-

lishments hardly accord with the stylistic canon of Expressionism. The graphic work of this painter, whom we regard for present purposes as a German artist since he was for long intimately connected with German art, oversteps the limits of Expressionism. Kandinsky's conversion to abstract art was completed between 1910 and 1913.

A work that is characteristic of this transition is the collection of poems entitled *Klänge (Sounds)*. A profusely illustrated quarto volume in purple boards, *Klänge* was published by Reinhard Piper in 1913. On his own admission the publisher was 'not exactly enthusiastic about this abstract art'.[31] Kandinsky writes as follows about the genesis of the book: 'My book *Klänge* was a modest example of composite work. I wrote the poems and "decorated" them with many woodcuts in colour and black and white. My publisher was pretty sceptical, but he had the courage to produce a de luxe edition; with special initial letters, handmade papier de *Hollande* – transparent – a rich binding with a gilt-impressed design and so on. In a word, a de luxe edition of 300 copies, signed and numbered by the author. But his courage was fully vindicated. The book was soon out of print. According to the terms of our contract neither he nor I were permitted to bring out a new impression.'[32]

The following quotations will give an idea of the nature of the prose poems which constitute the text:

'Gesicht.
Ferne.
Wolke.'

('Face. / Distance. / Cloud.')

'Eine Frau, die mager ist und nicht jung, die ein Tuch auf dem Kopf hat, welches wie ein Schild über dem Gesichte steht und das Gesicht in Schatten läßt.' ('A woman who is thin and not young, who has a kerchief over her head, which stands above her face like a shield and leaves her face in shadow'.)

To class writing of this kind as 'one of the pioneer works in the poetry' of the century, as has sometimes been done,[33] is certainly mistaken and indicates a biassed and subjective judgment. Taking the poems all in all, it is only too obvious that random elements have been linked by free association and thought abrogated. And Arp's statement that a breath blows 'through these poems from eternally unfathomable depths'[34] would seem to be an example of the kind of obscurity that invents profundity where none exists.

Viewed as a piece of book design, however, *Klänge* has every claim to be regarded as one of the most remarkable illustrated books of the Expressionist period. The very layout of the page shows notable skill, the rhythmic ten-

Siebzehntes Kapitel

Kandide kommt mit seinem Bedienten nach Eldorado.
Was sie da sahen

Wie sie über die Grenzen der Langohren waren, sagte Kakambo zu Kandide: „Sie sehen wohl, diese Hälfte der Erdkugel ist so wenig 'nen Pfifferling wert wie jene. Das Gescheiteste wäre, wir gingen wieder nach Europa, und das je eher, je besser."
Kandide: „Wieder nach Europa? Und wo denn hin? Nach Westfalen? Da schlagen Bulgaren und Abaren tot, was lebenden Odem hat; nach Portugal? Da werde ich verbrannt; und bleiben wir hier, so sind wir keinen Augenblick sicher, gespießt und aufgezehrt zu werden."
Kakambo: „I wissen Sie was! so wollen wir nach Karolina gehen. Dort finden wir Engländer, die ziehen durch die ganze Welt. Helfen tun uns die gewiß; 's sind gar gute Geschöpfe, und Gott wird uns auch beistehen."
Nach Karolina zu kommen, war so leicht eben nicht. Nach welcher Seite sie ihre Richtung nehmen mußten, wußten sie wohl so ungefähr; allein von allen Seiten her türmten sich ihnen schreckliche Hindernisse entgegen; Gebirge, Flüsse, Abgründe, Straßenräuber und Wilde. Endlich gelangten sie an das Ufer eines kleinen Flusses, das mit Kokusbäumen besetzt war. Da fanden sie wieder Nahrung ihres Lebens und ihrer Hoffnung.

45

Paul Klee: illustration to chapter 17 of *Kandide oder die beste Welt* by Voltaire. Munich: Kurt Wolff Verlag, 1920. Typeface: Unger-Fraktur. Klee made the twenty-six pen-and-ink drawings in 1911. 232 × 193 mm. [176]

sion between woodcut and type matter – a pleasant and legible roman face – is equally well planned, while the design is enhanced by a generous use of blank white areas where there is no type. After the books of the Jugendstil this is the first book of the Expressionist period to have been composed as an entity in all its parts, right through from the type, its size and spacing, to the whole type area, the illustrations and the binding.

The illustrations (twelve colour and forty-three black-and-white woodcuts), freely related to the text in a decora-

tive rather than an illustrative association, exemplify Kandinsky's development up to 1913. This emerges the more clearly since horsemen appear in all the woodcuts and are represented according to the degree of abstraction, lyrically or dramatically, in a fairy-tale manner or chaotically, in a concretely visual idiom or in an abstract sign-language. Some of the woodcuts in their fairy-tale, folkloric character betray their descent from the Jugendstil; these include 'Reiter in der Schlucht' ('Reiterweg') ('Horseman in the Ravine') and 'Reiter und Reiterin in roter Landschaft' ('Horseman and Horsewoman in Red Landscape'); others are purely Expressionist in approach. One such is the four-colour woodcut 'Lyrisches' ('Lyrical'). A horseman and his mount, its body stretched in full gallop, are simply suggested in a few lines grained into gleaming white and held suspended in colour surfaces. Here is none of the heaviness and austerity of the woodcut technique: the effect of the plate is of a drawing tinted in watercolour. This and similar plates link the book with Expressionist illustration, although many of the woodcuts in *Klänge* also show that the stylistic principle of the works is abstraction, that form and colour in absolute purity, freed from all subservience to the object, are conceived as sound and rhythm. These woodcuts of dream-landscapes are nothing if not graphic equivalents of Kandinsky's poems.

Klee

Paul Klee's work inhabits the fluid borderland between dream and reality, between abstract, dematerialized generalization and figurative concreteness.

Foreign literature was not his line. Yet we are indebted to Klee for two illustrated books, Voltaire's *Kandide*[35] and Corrinth's *Potsdamer Platz*. Theodor Däubler's book *Mit silberner Sichel* with etchings by Klee was announced in several of Gurlitt's prospectuses; but it never appeared, or at any rate not with Klee's illustrations.

Klee's twenty-six pen-and-ink drawings to Voltaire were executed in 1911. He refers in his diary to the difficulty of the work. But he also admits: 'Following his [Candide's] paths, I found many a weight was shifted, which previously had been in its proper place, as was indispensable to my equilibrium; perhaps I actually recovered my real self at this point ...'[36] It is hard to determine what Klee meant by this. Had he recognized the fantastic as one of his essential strengths? Had he discovered new potentialities in drawing? At all events, the rudiments of this fine, web-like style of drawing are found in a few examples as early as 1909; and it reappears later in greatly altered form in certain plates of *c*. 1912/13. This floating line that touches the leaves like a fine bloom is at its most distinctive in the illustrations to *Candide*. It never occurs again in Klee's work.

Klee made the drawings to *Candide* before the summer of 1911, but they did not appear until much later, in 1920 – the year in which Gropius called the artist to the Bauhaus in Weimar – when they were published by Kurt Wolff.

Like many of Voltaire's philosophical tales, *Candide* is concerned with the problem of the conditions under which human beings may find happiness. All the calamities that life in Voltaire's day could unleash befall the simple-hearted Candide. At the end, the woman whom the writer calls simply 'la vieille' reviews the terrible misfortunes that Candide and his little band have suffered, among them assault, running the gauntlet, *auto-da-fé*, torture, work in the galleys. And yet, as Candide so agreeably concludes '. . . il faut cultiver notre jardin'. Paul Klee interpreted Candide in his own way, although his picture is ironical and comic like Voltaire's. A comparison between text and pen-and-ink drawings shows that Klee's illustrations are highly individual. Certain plates, such as that to Chapter 18, depicting the carriage drawn by six sheep which conveys Candide to the king of Eldorado, and that to Chapter 9, in which the hero slays the Jew and the Great Inquisitor, follow the text exactly. Others, however, are free variations on the theme; thus, in the drawing to Chapter 8, Candide, finding Cunégonde after a long search, embraces her tempestuously, though this does not happen at this point in the text. Klee sometimes selected unimportant incidents, though the passages he chose are always ones that strongly invite illustration. The gaunt, ghost-like figures are drawn in an incorporeal manner. The term line is useless to describe these works; phrases like toneless, discontinuous strokes, perceptibly overlapping box shapes, clusters of hatching like twisted thread, side by side and one on top of the other, may be rather more helpful. Some very distant influence may perhaps derive from James Ensor. The fragile, thread-like, thin configurations create no space on the paper, instead they spin a droll kind of ornament. The magical poetry, a continuing principle in Klee's works, is felt in many of the plates, and is often tinged with irony as, for example, in the plate which shows Candide in the boat with Cacampo. A plate such as this adumbrates the whole of the later Klee. The formal elements harmonize fully with the spirit of the writing. Yet it is remarkable that Klee's drawing of many of the figures, particularly that of Candide himself, suggests puppets worked by wires. This is most marked in the drawing to Chapter 19, which shows Candide and Cacampo with the mutilated Negro lying on the ground minus his left leg and right hand. The left-hand figure is drawn so that it appears to be suspended on wires like a real puppet. Klee's reading of the story, obviously intuitive, made him able to illustrate one of the crucial principles of Voltaire's writing, of which Victor Klemperer wrote that it is a puppeteer's art and is in fact seen at its finest in *Candide*: 'Candide, unencumbered by philosophy, his optimistic friend, his pessimistic friend, his beloved, her proudly aristocratic brother – all are puppets, they are able to endure the most dreadful disasters, the most terrible mutilations, they may be on the verge of death, yet they always spring up again . . .'.[37] Paul Klee's drawings show just such luckless creatures, droll, grotesque puppets, a visual allegory of Voltaire's story.

When at last it came to printing the book, in February and March 1920, Klee was much concerned about the typographic layout. The fragile drawings needed support from the letterpress, needed to be matched by a warm, decorative type and would show to advantage only if delicately harmonized with the type matter. Kurt Wolff found the balance that was needed. The choice of Unger-Fraktur was in itself a happy one and Klee was well satisfied. We know from letters to his publisher how much it mattered to him that a book should be well made. Thus, on 26 February 1920 he wrote: 'I just think that the chapter-headings are rather too prominent, their heaviness is obtrusive and rather disturbing beside the illustrations. Would it not be possible to try keeping the type for 'Erstes Kapitel' [Chapter One] but to treat the short indications of contents more as sub-titles and if it is unsuitable to print them in a smaller size than the text, then they should at least be the same size.'[38] Then follows a sketch in which Klee defines the relationship between drawing and type. Later, in a letter of 17 March 1920, he wrote of a 'slight disharmony' that had resulted from '3 different widths' in the type area.[39]

The second work that Klee illustrated appeared in the same year, 1920. His ten lithographs to the 'ecstatic visions' of Curt Corrinth, executed in 1918/19, were published by the Georg Müller Verlag, Munich. Corrinth's Expressionist tale appeared under the title *Potsdamer Platz oder Die Nächte des Neuen Messias* (*Potsdamer Platz or the Nights of the New Messiah*). The typography of the little volume presented no difficulty, for the lithographs took their place as full-page plates.

The theme of Corrinth's text is the relationship between the sexes, woman's salvation through sex – vital and mythical. Paul Klee produced lithographs that reflect the spirit of the writing and illustrate concrete passages in the text, often in the manner of an arabesque, organic diagram that stems the erotic, torrential stream of words. The most striking is the illustration with Corrinth's title 'Du Starker – o – schön du!' (Thou strong, oh thou beautiful!). The vital clusters of lines, laid crosswise, move with jerky zig-zag lines into the vibrating curves of a female body. In content – but certainly not in the style of the drawing – the plate resembles Kokoschka's drawings for *Mörder, Hoffnung der Frauen*.

Both sets of illustrations are examples of a variant of the Expressionist art of illustration which combines fantastic and daemonic figuration with an abstract play of forms. Klee's desire to dissolve objective appearances grows stronger in his lithographs to Corrinth's story.

In contrast to Kokoschka's and Beckmann's styles Klee's style of illustration attracted no school of followers during the Expressionist period. Closest to Klee was Alfred Kubin, who greatly admired him, but after a short encounter his drawing moved in a totally different direction.

Beckmann

The crucial transformation in Max Beckmann's art, through which he discovered his own identity, was brought about by the upheavals of the war. The break came in 1917.

At about this time, between 1915 and 1924, Beckmann did his best graphic work. In addition to book illustrations this includes the portfolios *Gesichter* (*Faces*; Munich, Piper, 1919), *Die Hölle* (*Hell*; Berlin, I. B. Neumann, 1919), *Jahrmarkt* (*Annual Fair*; Munich, Piper, 1922) and *Berliner Reise* (*Berlin Journey*; Berlin, I. B. Neumann, 1922).

Beckmann was attracted to illustration early; by 1914 he had done lithographs to the New Testament, to songs by Johannes Guthmann and to Dostoyevsky's *Das Bad der Sträflinge*. As regards interpretation and technique these works are related to Impressionist draughtsmanship and recall Lovis Corinth and Max Slevogt. Altogether Beckmann illustrated eleven literary texts, four during his Expressionist period. These are Edschmid's *Die Fürstin* (*The Princess*), Braunbehrens's *Die Stadtnacht* (*City Night*), Brentano's *Fanferlieschen* and his own comedy *Ebbi* – which was printed in an edition limited to thirty-three copies at the Johannes-Presse in Vienna. The plates to *Die Fürstin*, *Die Stadtnacht* and to *Fanferlieschen*, together with the lithographs to *Apokalypse* (1943), and his drawings to Goethe's *Faust*, *Part II* (begun in 1943) represent Beckmann's greatest successes as an illustrator.

The etchings to Kasimir Edschmid's novella *Die Fürstin* (Weimar, Kiepenheuer, 1918) are the first in the short series of Beckmann's Expressionist illustrations. Edschmid's theme is life lived furiously, frantically. The writer's language is extravagant, though terse, but over-inflamed by emotions, passions and moods. Beckmann's etchings are severe line drawings; there is not the slightest hint of the soft, painterly tone that characterizes Kokoschka's illustrations after his drawings to *Mörder, Hoffnung der Frauen*. Every stroke of the etchings goes to create figure and space. The surfaces are densely packed: heads, bodies and limbs, intersecting and superimposed, produce a sense of plagued, frightening and endangered life. As with Kokoschka, Beckmann's art is already an 'assertion of self in time against time'.[40] Thus, again and again the artist managed to slip a self-portrait into his illustrations. His motive was not vanity but commitment. In criticism Beckmann was not impartial and dry or aggressive and assertive like George Grosz or Otto Dix; he was passionately interested, involving his ego in his judgment, illustrating it in terms of self. This egocentric view of the world, on which the Expressionists insisted too uncompromisingly, was later to divorce Beckmann from the artists of Neue Sachlichkeit (the New Objectivity) and from the social critics who represented verism. The attitude is quite clearly present in the etchings to *Die Fürstin*, although it did not come fully into play until *Die Stadtnacht* and the large portfolios. The etchings to Edschmid contain motifs from Beckmann's unfinished painting *Auferstehung* (*Resurrection*), begun in 1916. The motif of the fifth plate also occurs in an almost similar composition in an etching of 1918 which also comes from the painting *Auferstehung* and is intended to sum up the painting in graphic terms.

In the six plates to *Die Fürstin* the cold metallic line of the etching needle matches the dramatic, angular formal idiom, that once only, in plate 4, gives way to lyricism, when the eye is allowed to roam among the hills of a landscape seen through a window.

Fanferlieschen and *Ebbi* were also illustrated with plates that show Beckmann to have been a sovereign master of etching. They appeared in 1924, the year in which Piper published a monograph on Beckmann by Curt Glaser, Julius Meier-Graefe, Wilhelm Fraenger and Wilhelm Hausenstein. These plates are more static, quieter, and it could also be said that the compositional structure is more economical, more reticent. About this time Beckmann developed a new attitude towards colour which he thenceforth used as 'a state of tension between two colours which exist independently below and above one another'.[41] It is quite possible that this manner of using colour also influenced Beckmann's graphic art, which is now conspicuous less for the knotted masses of figures than for the deliberate use of empty spaces. The Expressionist exuberance has gone. This is particularly so in the case of certain plates to Brentano's fairy-story of Fanferlieschen Schönefüßchen, a tale of irony and fantasy, of marvels and horrors, to the humanist concern of which Beckmann gave special emphasis. 'Die fliegende Kirche' ('The Flying Church') is one of the artist's finest etchings.

Beckmann's approach to a text may be studied from his lithographs to Lili von Braunbehrens's poems *Die Stadtnacht*. The initiative for this book came from the painter himself. He sent the poems to Reinhard Piper and submitted his proposal for an edition to contain his lithographs.[42] Comparison between the text and the image shows that the lithographs take verses or snatches of verses, give them visual form in the drawing and continue and condense in the image what has been enunciated in the word. Thus indeed it is difficult without the verse to identify the subject of the plates; however, a straightforward transposition of the poet's word and the atmosphere it evokes into optically visual equivalents does not exhaust the sense of the lithographs; Beckmann both illustrates and interprets. The lithograph to 'Das Trinklied' ('Drinking Song') shows four men huddled closely round a table: two consume a joint, the others revive themselves with champagne. The poet's text runs: 'Drink up, drink! I have not spared the roast!' This is the concrete reference to the text; there is no other clue to the meaning of the plate, which exists on its own account. 'The sharp-edged style of our machine-age, which seeks to burn out all remnants of the Baroque, inscribed the details', observed Julius Meier-Graefe[43] of graphic works that are very close in feeling to these plates. Beckmann presents the lavish and spendthrift life of the rich in the post-war period with critical irony. Most of the lithographs to *Die Stadtnacht* contain something of the dangerous, haunted atmosphere of the metropolitan underworld of the time. Beckmann is close to Grosz and Dix in such plates, although their cold aloofness was alien to him, as is shown by the observing, calculating self-portrait that illustrates the poem 'Verbitterung' ('Embitterment'). Beckmann depicts himself in profile in front of the façade of a house that plunges obliquely into the centre of the plate; he sits on a chair, at his shoulder is a cat that has been interpreted as a 'symbol of introverted inaccessibility'.[44] The concrete point of departure for this plate is the line: 'Kocht was ihr wollt aus meiner Grimasse!' ('Make what you like of my grimace!'). The twenty-year-old poet was obviously

not thinking of Beckmann, but the lithograph shows the artist's position in relation to the text he was illustrating: the words provided no more than the spark and the material for the realization of his own ideas and imaginings. His approach to a text remained the same throughout his life: even the late drawings to *Faust* are interpretations, confessions, declarations and judgments stemming from a highly personal vision. The lithograph to 'Vorstadtmorgen' ('Suburb: Morning') adheres more closely to the text: it shows two workmen in a railway compartment; through the window can be seen the 'black houses, pitiless' of the poem; they come very close, as though the houses, the street lamp and the sickle moon were inside the train. The poem ends:

'Schleppt der Zug uns noch halb schlafend / In die Vorstadt, / Die vom Nachtdienst abzulösen.' ('The train drags us, still half asleep / into the suburb / to relieve it from night duty'.)

The same oblique, vitalizing composition is seen in the lithograph to this poem. The lithograph to the poem 'Möbliert' ('Furnished') is particularly disturbing. The material presence of the volumes could hardly be sharper: in the centre, dominating the whole space, is the horn of a gramophone that a little girl on the right is winding; under the mouth of the horn a woman lies sprawled on her stomach on a divan, her legs in the air kicking the rim of the horn, while dashing against it from above is an elliptical form which turns out to be a tray; this is carried by a man and two fish lie on it; the space-engulfing rim of the horn is wedged in by diagonals, angles and triangles. This creates a sense of an oppressively small space in which no-one can move but which can be filled with abounding life: furnished. The poet writes:

'Die blonde kleine Tochter dreht lächelnd am Grammophon: / Der alte Trichter päkert einen süßen Walzer, / Und Hering wird von Jemand aufgetragen.'

('The little fair daughter, smiling, winds the gramophone; / the old horn clacks out a sweet waltz, / and someone brings in herrings'.)

The last plate, 'Die Kranke' ('The sick Woman'), may perhaps reflect the poet's own fate. Reinhard Piper recalls[45] how, almost blind, she would scratch her little poems on to an aluminium tablet, usually sitting up in bed with moonlight streaming into her dark room. So each plate reflects, on the one hand, Lili von Braunbehrens's poem and on the other Beckmann's experience of the metropolis, sparked into creative life by the poems. The illustrator transposes the poet's tempered Expressionism into a verism containing a strong current of social criticism. One can only regret that an ill-chosen gothic type prevented this important edition from achieving the perfect integration of image and typography that we prize so highly in the great examples of book design.

Meidner

Ludwig Meidner with his two-fold talent as writer and draughtsman is *the* representative Expressionist.

After Kokoschka, it is to Meidner that we owe the most important portraits of the generation of Expressionist writers, to which he himself – by virtue in particular of his books *Im Nacken das Sternemeer* (*Behind one the Sea of Stars*, 1918) and *Septemberschrei* (*September Cry*) – very much belongs. These works are personal admissions, clothed in expressive verbal formulas, 'ardent confessions, stammering transports of an ecstatic man, solitary in the midst of the crowd, his ears ringing with its cries, suffering from its griefs …'[46] Both books were illustrated. The drawing for *Sternemeer* were done in 1915 and 1916, the plates to *Septemberschrei* in the autumn and winter of 1917 and at the beginning of 1918. The first book, accepted for publication by Kurt Wolff, is not strictly speaking illustrated. In a letter to the publisher[47] Meidner himself writes of the 'graphic decoration'. The drawings depict variously gesturing figures, figures of apostles, praying figures, entreating figures, with a self-portrait among them. The excessively long and attenuated hands, arms and legs exist side by side with thick-set, angular, vigorous forms and gathered bodies which suggest rustic Baroque as well as the Expressionist idiom. Meidner produced many similar graphic decorations for books, among them drawings to Mynona's grotesque tale *Schwarz-Weiß-Rot* (*Black, White, Red*) of 1916, and to Psalm 69 (1923).

An unusual piece of book production was the facsimile reprint of the 1757 edition of Klopstock's tragedy *Der Tod Adams* (*The Death of Adam*) into which were inserted five original etchings by Meidner. The book was published in 1924 by the Pontos Verlag in Freiburg im Breisgau.

The etchings to *Die Feuerprobe* (*The Ordeal*) by Ernst Weiß (1923) reveal a changed Meidner, the darting lines, inherited from Van Gogh, express neither excitation nor passion.

But Meidner the Expressionist was the right artist to decorate the title-pages of many little volumes, the texts of which were designed to make positive and topical impacts.

He made many drawings for bindings, mainly for the two series 'Lyrische Flugblätter' (Alfred Richard Meyer) and 'Umsturz und Aufbau' (Rowohlt). He did drawings for the title-pages of works by Arno Nadel, Rudolf Leonhard, Alfred Richard Meyer, Johannes R. Becher, Walter Hasenclever, Gottfried Benn and Paul Zech. They usually reflected the theme of the text and their vigorous, restless lines had all the impact of beacons. Meidner's many title-pages succeeded in producing a measure of agitation on behalf of humanist and even, on occasion, of revolutionary, proletarian ideas.

The headstrong *élan* of his art expressed itself again in *Septemberschrei* published by Paul Cassirer in 1920. The drawings display the whole panorama of the features that characterize Meidner. They are dominated by an ecstasy that bursts forth in barbaric ferocity. Houses rise reeling out of the ground as though shaken by an earthquake, suns explode like shells, corpses are hurled into a landscape, stretched out before shattering buildings, bodies, drawn in a few lines, burrow into the ground, hands gesticulate and speak. No other artist could draw such things as these. And as a sign of impending doom the scythe over the water, the ships, the houses, over the *civitas urbana*, it is grasped by a powerful fist growing out of an endless arm; the arm belongs to the body whose head has been flung to the bottom of the picture – and from the head stare the artist's own features. Such plates no longer express the romantic discontent voiced in the early ones; they signify rebellion, tumult. Their suggestive power stems from the antithesis, welded into a refractory unity, between a verism that lays bare a terrifyingly exaggerated truth and a visionary gaze that is ever fixed on promise and prophecy. In this respect these drawings express both the terrors of the war and the artist's premonitions of radical social change.

A style related to that of Meidner appears in the work of Richard Janthur and Jakob Steinhardt before the First World War. The three painters joined forces in 1912 and formed the group known as Die Pathetiker (Pathetic Ones), exhibiting in the same year at Herwarth Walden's gallery. This was Meidner's great moment: he was recognized as the leading spirit of this group, appreciated and soon acclaimed as a celebrity. Meidner's style as a draughtsman affected other artists. The best known is Conrad Felixmüller, who visited Meidner in 1915 and was deeply influenced by him.

Ludwig Meidner: one of fourteen lithographs to his book *Septemberschrei*. Berlin: Paul Cassirer, 1920. 201 × 144 mm. [234]

Occasional works with illustrations

The Expressionist painters had a strong feeling for the decoration of their own publications, for reasons, of course, of self-display; yet in most cases traditional book decoration was entirely alien to them and they had little sense of decorative book design (this also explains why, for example, in contrast to the ornamentation of the Jugendstil book, no specifically Expressionist ornament emerged). As

Arp, Kandinsky, Kokoschka and Meidner illustrated their own writings, so did others, particularly the artists of Die Brücke, design their programmes, catalogues, biographies and catalogues raisonnés, so that writings of this sort did after all offer the masters of Expressionism the all too rare opportunity of putting their skills as book artists and illustrators to the test. Thus catalogues served to display Expressionist designs for wrappers and bindings. The 'Bücher der Galerie Goyert' in Cologne are important in this connection: they are catalogues printed on the cheapest paper, but with original woodcuts on the jackets. Franz Maria Jansen and Max Pechstein are represented, as is Christian Rohlfs (Book V, 1922), whose sign-like woodcut for the Goyert catalogue is the only one of the 185 items constituting his graphic *œuvre*[48] that in any sense serves a bookish purpose. The *salon* Neue Kunst Hans Goltz in Munich also occasionally used woodcuts printed from the block on the jackets of its catalogues. A fine example is the publication for the 46th Exhibition which was devoted to the Expressionist woodcut and brought together 287 sheets (June/July 1918); it has a woodcut on the title-page by Georg Schrimpf. The catalogue of the Kandinsky exhibition arranged by Goltz in 1912 elicited an illustration drawn by the artist specially for the cover. A cover of outstanding character, however, is that of the Kirchner catalogue of the Galerie Ludwig Schames (Frankfurt am Main, 1919) on which image and type form a perfect union. This was Kirchner's special achievement: in the marrying of woodcut image and woodcut lettering he was unsurpassed. Among the best examples of this are the invitation cards and the catalogues of the various Die Brücke exhibitions (Dresden 1906, Hamburg 1912, Berlin 1912) and the list of members of Die Brücke, a single sheet folded into five issued in 1909.[49] The other artists of Die Brücke also showed themselves to be masterly designers in this sphere: Erich Heckel demonstrated his talent on the cover of the first of the group's catalogue to contain woodcut illustrations; this appeared in September 1910 for the exhibition at the Galerie Arnold in Dresden. The woodcut titles to the annual portfolios of Die Brücke (1906–12) gave the artists an opportunity of integrating lettering and image into a satisfying whole, often in the style of early broadsheets.

Understandably enough, the design of the basic documents of the Expressionist painters provided a powerful incentive. These include the almanac *Der Blaue Reiter* (Munich 1912) and the *Chronik der Künstlergemeinschaft Brücke* (1913). *Der Blaue Reiter* was published by Piper and even its exterior is striking, with Kandinsky's coloured illustration on the cover; the de luxe edition of this programmatic

Franz Maria Jansen: woodcut from cover of Book VI of the
Galerie Goyert. Cologne, 1922. 220×160 mm.

Christian Rohlfs: woodcut from cover of Book V of the Galerie
Goyert. Cologne, 1922. 210×139 mm.

Ernst Ludwig Kirchner: woodcut cover design
for the catalogue of the exhibition of his work at the
Galerie Schames, 1919. 173 × 132 mm.

Ernst Ludwig Kirchner: woodcut design for the title-page
of the second catalogue of *Die Brücke* exhibition at the Galerie
Commeter, Hamburg, 1912. Woodcut 155 × 59 mm.

Above, left   Erich Heckel: woodcut title of the 5th Annual Portfolio of Die Brücke (devoted to Ernst Ludwig Kirchner), 1910. 300 × 400 mm.

Left   Max Pechstein: woodcut title of the 6th Annual Portfolio of Die Brücke (devoted to Erich Heckel), 1911. 375 × 305 mm.

Above   Otto Mueller: woodcut title of the 7th Annual Portfolio of Die Brücke (devoted to Max Pechstein), 1912. 380 × 305 mm.

Opposite   From the *Chronik der Künstlergemeinschaft Brücke* (*Chronicle of the Brücke Group of Artists*): woodcuts by Ernst Ludwig Kirchner and Karl Schmidt-Rottluff, 1913. 320 × 255 mm.

booklet contains two additional hand-coloured plates by Kandinsky and Marc; the initials were by Marc and Arp.

That the chronicle of Die Brücke, which was the work of Kirchner, caused disagreement among the other members of the group and that it broke up as a result is familiar history. Later and without the consent of the other artists, Kirchner issued a few copies of the *Chronik*. This privately printed edition contains twenty-two pages and a woodcut by Kirchner on the title page. The first three pages are celebrated: each has two small woodcuts by Kirchner, Schmidt-Rottluff and Heckel respectively; they were placed on the page diagonally opposite one another, a woodcut in each top left and bottom right corner of the type area, forming an effectively taut relationship. These three pages contain Kirchner's *Chronik*; the others carry two articles by Kirchner, 'Über die Malerei' ('On Painting') and 'Über die

Graphik' ('On Graphic Art'), and lists of the friends and members of Die Brücke. The *Chronik* was reprinted for the first time in 1948, in the catalogue of the exibition *Paula Modersohn und die Maler der Brücke* organized by the Kunsthalle in Berne. Another project of the artists of Die Brücke was a jointly written and illustrated book, *Odi profanum vulgus*,[50] a *livre d'artiste* in which much space was to be devoted to protest against philistine bourgeois disregard of their art. It cannot now be ascertained which of the members of Die Brücke proposed this title. At all events the group provided themselves with a book measuring about 18 × 22 cm. on which they worked together. Individual painters would make a drawing or watercolour for it and prints were also inserted. When the group broke up in 1913 the book was handed to Erich Heckel for safe-keeping. In 1944 his Berlin studio was destroyed by bombs and the unique copy of *Odi profanum vulgus* perished.

Im Jahre 1902 lernten sich die Maler Bleyl und Kirchner in Dresden kennen. Durch seinen Bruder, einen Freund von Kirchner, kam Heckel hinzu. Heckel brachte Schmidt-Rottluff mit, den er von Chemnitz her kannte. In Kirchners Atelier kam man zum Arbeiten zusammen. Man hatte hier die Möglichkeit, den Akt, die Grundlage aller bildenden Kunst, in freier Natürlichkeit zu studieren. Aus dem Zeichnen auf dieser Grundlage ergab sich das allen gemeinsame Gefühl, aus dem Leben die Anregung zum Schaffen zu nehmen und sich dem Erlebnis unterzuordnen. In einem Buch "Odi profanum" zeichneten und schrieben die einzelnen nebeneinander ihre Ideen nieder und verglichen dadurch ihre Eigenart. So wuchsen sie ganz von selbst zu einer Gruppe zusammen, die den Namen "Brücke" erhielt. Einer regte den andern an. Kirchner brachte den Holzschnitt aus Süddeutschland mit, den er, durch die alten Schnitte in Nürnberg angeregt, wieder aufgenommen hatte. Heckel schnitzte wieder Holzfiguren; Kirchner bereicherte diese Technik in den seinen durch die Bemalung und suchte in Stein und Zinnguss den Rhythmus der geschlossenen Form. Schmidt-Rottluff machte die ersten Lithos auf dem Stein. Die erste Ausstellung der Gruppe fand in eigenen Räumen in Dresden statt; sie fand keine Anerkennung. Dresden gab aber durch die landschaftlichen Reize und seine alte Kultur viele Anregung. Hier fand "Brücke" auch die ersten kunstgeschichtlichen Stützpunkte in Cranach, Beham und andern deutschen Meistern des Mittelalters. Bei Gelegenheit einer Ausstellung von Amiet in Dresden wurde dieser

zum Mitglied von "Brücke" ernannt. Ihm folgte 1905 Nolde. Seine phantastische Eigenart gab eine neue Note in "Brücke", er bereicherte unsere Ausstellungen durch die interessante Technik seiner Radierung und lernte die unseres Holzschnittes kennen. Auf seine Einladung ging Schmidt-Rottluff zu ihm nach Alsen. Später gingen Schmidt-Rottluff und Heckel nach Dangast. Die harte Luft der Nordsee brachte besonders bei Schmidt-Rottluff einen monumentalen Impressionismus hervor. Währenddessen führte Kirchner in Dresden die geschlossene Komposition weiter: er fand im ethnographischen Museum in der Negerplastik und den Balkenschnitzereien der Südsee eine Parallele zu seinem eigenen Schaffen. Das Bestreben, von der akademischen Sterilität frei zu werden, führte Pechstein zu "Brücke". Kirchner und Pechstein gingen nach Gollverode, um gemeinsam zu arbeiten. Im Salon Richter in Dresden fand die Ausstellung der "Brücke" mit den neuen Mitgliedern statt. Die Ausstellung machte einen grossen Eindruck auf die jungen Künstler in Dresden. Heckel und Kirchner versuchten die neue Malerei mit dem Raum in Einklang zu bringen. Kirchner stattete seine Räume mit Wandmalereien und Batiks aus, an denen Heckel mitarbeitete. 1907 trat Nolde aus "Brücke" aus. Heckel und Kirchner gingen an die Moritzburger Seen, um den Akt im Freien zu studieren. Schmidt-Rottluff arbeitete in Dangast an der Vollendung seines Farbenrhythmus. Heckel ging nach Italien und brachte die Anregung der etruskischen Kunst. Pechstein ging in dekorativen Aufträgen nach Berlin. Er versuchte die neue Malerei in die Sezession zu bringen. Kirchner fand in Dresden den Handdruck

der Lithographie. Bleyl, der sich der Lehrtätigkeit zugewandt hatte, trat aus "Brücke" 1909 aus. Pechstein ging nach Dangast zu Heckel. Im selben Jahre kamen beide zu Kirchner nach Moritzburg, um an den Seen Akt zu malen. 1910 wurde durch die Zurückweisung der jüngeren deutschen Maler in der alten Sezession die Gründung der "Neuen Sezession" hervorgerufen. Um die Stellung Pechsteins in der neuen Sezession zu stützen, wurden Heckel, Kirchner und Schmidt-Rottluff auch dort Mitglieder. In der ersten Ausstellung der N.S. lernten sie Mueller kennen. In seinem Atelier fanden sie die Cranachsche Venus, die sie selbst sehr schätzten, wieder. Die sinnliche Harmonie seines Lebens mit dem Werk machte Mueller zu einem selbstverständlichen Mitglied von "Brücke". Er brachte uns den Reiz der Leimfarbe. Um die Bestrebungen von "Brücke" rein zu erhalten, traten die Mitglieder der "Brücke" aus der neuen Sezession aus. Sie gaben sich gegenseitig das Versprechen, nur gemeinsam in der "Sezession" in Berlin auszustellen. Es folgte eine Ausstellung der "Brücke" in sämtlichen Räumen des Kunstsalons Gurlitt. Pechstein brach das Vertrauen der Gruppe, wurde Mitglied der Sezession und wurde ausgeschlossen. Der Sonderbund lud "Brücke" 1912 zu seiner Cölner Ausstellung ein und übertrug Heckel und Kirchner die Ausmalung der darin befindlichen Kapelle. Die Mehrzahl der Mitglieder der "Brücke" ist jetzt in Berlin. "Brücke" hat auch hier ihren internen Charakter beibehalten. Innerlich zusammengewachsen, strahlt sie die neuen Arbeitswerte auf das moderne Kunstschaffen in Deutschland aus. Unbeeinflusst durch die heutigen Strömungen, Kubismus, Futurismus usw., kämpft sie für eine menschliche Kultur, die der Boden einer wirklichen Kunst ist. Diesen Bestrebungen verdankt "Brücke" ihre heutige Stellung im Kunstleben. E. L. Kirchner.

Page from the *Chronik der Künstlergemeinschaft Brücke*: woodcuts by Erich Heckel, 1913. 320 × 255 mm.

The Expressionists bestowed much loving care on the design of their first biographies and *œuvre* catalogues, which appeared before the reputations and standing of the artists had been firmly established. Not the least of the uses of the catalogues and biographies lay in proving the respectability of an artistic *œuvre* that was the subject of violent controversy, and indeed of hostility. Some of these books are pieces of solid and sober book-making. The work of Kandinsky and Munch is slighter. Kandinsky contributed an illustration for the binding of his biography by Hugo Zehder published by Kaemmerer in Dresden in 1920. Edvard Munch was even more reserved: the design of the two volumes containing Gustav Schiefler's catalogue of his graphic work to 1926 bears no trace of the artist's influence apart from the few original etchings which have nothing to do with the design of the book. Although a few of Munch's prints were inspired by works of Ibsen, he never illustrated literary texts. This is strange, to say the least, since his friend Stanislaw Przybyszewski wrote a few novels – *Totenmesse* (*Mass for the Dead*), 1893; *Totentanz der Liebe* (*Love's Dance of Death*), 1902; *Der Schrei* (*The Cry*), 1918 – which in atmosphere, theme and, indeed, subject, closely reflected Munch's world. This, presumably, is an inverted case of a writer who was decisively and lastingly influenced by a visual artist.[51] Edvard Munch's suite of lithographs *Alfa og Omega* (Copenhagen, 1909) is far removed from Expressionism in character.

The decoration of the two volumes which comprise Gustav Schiefler's catalogue of the graphic work of Emil Nolde (Berlin, 1911 and 1927) is therefore all the more illuminating in this respect. The many woodcuts show that Nolde possessed the talent and originality to become a book-designer of distinction; but he never had a chance to illustrate a literary text (he made a single suite of woodcuts for a fairy-tale). Nolde himself cut many borders and vignettes for Schiefler's *catalogue raisonné*: fabulous beasts, trees, male and female heads, dancers, steamers and animals people the pages, little masterpieces of Expressionist book decoration. In these small decorations, as in his large sheets, Nolde handled the knife with such vehemence that the lines and surfaces splintered in the soft wood, producing painterly effects in the process. Yet the severely simplifying clarity of his technique is the predominant feature in the woodcuts for these books. The unity of the page was emphasized by the choice of an old Schwabacher, a typeface that is found in Gothic woodcuts, occurs often during the last quarter of the fifteenth century and a century later quickly became the favoured type for the books and pamphlets of the Reformation. In reviving a Gothic tradition, the Expressionists also frequently and with varying degrees of success sought to establish a unity between the arched and rounded Schwabacher letter and the woodcut image. This unity of style is achieved in Nolde's *œuvre* catalogue (particularly in Vol. 2).

Max Pechstein and Karl Schmidt-Rottluff too influenced the design of their *œuvre* catalogues. Pechstein designed the binding, end-papers, title-page and various vignettes for Paul Fechter's catalogue of his graphic work (Berlin, Gurlitt, 1921). Schmidt-Rottluff decorated Rosa Schapire's *catalogue raisonné* of his graphic art (Berlin, Euphorion-Verlag, 1924) with a cover design and nine hand-printed woodcuts.

Ernst Ludwig Kirchner's design for his *œuvre* catalogues and monographs is also outstanding, although they did not equal the Nolde catalogue in beauty and consistency. Kirchner designed the binding and preliminaries for Will Grohmann's book on his drawings (Dresden, Ernst Arnold, 1925) and also contributed a few woodcuts. A year later the same writer published the first monograph on Kirchner (Munich, Kurt Wolff, 1926); Kirchner did the cover design, contributed five original woodcuts and took over the whole of the typographical design. Finally, he decorated Schiefler's catalogue of his graphic works (Berlin, Euphorion-Verlag, 1926) with fifty-two woodcuts, four of which were in colour; he was also responsible for the design of the binding and general *mise en page*.

These Expressionist artists gave their attention to the artistic aspects of their biographies and *œuvre* catalogues and in doing so created fine books of high quality and considerable originality.

1911

4 **Fauſt.** Der Oberkörper eines am Pult ſitzenden Mannes on der Seite, nach r., das Geſicht dem Beſchauer zugewandt). ie l. Hand ſtützt die l. Backe, die r. liegt auf dem Pult. Halb= ſchloſſene Augen in tiefen Höhlen; ſchmale zuſammengepreßte ppen. Dunkler Kragen auf hellerem Mantel. Umrahmungs= ie von nicht geradlinig gezogenem Strich.   150×105/7

Weißer Hintergrund hinter dem Kopf
    Wenige Probedrucke

I Der Hintergrund iſt getönt am Bildrand r. mit vertikalem Streif, in der Bildecke l. o. mit wolkigen Ballen
    Wenige Probedrucke

I Der Hintergrund in noch ſtärkeres Dunkel gelegt, dergeſtalt, daß ſich die Schattenpartien oberhalb des Scheitels von r. und l. bis auf 5 mm nähern.
a) Wenige Probedrucke
b) Auflage von 20 numerierten und ſignierten Exemplaren

5 **Der Pflüger.** Ein von rückwärts geſehener Bauer, der nter dem Pfluge geht. Das Geſpann beſteht aus einem Brau= n (l.) und einem Schimmel (r.). Helle Ackerfurchen, dunkles eld. Vögel am Himmel. Umrahmungslinie.   150×105/7

126 „**Getreu**". Profilkopf eines Mannes (nach r.) mit reſigniert=edlem Ausdruck. Das mit breiten Umrißlinien um= zogene Geſicht, von mützenartig auf dem Scheitel liegendem und tief in die Stirn herabreichendem Haar gekrönt, löſt ſich aus dem Dunkel des Bildrandes l. los und wird durch eine breite helle Hintergrundzone vom Dunkel des Bildrandes r. geſchieden. Über dem u. Bildrand ein längliches helles Viereck, gleichſam zur Aufnahme einer Inſchrift beſtimmt.   185×115

a) Einige Probedrucke.
b) Auflage von 50 Exemplaren; Stock vernichtet.

1917

127 **Kerzentänzerinnen.** Auf dem Fußboden ſtehen flak= kernde Kerzen in Leuchtern. Zwiſchen ihnen tanzen zwei Mäd= chen: die Oberkörper und die Beine ſind nackt, die Hüften mit einem kurzen längsgeſtreiften flatternden Röckchen umgürtet. Die eine (links) erhebt die Hände in die Luft und wirft den von dunklem Haar umwallten Kopf ſeitlich zurück; die zweite (rechts) verſchränkt die Hände oberhalb der Brüſte und reckt den Kopf in die Bildecke r. o.   300×235/40

Emil Nolde: woodcut illustrations to *Das graphische Werk von Emil Nolde 1910–1925* by Gustav Schiefler. Berlin: Euphorion-Verlag, 1927. 56×116 mm; 57×116 mm. [250]

W Grohmann
Kirchner-Zeichnungen
100 Tafeln und zahlreiche Holzschnitte im Text
Arnolds Graphische Bücher
Zweite Folge   Band 6
Verlag Ernst Arnold
Dresden   1925

Ernst Ludwig Kirchner: title-page of *Kirchner-Zeichnungen* by
Will Grohmann. Dresden: Verlag Ernst Arnold, 1925.
263 × 204 mm.

DER NEUE CLUB
NEOPATHETISCHES CABARET

8. Abend. **Sonnabend, den 16. Dezember 1911.**
Oberer Saal (Café Kutschera) Kurfürstendamm 208-9 pkt. 8 Uhr.

▢ ▢ ▢

André Gide: Die irdische Nahrung (übertragen von F. Abraham).
Georg Heym: Der Garten der Irren.
Einstein: Stücke aus „Bebuquin".
Jakob van Hoddis: Fragment aus den Lebensbeschreibungen unheilbarer Moralisten.
Debussy: Danse sacrée — Danse profane.
(Marie Zweig.)

Erich Unger.
Robert Jentsch: Gedichte.
(John Höxter.)

Golo Gangi
Rudolf Kurtz: Séance.
(Ludwig Hardt.)
W. S. Ghuttman: Der Weltbrand.
Mynona: Neue Grotesken.
Herr Gottlob Leider: Wir können Gott leichter lieben als erkennen.
Herwarth Walden: Klaviermusik.
Das Loch.
Schattendrama von Achim von Arnim. Figuren von Engert.

▢ ▢ ▢

Billets à 1,25 Mk. im Café des Westens und Café Kutschera sowie
an der Abendkasse.

▢ ▢ ▢

Geschäftsstelle des NEUEN CLUBS: Erich Unger, Sigismundshof 21

Karl Schmidt-Rottluff: title design to the programme for an
entertainment ('Neopathetisches Cabaret') in Berlin, 1911.
47 × 168 mm.

1 An illustration by Otto Mueller to Max Brod's *Aus einer Nähstube* is reproduced in the almanac *Vierzig Jahre Kiepenheuer 1910–1950*, Weimar. 1951 (p. 191). According to the press the book was not published.

2 Nell Walden, 'Kokoschka und der Sturm-Kreis', in *Expressionismus. Aufzeichnungen und Erinnerungen der Zeitgenossen*, ed. P. Raabe, Freiburg im Breisgau, 1965, p. 132.

3 Hans Kaufmann, *Krisen und Wandlungen der deutschen Literatur von Wedekind bis Feuchtwanger*, Berlin and Weimar, 1966, p. 262.

4 See *Kunstblatt*, vol. I, 1917, p. 314.

5 As far as I can tell, Werner Haftmann was the first to use this concept in connection with Kokoschka's art. See his *Painting in the Twentieth Century*, 2nd edition, London and New York, 1965, vol. I, pp. 133–34.

6 Oskar Kokoschka, 'Von der Natur der Gesichte', lecture given in 1912, first published in *Genius*, 1919. Cited after Kokoschka, 'Die Wahrheit ist unteilbar', *Schriften des Museums des 20. Jahrhunderts*, 1, Vienna, 1966, p. 7.

7 C. G. Heise, 'Kokoschka's Zeichenstil', in *I. Internationale der Zeichnung. Eine Ausstellung der Stadt Darmstadt*, 1964, p. 273.

8 Information supplied by Heckel in a letter to the author dated 29 February 1968.

9 Oscar Wilde, *The Letters*, ed. Rupert Hart-Davis, 1962, p. 654.

10 *Das Kunstblatt*, vol. 2, 1918, p. 284.

11 Cited after A. Dube-Heynig, *E. L. Kirchner – Graphik*, Munich, 1961, p. 58. Edition in English 1966.

12 A. Dube-Heynig, loc. cit.

13 L. Grisebach, *E. L. Kirchners 'Davoser Tagebuch'*, Cologne, 1968, p. 62.

14 Cf. Kurt Wolff, *Briefwechsel eines Verlegers 1911–1963*, ed. B. Zeller and E. Otten, Frankfurt am Main, 1966, p. 391.

15 Wolff, op. cit., p. 392.

16 Wolff, loc. cit.

17 Wolff, op. cit., p. 423.

18 Dube-Heynig, op. cit., p. 96.

19 Wolff, op. cit., p. 425.

20 Wolff, loc. cit.

21 Wolff, op. cit., p. 429.

22 Wolff, loc. cit.

23 Wolff, op. cit., p. 432.

24 Wolff, op. cit., p. 403.

25 Wolff, op. cit., p. 407.

26 C. Glaser, 'Ein Holzschnittbuch von Ludwig Kirchner', in *1925. Ein Almanach für Kunst und Dichtung aus dem Kurt Wolff Verlag*, Leipzig, p. 90.

27 Walter Heymann, *Max Pechstein*, Munich, 1912.

28 Cf. Pechstein's illuminating essay in the collected volume *Schöpferische Konfession* ('Tribüne der Kunst und Zeit', no. 13), Berlin, 1920.

29 Paul Ferdinand Schmidt, *Geschichte der modernen Malerei*, Stuttgart, 1957, p. 216.

30 For the November Group see *Zehn Jahre Novembergruppe*, Berlin, 1928; *Manifeste Manifeste 1905–1933*, collected and edited by Diether Schmidt, Dresden, 1965; Lothar Lang, *Das Bauhaus 1919–1933, Idee und Wirklichkeit*, Berlin, 1965; Helga Kliemann, *Die Novembergruppe*, Berlin, 1969.

31 Reinhard Piper, *Mein Leben als Verleger*, Munich, 1964, p. 299.

32 Kandinsky, in *XXᵉ Siècle*, no. 3, 1938; Max Bill, *Kandinsky, Essays über Kunst und Künstler*, Stuttgart, 1955, p. 217.

33 Cf. Kurt Leonhard, *Moderne Lyrik*, Bremen, 1963, p. 216.

34 Hans Arp, 'Der Dichter Kandinsky' in *Kandinsky*, ed. Max Bill, Paris, 1951.

35 Contrary to the usual German practice, Klee chose to spell Candide with a K.

36 *The Diaries of Paul Klee*, edited, with an introduction, by Felix Klee, London, 1965, p. 258.

37 Victor Klemperer, 'Voltaire und seine kleinen Romane' in *Voltaire: Sämtliche Romane und Erzählungen* (2 vols.), vol. 1, Leipzig, 1964 (Sammlung Dieterich, vol. 58/59, pp. XXXVf.

38 Kurt Wolff, *Briefwechsel eines Verlegers 1911–1963*, Frankfurt am Main, 1966, p. 358.

39 Kurt Wolff, loc. cit.

40 Alfred Hentzen in an address at the annual meeting of the Beckmann-Gesellschaft in Munich and Ohlstedt, 1965.

41 Erhard Göpel, 'Beckmanns Farbe', in *Blick auf Beckmann*, Munich, 1962, p. 134.

42 Reinhard Piper, *Mein Leben als Verleger*, Munich, 1964, p. 326.

43 *Gesichter*, 13th publication of the Marées-Gesellschaft, Munich 1919, edited and with an introduction by Julius Meier-Graefe, p. 8.

44 Lothar-Günther Buchheim, *Max Beckmann*, Feldafing, 1959, p. 105.

45 R. Piper, op. cit., p. 326.

46 Lothar Brieger, 'Ludwig Meidner', in *Junge Kunst*, vol. 4, Leipzig, 1919, p. 5.

47 Kurt Wolff, op. cit., p. 191.

48 Paul Vogt, *Christian Rohlfs – Das grafische Werk*, Recklinghausen, 1960.

49 Not recorded by Schiefler. Cf. *Brücke-Museum. Verzeichnis der zur Eröffnung ausgestellten Werke*, Berlin, September 1967, cat. no. 118.

50 All my information about this book is contained in a letter to me from Erich Heckel dated 28 May 1967. Günter Krüger mentions a second volume of *Odi profanum vulgus*, the items in which are dated c. 1906; see his 'Fritz Bleyl. Beiträge zum Werden und Zusammenschluß der Künstlergruppe Brücke', in *Brücke-Archiv*, nos. 2/3, Berlin (West), 1968/69, p. 40.

51 See Marianne Brosemann, 'Notizen zu Munch und der zeitgenössischen Literatur', in *E. M. Staatliches Museum zu Berlin. Ausstellung des Berliner Kupferstichkabinetts*, 1963/64.

IV. Writers as illustrators

German Expressionism is characterized not only by a duality in the arts – in the sense that there was a close interplay between literature and visual art – but also by the fact that many of the artists were gifted in both fields, some impressively so. Oskar Kokoschka and Ernst Barlach are the archetypes; among the many others one might mention Hans Arp, Wassily Kandinsky, Ludwig Meidner and Karl Jakob Hirsch. In addition to these artists who, with widely varying literary ability, made an occasional appearance in print, there were writers who illustrated their works – though often only the title-pages – with drawings of their own. Among them were the poet Wilhelm Klemm, Walter Mehring, a versatile writer and essayist, and, of course, the poet Else Lasker-Schüler. Such people were the descendants of certain writers typical of the culture-loving eighteenth and nineteenth centuries, for whom drawing was an accepted part of a cultivated general education; some of these writers occasionally decorated their works with their own drawings: Clemens von Brentano, for example, produced a folded, engraved frontispiece for his rare little work, *Der Philister vor, in und nach der Geschichte* (*The Philistine before, in and after History*; Berlin, 1811), and fourteen lithographed plates designed by himself and drawn on stone by Strixner for his book of fairy-tales, *Gockel, Hinkel, Gackeleia* (Frankfurt, 1838).

Barlach and Kokoschka among the artists of Expressionism produced important literary work. Among the writers mention has been made of Klemm, Mehring and Lasker-Schüler. Walter Mehring designed many drawings for jackets; he also did text drawings for a few volumes, including *Europäische Nächte* (*European Nights*; Berlin, 1924) and *Westnordwestviertelwest* (*Westnorthwest, Quarter West*; Berlin, 1925). But these are not Expressionist drawings in the strict sense. In terms of quantity Wilhelm Klemm was a more modest illustrator: he designed title-pages for several of his volumes – *Aufforderung* (*Challenge*; Berlin, 1917) and *Traumschutt* (*Dream Ruins*; Hanover, 1920); the additional decoration that occurs in the volume of verse entitled *Aufforderung* is unusual. Klemm's few drawings are remarkably reminiscent of the style of Lasker-Schüler. Of all the Expressionist poets Else Lasker-Schüler was the only true illustrator. Her writing anticipated elements of the Expressionist lyric long before 1910.[1] Her frightened magnification of her individual destiny into a cosmic situation and her consequent confusion of personal feelings with the character of a whole epoch are typical of the in-

tellectual attitude of the Expressionists. Literary critics are unanimous in their unwillingness to classify Else Lasker-Schüler as Expressionist in every sense. Despite many important points of similarity, there are significant differences, in particular the romantic element[2] in her writing. This sprang from the poet's philosophy of life and is expressed mainly in a fantasy pervaded by the world of fairy-tale and myth, in figures drawn from the Bible and from oriental fairy-tales. Else Lasker-Schüler's significance as an artist was recognized early and highly respected. By

1910 Karl Kraus was already writing of the 'most powerful and most unusual lyrical figure in modern Germany'.[3] Kasimir Edschmid and Gottfried Benn called her 'one of the greatest women poets', indeed, 'the greatest woman lyric poet Germany has ever had'.[4] Albert Einstein wrote of an 'inspired poet'.[5] In 1932 she was awarded the Kleist Prize for the 'timeless quality of her writing, which includes many verses which equal the definitive works of our greatest German masters'. In her way of life this woman came to personify the Expressionist group of artists. She knew, admired and respected Gottfried Benn, Georg Trakl, Franz Werfel, Hans Ehrenbaum-Degele, Ernst Toller, Erich Mühsam, John Heartfield, Wieland Herzfelde, George Grosz, Oskar Kokoschka, Franz Marc,

Adolf Loos, Karl Kraus, Kurt Wolff, Albert Ehrenstein, Paul Zech, Peter Baum, Peter Hille, Richard Dehmel, Theodor Däubler and many others; she married Georg Levin (her second husband) and renamed him Herwarth Walden. She gave them all fantastic names, appointing them princes and potentates of her imaginary kingdom, dedicated her poetry and prose to them, celebrated some of them in her verse.

Else Lasker-Schüler first wanted to be a painter,[6] but her poetic talent proved the stronger force. In certain of her books, however, verse and drawing are of equal quality and ideally complement one another. *Styx*, her first book, was published by Axel Juncker in Berlin in 1902. It contained vignettes by the industrious Jugendstil illustrator

Else Lasker-Schüler: lithographs to her volume of poems
Theben. Berlin: Querschnitt-Verlag, 1923 ('Flechtheim-Druck',
no. 24). Edition of 250 copies, of which 50 are coloured.
235 × 156 mm; 220 × 157 mm; 235 × 130 mm. [217]

Fidus (Hugo Höppner) who also did the title decoration of the naked dancing child. During the following years the artist illustrated many of her own books with title decorations and plates. Among them are the prose works *Mein Herz* (*My Heart*; 1912, second impression 1920), *Der Prinz von Theben* (*The Prince of Thebes*; 1914, second impression 1920) and *Der Malik* (1919). Her masterpiece, however, *Theben – Gedichte und Lithographien* (*Thebes – Poems and Lithographs*), a perfectly integrated unity of word and image, was published in 1923 as the 24th Flechtheim-Druck (Querschnitt-Verlag, Frankfurt am Main) in an edition limited to 250 numbered copies. Opposite the ten poems are ten drawings, the words and images drawn on the stone by the artist, printed on a hand-press and bound in the manner of a block book. The lithographs in the first fifty copies were coloured by hand. Sometimes the drawings transpose the core of the poem into an optical image; sometimes, however, the word-poems are accompanied by a 'linear poem', a drawing that matches the spirit and atmosphere of the poem, but not its text.

Lasker-Schüler's drawings cannot be compared with any graphic work of those years, their character is not Expressionist in the usual sense. The figures, their bodies often elongated, are 'romantic', usually visionary types, sleep-walking creatures, drawn naively but with compelling sensibility, formed of lines that lead a life of their own. The scenes and figures are often oriental in appearance. The drawings are, in the true sense of the word, a handwriting; they are subject to no law, traditional or new-found, they are not formed as graphic configurations, but are actually written. They are the expressions of a fantastic, visual world of imagination that is not adequately conveyed by the language of poetry alone. Klabund once wrote that her art was emotionally related to 'that of her friend, the Blauer Reiter, Franz Marc',[7] who for his part was deeply impressed by the poet's drawings. The common ground was one of sentiment and the underlying psychic atmosphere; their style of drawing is quite dissimilar. Curiously enough, however, there is an element of caricature in Lasker-Schüler's drawings; it does not, indeed, give the object a gay or even a comical character, let alone lift it into the realm of satire, but gives it that abbreviated appearance that is so much a part of caricature. She must have sensed this herself, for she uses the word 'Carrikatur' – in connection with her portrait drawings – in a letter to Kurt Wolff, the publisher.[8] The peculiar thing is that Lasker-Schüler's style as a draughtsman – in contrast to her poetic style – underwent no change over the years. She was from the beginning a 'finished' draughtsman. Her early drawings have, there-

fore, the same linear quality, the same characteristic features, the same compositional use of many figures seeming to seek safety in numbers, as the later sheets, and, indeed, as the very late drawing for *Das Hebräerland* (*The Land of the Hebrews*; Zürich, 1937) and *Mein blaues Klavier* (*My Blue Piano*; Jerusalem, 1943). Illustrative drawing was a field in which the artist's inexhaustible talent could disport itself with joy and satisfaction without discovering anything really new. In other words these illustrations are dilettante in character; but their dilettantism is that of an unusually talented and highly cultivated woman.

Else Lasker-Schüler was an exceptional case in the realm of book illustration. No other contemporary writer produced graphic work that can be compared in importance with hers. The most nearly comparable was Paul Scheerbart (1863–1915), older than she, a writer of fantastic and comical tales, who also made drawings for some of his books. We have to go back to E. T. A. Hoffmann (1776–1822) to find a parallel case; Hoffmann drew and engraved frontispieces and illustrations to some of his books. Thus the *Kinder-Mährchen* by Contessa, De la Motte Fouqué and Hoffmann, a charming small octavo two-volume set published in Berlin in 1816 and 1817, has six copper-plate engravings and six vignettes by E. T. A. Hoffmann. What is remarkable is that often E. T. A. Hoffmann's drawings also contain elements of caricature – although with him they directly reflect the text and are more pronounced than in the drawings of Lasker-Schüler, whose verses contain the merest hint of caricature. The art of the book in the Expressionist period was greatly enriched by Else Lasker-Schüler's illustrations, yet as regards the graphic style of Expressionism they were no more than a passing incident.

1 See Hans Kaufmann, *Krisen und Wandlungen der deutschen Literatur von Wedekind bis Feuchtwanger*, Berlin and Weimar, 1966, p. 199.
2 Gerhard Moerner was the first to draw attention to it. See *Das literarische Echo. Halbmonatsschrift für Literaturfreunde*, ed. E. Heilborn, vol. 15, no. 10 (1913), col. 702.
3 *Die Fackel*, vol. XII, no. 313/4 (1910), p. 36 (footnote).
4 Edschmid is cited from *Expressionismus. Der Kampf um eine literarische Bewegung*, ed. P. Raabe, Munich, 1965, p. 105f. For Benn see *Gesammelte Werke*, vol. I (*Essays, Reden, Vorträge*), Wiesbaden, 1959, p. 538.
5 See Publications of the Leo Baeck Institute of Jews from Germany, *Bulletin No. 7*, Tel Aviv, 1959, p. 165.
6 For the poet's biography see Margarete Kupper, 'Else Lasker-Schüler', in *Nachrichten aus dem Kösel-Verlag. Sonderheft für Else Lasker-Schüler*, Munich, December 1965. Reprinted in E. Lasker-Schüler, *Sämtliche Gedichte*, Munich, 1966, p. 291ff.
7 Notice in the journal *Revolution*, Munich, 1913, no. 1.
8 Kurt Wolff, *Briefwechsel eines Verlegers. 1911–1963*, Frankfurt am Main, 1966, p. 80.

V. Excursus on Kubin, Barlach and Masereel

In the years between 1907 and 1927 Expressionist book illustration was one among many styles available to artists decorating or illustrating literary texts. One need only recall the work of Emil Preetorius (Chamisso's *Peter Schlemihl*, Munich, Hans von Weber, 1907); Max Slevogt's illustrations to *Lederstrumpf* – James Fenimore Cooper's *Leatherstocking Tales* (Berlin, Pan-Presse, 1909) and his lithographs to Cellini (Berlin, Bruno Cassirer, 1914); Lovis Corinth's lithographs to *Das Buch Judith* (*The Book of Judith*; Berlin, Pan-Presse, 1910); and Hans Meid's lithographs to Schiller's *Wallenstein* (for the Maximilian Gesellschaft, 1914) – none of them artists in any way connected with Expressionism. The work of Lovis Corinth alone met the challenge of Expressionism. His late work came briefly into contact with the new movement, although Corinth's expressiveness must not be confused with Expressionism. The case of Alfred Kubin, Ernst Barlach and Frans Masereel is different. Kubin made his début as an illustrator in 1909 with drawings to his fantastic novel *Die andere Seite* (*The other Side*) and illustrations to Edgar Allan Poe's *Das schwatzende Herz und andere Novellen* (*The Tell-tale Heart, etc.*) – both published by Georg Müller, Munich and Leipzig – and his importance was felt immediately. By the time Barlach's first work was produced the Expressionist period had begun; his plates to *Die Steppenfahrt* (*Journey in the Steppes*), published in the journal *Kunst und Künstler*, date from 1912, as do the twenty-seven lithographs to his drama *Der tote Tag* (*The Dead Day*), published by Paul Cassirer as the tenth publication of the Pan-Presse). Masereel followed three years later: four books containing decorations by him appeared in Paris in 1915; they include *La Belgique envahie* by Roland de Marés (Georges Crès & Cie.) with drawings; his first woodcut book illustrations appeared in 1917 in *Quinze Poèmes* by Emile Verhaeren, also published by Georges Crès & Cie.

Stylistically Barlach, Kubin and Masereel cannot be regarded as Expressionists. Many art historians have nevertheless treated them as Expressionist artists, though sometimes admitting that they stood outside the mainstream.[1] Extreme caution and many provisos are called for if they are to be so included, for the differences that separate these three artists from Expressionism are great.

At first strongly affected by the graphic art of Klinger, ALFRED KUBIN succumbed to the spell of the fantastic vision of such artists as Ensor, Feininger and Klee. Expressionist influences are visible for the few years during which

Kubin belonged to the Blauer Reiter. But Kubin himself was an influence, on Klee in particular. Despite his hermit's existence, the bourgeois avant-garde accepted him as one of their own: as late as 1919 he was considered for the job of designing the sets for the Expressionist film *Das Kabinett des Dr. Caligari* (script by Hans Janowitz and Carl Mayer, producer Robert Wiene), but the commission went to the architects Hermann Warm, Walter Röhrig and Walter Reimann. Certain pieces by Kubin of *c.* 1912 – e.g. *Lebhafter Disput* (*Lively Dispute*), in pen-and-Indian-ink, and *Geflüster ums Haus* (*Whispering round the House*), in pen-and-Indian-ink and watercolour – both in the Collection A. Samhaber, Wernstein – are distinguished by the same fantastic and grotesque humour that appears in Paul Klee's work as early as 1909 and constitutes the stock in trade of the figures

Alfred Kubin: lithograph 'In memoriam Dostoyevsky. An der Grenze' ('At the Border'), 1919. 410 × 310 mm.

Ernst Barlach: woodcut to *Der Kopf* by Reinhold von Walter.
Berlin: Pan-Presse (Paul Cassirer), 1919. 137 × 140 mm.

in his illustrations to Voltaire's *Candide* of 1910. Though proof is impossible, the presumption must certainly be that in these works Kubin was influenced by Klee, whom he much admired. However, there is no sign of such contacts in his illustrations. Kubin's language of extremely fine and concentrated sets of lines realizes and evokes a fantastic world full of visions which has nothing to do with the Expressionist image of the world. These drawings are far removed in character from the handwriting that typifies so many Expressionists: hectic in its speed, charged with energy and often apparently impelled by convulsive spasms.

The case of ERNST BARLACH is different. His contact with Expressionism was closer and is therefore visible in his work. We know, however, from the sculptor's own statements that he wanted nothing to do with Expressionism; he roundly dismissed Kandinsky's work and took a sceptical view of the literary work of his friend Däubler. In fact the only contemporaries whom he admired were Käthe Kollwitz and Alfred Kubin. The opinions of art-historians vary as to whether Barlach belonged to the Expressionist movement, even if only briefly and distantly. As early as

1922 Julius Bab wrote of an Expressionism 'beyond all fashion and full of urgency'[2] – though it is true that he was discussing Barlach's dramas. Later, indeed quite recent, writers describe his art as Expressionist 'in the original sense',[3] regard it as a realistic variant,[4] while others deny that the artist's work belongs to Expressionism.[5] Ernst Barlach's work does indeed lack such specific principles of Expressionist art as the ecstatic manner, eruptive, exploded forms, the feverishly inflamed excitability and the wild cry of the blind, aimless insurrectionist. To the Expressionist 'nonform' Barlach opposes forms, the passionate quality of which is marked by their regular commitment to the material. The dramatic vitality of his lines, so different from the delicate sensitivity and visionary character of Kubin's linear art, produces great vaulting forms that root the figures strongly and firmly to the ground; in his graphic work, as in his sculpture, details are subservient to the integrated formal whole. Barlach had a sense of the cosmic and of terror, wrote the poet Theodor Däubler. His words sum up the problem of the philosophy contained in Barlach's art which points to an ultimate, yet leaves unanswered more questions than it answers. What is certain is that the human figures which, as Barlach said himself, became his natural idiom in both sculpture and graphic art, ring with the voice of the people, a people that endures suffering, that is strong and vigorous, visionary and at times rises in a frenzy of rage. To this extent Barlach's figures have only a vague social intention and no class connotations. This might be regarded as his point of contact with Expressionism, although, as we have already remarked, to force him into this movement would be to do him violence. Nevertheless one is struck in his illustrations, most of which were done during his Güstrow period, by certain elements that suggest at least some proximity to Expressionism. For example, the ten robust woodcuts to Reinhold von Walter's poem *Der Kopf* (*The Head*; Berlin, Paul Cassirer, 1919, 16th publication of the Pan-Presse) contain grotesque elements and are Expressionist in atmosphere. The work is one of the masterpieces of modern German book art: the woodcuts and the type matter, closely set in Rudolf Koch's gothicizing Maximilian type, combine to form an integrated whole that was rare at that period. Barlach produced work that resembled the terse, abbreviated idiom of the Expressionist woodcut on other occasions, for example in his plates to Goethe's *Walpurgisnacht* (*Walpurgis-night*; Berlin, Paul Cassirer, 1923) and in those to Schiller's poem *An die Freude* (*To Joy*; Berlin, Paul Cassirer, 1927). These are mere resemblances that may spring from his love of visual intensity and of simplified forms designed to convey gathered energy. As regards ideas and ideals there was no common ground between Barlach and the Expressionists. Barlach's contact with the movement was tangential.

The case of FRANS MASEREEL, the Flemish woodcut artist, whose reputation was on his own admission established in Germany with the help of the German publisher Kurt Wolff, is similar. They have, indeed, certain external features in common: the pointed expressiveness and dynamism of the utterance, the simultaneity of the many scenes on a single sheet (a device Masereel shared with the Futurists too), the interlocking of cubic and angular fields. Pierre Vorms writes of the 'almost Expressionist vision of certain sketches', especially in the year 1924.[6] And as early as 1920 Kasimir Edschmid referred to the 'ecstatic rage' with which Masereel loaded his drawings and woodcuts.[7] The illustrated books and celebrated philosophical-sociological novels in pictures of the 1920s contain many plates that are more or less Expressionist in character. We may mention individual works in *Das Stundenbuch* (*Book of Hours*; Munich, Kurt Wolff Verlag, 1920) and particularly in *Die Idee* (*The Idea*; Munich, Kurt Wolff Verlag, 1924), notably also *Un fait divers* (Geneva, Editions du Sablier, 1920), his drawings to *Groteskfilm* (Berlin, I. B. Neumann, 1921), his illustrations to Leonhard Frank's novel *Die Mutter* (*The Mother*; Zürich, Max Rascher Verlag A.G., 1919), to Carl Sternheim's *Chronik von des zwanzigsten Jahrhunderts Beginn* (*Chronicle of the Beginning of the Twentieth Century*; Munich, Drei Masken Verlag, 1922) and to *Fairfax* (Berlin, Düsseldorf and Frankfurt am Main, Galerie Flechtheim, 1922). There are many other examples. They show that Masereel was sensitive to the artistic influences of his day, which, as regards the woodcut, came mainly from German Expressionism. He borrowed several of its formative means, with the result that, for some years at least, his work bore an outward resemblance to that of the Expressionists. The idea of the format of his novels in pictures also presupposes certain connections with Expressionism. *La Ville* with its hundred plates (Paris, Editions Albert Morancé, 1925) is not a true novel in pictures in the way that *Die Idee* (*The Idea*), for example, is. It is rather a psychological and sociological study of the city, an X-ray film of contemporary civilization, a world of almost brutal imagination, viewed, as Thomas Mann remarked, 'with a censorious and a compassionate eye'.[8] Yet it presents an almost 'classic' parallel to Expressionism: *La Ville* is the metropolis. Structurally too, with its images in sequence, it breathes the spirit of the movement. A terrible tension governs these images; the surfaces are loaded with figures, buildings and objects in Masereel's usual way, all too densely packed. This art is

Frans Masereel: woodcut to *Die Mutter* by Leonhard Frank. Zürich: Max Rascher, 1919. Sheet size 235 × 185 mm.

overcharged. The fighting heart unburdens itself. The city whose character Masereel lays bare is no random community; it possesses nothing of the sleepy country town where petty-bourgeois romanticism takes architecture and intellect alike in its toils. Masereel gives us a glimpse of a typical city, an industrial metropolis of the late bourgeois era. Here are clashing contrasts, shattering confrontations: riots in the abysses that are the streets, reducing the individual to a nonentity, dejection and oppression in shabby apartments where loneliness gnaws at the soul; department store and dictating room, money-market and parade ground; hospital and wedding and funeral; power-station and anatomy lecture-theatre; assault, rape and murder, prostitution and love; prison and court-room; motor-cars and horse-drawn cabs; steel-works and a human birth; parliament and circus; backgammon and fireworks; a public execution and orgies in high society; credulous faces

Frans Masereel: from the woodcut book *Die Idee*. Paris.
Edition Ollendorf, 1920; Munich: Kurt Wolff-Verlag, 1924.
88 × 65 mm.

and fingers pointing prophetically in popular assemblies and gunshots at a demonstration; a suburban bar and a fancy-dress ball; factories spewing out men, done in, hungry for bread and a moment's love; a man hanged among bourgeois furnishings and a garret philosopher lost in thought; but also a vast procession of people raising the symbolic banner, sweeping aside all obstacles in its path – proletarians of the world unite! This is the pictorial vocabulary of Expressionism. It is also the pictorial world of George Grosz. And yet how different! Masereel's universalizing use of flat surfaces, his suggestive release of dynamic forces, caught in the soft wood, full of mysterious and perennially seductive paradoxes, shapes revolutionary ideas. Masereel emerges as the unsurpassed diagnostician of social conditions during the first third of the century. Stefan Zweig compared him in this respect with Balzac.

Masereel's woodcuts do not simply raise an outcry or utter their passionate protest; they do more. Masereel seeks the meaning of life and his declared aim is to discover the deepest forces motivating human society. Long and hard though the road to freedom may be, in Masereel's work man always escapes at last from the agony of slavery and emerges victorious. The revolutionary ideal – the proletariat-social idea – forms the core of his art. It is this more than anything that separates this artist from the Expressionists, and his work that exposes the historical limitations of the whole Expressionist movement.

Despite several formal features in common, ideological motives kept Kubin, Barlach and especially Masereel far removed from Expressionism. No art-historian would deny that they remained independent of all the artistic movements of their time. Expressionist elements in their works, far more pronounced in that of Barlach and Masereel than in that of Kubin, indicate merely that their philosophical and artistic consciousness was fluid and open, was prepared to respond critically to suggestions, to test and evaluate them, but was secure enough in itself to pursue a line of artistic activity, once found and adopted, without deviating. Thus, though there were points of contact between Kubin, Barlach, Masereel and Expressionism, they remained tangential.

1 See G. F. Hartlaub, *Die Graphik des Expressionismus in Deutschland*, Stuttgart, 1947; B. S. Myers, *Expressionism, a Generation in Revolt*, London, 1957, and New York, 1963 (as *The German Expressionists ...*); L. G. Buchheim, *Graphik des Expressionismus*, Feldafing, 1959; G. K. Schauer, *Deutsche Buchkunst 1890–1960*, Hamburg, 1963.
2 J. Bab, *Chronik des deutschen Dramas*, part 4, Berlin, 1922, p. 106.
3 P. Raabe, *Der Ausgang des Expressionismus*, Biberach, 1966, p. 20.
4 P. H. Feist, 'Käthe Kollwitz – eine große sozialistische Realistin', in *Einheit*, no. 6, 1967, p. 760.
5 See H. Lüdecke, 'Barlach und die Einsamkeit', in *Ernst Barlach* (exhibition catalogue), Deutsche Akademie der Künste, Berlin, 1951/52; E. Jansen, *Ernst Barlach, Prosa aus vier Jahrzehnten*, Berlin, 1963 (postscript).
6 *Frans Masereel. Mit Beiträgen von S. Zweig, P. Vorms, G. Pommeranz-Liedtke und einer Bibliographie von H. C. v. d. Gabelentz*, Dresden, 1959, p. 44.
7 *Frans Masereel: Politische Zeichnungen* (introduction by K. Edschmid), 'Tribüne der Kunst und Zeit', X, Berlin, 1920, p. 8.
8 See Thomas Mann's introduction to *Das Stundenbuch*. Cited from Thomas Mann, *Gesammelte Werke*, vol. XI, Berlin and Weimar, 1965, p. 596.

VI. Periodicals

The Expressionist era was very much that of the periodical. Paul Raabe has recorded a hundred titles published between 1910 and 1921, many of them new and short-lived, and copies of them are now extremely rare. Some of these are listed below.[1] Many of these journals subsisted on contemporary art, and came into existence along with new trends; indeed, they were often edited by men of letters. We owe it in no small measure to their existence that poems, prose, drama and the graphic art of these decades survived in large quantities and could be collected without delay, thus cumulatively providing a faithful chronicle of all the literary and artistic movements of the time. These papers were, however, no mere repositories; they were primarily organs of the Expressionist movement itself, which it had created for the purpose of communicating its new ideas on art to an interested public and pressing them home with great vigour in pamphlets, manifestos and artistic work. This kind of publication – overt and deliberate literary influences – belonged to a tradition that went back to the Enlightenment in Germany: Wieland's *Der Teutsche Merkur*, Schiller's *Die Horen*, and *Das Athenäum* edited by the brothers Schlegel all belonged to the same lineage.

The Expressionist periodicals varied enormously in form and composition. Many of them were mainly literary like *Die weißen Blätter* (1913–21), edited principally by René Schickele, in which graphic contributions (by Grossmann, Oppenheimer and others) were few. Besides these there were many journals which exemplified the unity of the Expressionist movement. They contained not only literary contributions but also many graphic ones, often in the form of original woodcuts. Such periodicals are examples of the friendly collaboration of an intellectual fraternity of Expressionist artists. Feuds and violent arguments were not excluded, indeed they were taken for granted; moreover, anyone who no longer agreed with the policy of a paper could easily move to another, or, in partnership with others who shared his views, found a new organ – and it mattered little if funds did not last for more than a couple of numbers.

First among the group of periodicals devoted jointly to art and literature were Herwarth Walden's *Der Sturm* and Franz Pfemfert's *Die Aktion*; and these then formed the pattern for many new ventures. There were, of course, also papers that served the visual arts only. These included *Der Fels* published in Passau by G. P. Wörlen, a broadsheet issued by a group of artists of the same name and printed di-

rect from the block in an edition limited to two hundred copies; and the serious collectors' journal *Die Schaffenden* edited from 1918 until 1932 by Paul Westheim (published first by Kiepenheuer and later by the Euphorion-Verlag). *Die Schaffenden* appeared in the form of a portfolio, each one (of an edition limited to 125–130 copies) containing up to twelve original prints signed by the artist, together with a brief introductory text. The declared aim of the journal was to provide a 'survey and guide to the graphic work of the present day'.[2] Not all the prints were Expressionist – furthermore Ernst Ludwig Kirchner contributed nothing; on the contrary it found room for every new movement and is thus comparable with the Bauhaus Port-

Broadsheet of the artists' group Der Fels. Woodcut by C. H. (?) Probably 1919. 390 × 325 mm.

folios (*Neue Europäische Grafik*; 1921–24) which present in a nutshell the whole conflicting panorama of the visual arts during the 1920s. *Die Schaffenden*, therefore, was not an exclusively Expressionist periodical.[3]

Brief mention may also be made of two art journals: *Genius* (1919–21), edited in Munich by C. G. Heise, H. Mardersteig and K. Pinthus; and *Das Kunstblatt* (1917–31) published in Potsdam under the editorship of Paul Westheim. Neither was in any special sense an Expressionist periodical, but both – particularly *Das Kunstblatt* – proved themselves extremely useful in clarifying the theory and extending the popularity of Expressionist art.

In Berlin periodicals that presented Expressionist literature and graphic art together included *Das neue Pathos* (1913–20), *Der Anbruch* (1918–22), *Freie Straße* (1915–18), *Der Bildermann* (1916), *Der Einzige* (1919–25), *Neue Blätter* (1912–13), *Die Bücherei Maiandros* (1912–14), *Die neue Bücherschau* (1919–29, started in Munich), and *Der Feuerreiter* (1921–24), also *EOS*, *Marsyas* and, of course, *Der Sturm* and *Die Aktion*. *Die rote Erde* (1919–23), *Kräfte* (1919), *Die Kündung* and *Der Sturmreiter* (1919–20) appeared in Hamburg. Nearby Kiel saw the publication of *Die schöne Rarität* (1917–19) and the little Baltic town of Wolgast that of *Agathon* (1917/18). Munich produced an imposing array of similar journals: *Münchner Blätter für Dichtung und Grafik* (1919), *Neue Erde* (1919), *Der Weg* (1919), *Bücherkiste* (1919–21), *Ararat* (1919–21), *Neue Kunst* (1913/14), *Revolution* (1913) and *Zeitecho* (1914–17). *Die Sichel* (1919–21) was published in Regensburg; *Das Tribunal* (1919–21) and *Die Dachstube* (1915–18) in Darmstadt; *Saturn* (1911–20) in Heidelberg; *Der Schrey* (1919) in Mannheim; *Der Strom* (1919/20) in Cologne; *Die Kugel* (1919/20) in Magdeburg; *Konstanz 1919* (1919/20) in Constance; *Das hohe Ufer* (1919–20) and *Der Zweemann* (1919/20) in Hanover. And finally Dresden was the home of *Neue Blätter für Kunst und Dichtung* (1918–20) and *Menschen* (1918–21).

One or two of these papers deserve a closer look. *Das neue Pathos* (1913–20), edited by Hans Ehrenbaum-Degele, Robert R. Schmidt, Ludwig Meidner and Paul Zech, belongs to the period of early Expressionism. Its fine typography (it is printed in an old Schwabacher face) and the many excellent impressions of original prints (etchings and woodcuts) are a delight to the reader. The edition was limited to one hundred numbered copies and later (1914), in Edition B, to 250 copies. *Der Anbruch* (1918–22, edited by Otto Schneider and I. B. Neumann) was presented in a less earnest guise; its character was emphatically that of a broadsheet and in common with almost all other Expressionist periodicals it proclaimed in emotional tones the birth of a new humanity. In an appeal to 'all artists, poets and musicians' published in the first number of the second volume (January 1919) Ludwig Meidner called for an end of exploiters and exploited: 'No longer shall the vast majority be forced to live in the most wretched, undignified and dishonourable conditions, while a tiny minority guzzles at an overloaded table. We must opt for socialism, for a universal and progressive socialization of the means of production that gives every human being work, leisure, bread, a home and the sense of a higher goal. Socialism must be our new creed!' This journal contains a large number of prints by contemporary artists, newly executed, including a woodcut by Erich Heckel illustrating Dostoyevsky.

Title-page of the fortnightly *Revolution*, with a woodcut by Richard Seewald. Munich, issue of 15 October 1913. 320 × 230 mm.

Similar to *Der Anbruch* in opinion and appearance was *Die rote Erde* (1919–23, published monthly by Karl Lorenz and Rosa Schapire) in Hamburg and containing many poems and plays by the editor Karl Lorenz. Its characteristic marriage of word and image was also a feature of the Regensburg journal *Die Sichel* (1919–21), published by a painter (Josef Achmann) and a poet (Georg Britting).

All these periodicals issued numerous graphic plates but no – or very few – illustrations. The same applies, with a few exceptions, to their great prototypes, *Der Sturm* and *Die Aktion*. We must discuss these journals in rather more detail, because, in the integration of print and text that they represent, they exerted a powerful influence on illustration and the modern arts of the book: in particular this meant a new co-ordination of text and image and novel typographical treatment of preliminaries and jackets. Furthermore, they stimulated publishers to seek the collaboration of Expressionist artists for the insides of books too, and they encouraged publishers to think of a new art of illustration. In this sense the free, non-illustrative prints that are the feature of most of these Expressionist journals can be regarded as illustrations in the widest meaning, as embellishing texts or providing visual equivalents of many different sorts by means of their most ingenious art. Co-ordination of image and text showed what could be done both in intensifying the effect of a page or double-spread and in opening it out and so making it appear more lively and more emotive – because physical (i.e. making its impact optically). The ideas that stemmed from this development were to bear fruit in the field of book illustration. Thus the symbiosis of literature and graphic art in the Expressionist journals should not be viewed in its narrow aspect of literary illustration; it should rather be seen as a broad trial ground for typographical ideas, in which the permutations of the relationships between types, type areas and image were tried out in a free play of talent with much intelligence and great ability. It should be mentioned in conclusion that the introduction of graphic art into literary periodicals, which had, of course, already begun and become quite usual in the Jugendstil period, is convincing proof of a confessed sympathy with the aims of the Expressionist writers. In this special sense also these papers may be called – in a very loose interpretation of the word of course – periodicals with illustrations, that is, prints that accompany words as a second voice, but do not refer concretely to a text. Pre-eminent among these periodicals were *Der Sturm* and *Die Aktion*.

Der Sturm was in fact a complex group, created, alone and unaided, by Herwarth Walden (1878–1941?). It in-

cluded the journal, a book-publishing house, a gallery (opened 12 March 1913), and later an art school and a theatre. The first number of the journal *Der Sturm* appeared in March 1910, it flourished for twenty-one years and ceased publication in 1932. The first issues contained early Expressionist lyric poetry and prose; from No. 8 onwards reproductions of contemporary art were included. However, No. 17 of 23 June 1910 was the first to contain a full-page illustration on the title, though the title-pages of earlier numbers had carried a few – artistically rather unsuccessful – drawings. In the same year Kokoschka took possession of the pages of *Der Sturm*. The first of his 'Menschenköpfe' ('Heads of People') – a series of portraits,

F. J. Bartels: title-page of the journal *Die Kugel*. Magdeburg, issue for January/February 1920. 326 × 240 mm.

powerfully expressed, profound in their psychological and artistic understanding – appeared on 19 May 1910 (Vol. 1, No. 12). This was the portrait of Karl Kraus; portraits of Adolf Loos, Herwarth Walden, Paul Scheerbart, Alfred Kerr, Richard Dehmel, Yvette Guilbert and others followed. No. 20 of 14 July 1910 contained Kokoschka's drama *Mörder, Hoffnung der Frauen* with the sensational illustrations with which Expressionist graphics were introduced into the pages of *Der Sturm*. All the masters of Expressionism without exception followed suit: Max Pechstein, Emil Nolde, Ernst Ludwig Kirchner, Erich Heckel, Karl Schmidt-Rottluff, Franz Marc, Wassily Kandinsky, August Macke, Paul Klee and others. For the artists the journal became the most important and the most lively of organs of propaganda. *Der Sturm* did not content itself with accepting their drawings and graphics; it opened its columns to their manifestos and theoretical statements.

In 1912 *Der Sturm* extended its field of vision and Picasso and Boccioni made their appearance. Expressionism was joined in its columns by Cubism, Futurism, Constructivism and Abstraction. The first non-representational drawing appeared in October 1912: it was reproduced on the title-page, the artist being Wassily Kandinsky.

The title-pages of *Der Sturm* are entirely typical of the development of the visual arts up to 1926. The first to appear were the founders and masters of Expressionism; in 1912 Walden opened his doors to the new phenomenon of abstract art, the various currents of which from 1919 onwards set the pattern for the visual art of his journal. Except for the contributions of Klee and Baumeister, and a few other artists, *Der Sturm* becomes uninteresting (as far as the visual arts concerned) after about 1919. The nadir was reached in 1925 with the title-pages of such artists as Hugo Scheiber underlining the downward path of this most important journal. Looking through the annual volumes one feels that *Der Sturm* continued for ten years too many. The journal had lost its position both in art and in the conflicting ideologies in society.

The case of *Die Aktion* is entirely different. The journal ran to twenty-two annual volumes from 1911 to 1932 and is the life's work of its editor Franz Pfemfert (1879–1954). Certainly some of the title-pages of this journal (specially those prior to 1917) are mere reflections of the art of those years, yet the interest of many of the titles is not solely artistic: their political message lends them added value and significance. *Die Aktion* was indeed more than just a literary paper, it aimed to use the means at its disposal to influence the class struggle; its position was leftist, to be more exact: it was pro-socialist. Pfemfert attacked Wilhelmian Germany and criticized the sated, parasitic middle class. *Die Aktion* therefore also lacked the salon-like exclusiveness which clung to a greater or lesser degree to Walden's *Der Sturm*; its character was very much that of a broadsheet. As early as 1913 (No. 34, 23 August) the title-page carried the portrait of August Bebel drawn by Mopp (Max Oppenheimer). No accident, but deliberate policy: one of the foremost organs of modern art chooses Germany's most popular workers' leader to adorn its title-page. And Vol. IV, No. 10 (7 March 1914) was expressly dedicated to Rosa

Woodcut by Erich Heckel
for the monthly *Der Anbruch* (Vol. 2, No. 1), Berlin, 1919.
400 × 270 mm.

Luxemburg; Lothar Homeyer's title design is a rejection of war – which Georg Walter Rößner's drawing in No. 3 of the same year (17 January 1914) had already portrayed as a detestable massacre. Once adopted, this anti-war attitude reappeared between 1914 and 1918. The notices of deaths are in themselves unequivocal protests: there is, for example, no 'fallen for Kaiser and Fatherland on the field of glory', but 'Rudolf Börsch, 20 years old, conscripted soldier, was killed in Galicia at the end of June' (No. 29/30, 24 July 1915, p. 369). The language of many of the title-page designs is equally unambiguous: Ludwig Meidner drew himself in a hospital ward which he saw as a place of death (No. 20/21, 15 May 1915); his dedication leaf for 1915 (No. 1/2, 2 January 1915) shows gun-barrels, débris and a woman crouching in a protective posture. No trace of heroism. *Die Aktion* was a centre of anti-war art. The journal later supported the Russian and Bavarian revolutions. Thus the title-page of No. 17/18 (4 May 1918) carries a woodcut by Conrad Felixmüller entitled 'Long live world revolution!'. As a kind of introduction to the leading article headed 'On Communism', in an issue (No. 37/38, 20 September 1919) which also carries a sympathetic article on the 'History of the Munich Commune of 1919', Eugen Hoffmann did a title woodcut of a worker. Like George Grosz, only with different artistic means, Felixmüller, Ebert and Noske advanced to the attack. The memorial issue for Rosa Luxemburg and Karl Liebknecht (Vol. IX, Nos. 2–5, 1 February 1919) became one of *Die Aktion*'s most important political publications. Rosa Luxemburg and Karl Liebknecht had been treacherously murdered on 15 January 1919. The announcement in *Die Aktion*, so prompt[4] and so impassioned, shows how closely the journal was involved with the young Communist movement. The issue contains texts by Luxemburg and Liebknecht, together with contributions by Franz Pfemfert – 'Unsterbliche' ('Immortals'); Johannes R. Becher – 'Weh' euch!' ('Woe betide you'); Carl Zuckmayer – 'Der Berliner Spartakusaufstand siegreich niedergeschlagen' ('The Spartacist Rising in Berlin victoriously crushed'); Yvan Goll – 'Zu Liebknechts Tod' ('On Liebknecht's Death'); Albert Ehrenstein – 'Urteil' ('Judgment') and others. There were drawings by Rüdiger Berlit, Karl Holtz and Karl Jakob Hirsch, who also drew the portrait of Liebknecht for the title-page. Felixmüller, the most important designer of the journal's title-pages, was now joined by other artists, including F. W. Seiwert, George Grosz, Frans Masereel, F. M. Jansen and Heinrich Hoerle.

The typography of both journals accorded perfectly with the concept of suggestion: both papers set out to work for the new art and, in the case of *Die Aktion*, for a new community of peoples. The title-page was therefore the object of special care and was designed to appeal in poster fashion. The front pages of *Die Aktion* always carried the title heading designed by Max Oppenheimer, below it a list of contents and then, dominating the page, a reproduction of a drawing or an original woodcut. Similarly with *Der Sturm*, which had been the first to introduce this form of title-page but continued it only until the eighteenth volume (1927/28): here the contrast between the title heading and the image was even greater than in *Die Aktion* because the title was set in a sober and functional roman. The editors themselves spoke about the significance of their journals. Thus, on 23 May 1914 Pfemfert wrote in

Title woodcut by Georg Schrimpf
for *Die Sichel* (Vol. 1, No. 3), Regensburg, September 1919.
246 × 185 mm.

his paper: 'The material that has been printed in my journal during the past three years is so valuable, so full of abounding life ... that future historians of the literature, art, politics and history of modern Germany will not put pen to paper without having studied *Die Aktion*.' And Herwarth Walden writing advertising copy in 1918: '...the volumes of *Der Sturm* provide a survey of the whole artistic development of modern times. All who wish to understand

VERLAG / DIE AKTION / BERLIN-WILMERSDORF HEFT 160 PFG.

Drawing by Karl Jakob Hirsch
on the title-page of the weekly *Die Aktion*, Berlin,
1 February 1919. 280 × 215 mm.

the emergence of Expressionism, its character and its significance, must rely upon the material that appears in *Der Sturm*. ... *Der Sturm* is the leading organ of the Expressionists.'[5]

Pfemfert and Walden did not exaggerate; their journals are among the most important ever produced by the German literary world and are full of graphic works by Expressionist artists. To the question of the extent to which these graphics took the form of literary illustration, the answer must be that *Der Sturm* was more fertile than *Die Aktion*, although it was the free print rather than illustration that gave both journals their character.

Die Aktion included illustrative works by: Else Lasker-Schüler – *Briefe und Bilder* (*Letters and Images*), from 11 October 1913 onwards; Rudolf Grossmann – to a poem by Kurt Adler, 'Das Lied der irren Frau' ('The Song of the Mad Woman'), 13 February 1915; Max Oppenheimer – to Ernst Stadler's 'Christi Kreuzigung' ('The Crucifixion of Christ'), 3 April 1915; Conrad Felixmüller – to Ludwig Rubiner's 'Der Kampf mit dem Engel' ('The Fight with the Angel'), 21 April 1917; Margarethe Goetz – to Max Brod's 'Der Genius des Krieges' ('The Genius of War'), 25 August 1917; Otto Freundlich – to the Communist Manifesto, 4 May 1918; and Hans Richter-Zürich – to Yvan Goll's 'Unterwelt' ('Underworld'), 29 December 1917. Else Lasker-Schüler's drawings are little decorative pieces, while Otto Freundlich's 'Volksblatt zum Kommunistischen Manifest', which appeared in the special issue devoted to Karl Marx, ignores the concrete class character of this epoch-making political programme and substitutes an Expressionist 'all men are brothers' sentimentality. Only in the drawings of Hans Richter-Zürich does *Die Aktion* distinguish itself with a weightier contribution to the art of illustration. His expressively dismembered, ecstatically dynamic drawings – perhaps inspired by Marc Chagall – are admirably suited to Yvan Goll's 'Unterwelt'.

Herwarth Walden's *Der Sturm* was of greater importance for the new illustrative art, thanks, in the main, to Oskar Kokoschka's illustrations (to the artist's drama *Mörder, Hoffnung der Frauen*, in No. 20, 1910; to Ehrenstein's *Tubutsch*, in No. 106, 1912; to Bohuslav Kokoschka's *Ein Vorfall* (*An Incident*) in the November 1916 issue. It also contained a woodcut by Franz Marc. And there were marginal drawings by Else Lasker-Schüler to her *Briefe nach Norwegen* (*Letters to Norway*; 1911) and a plate by Ludwig Meidner to Paul Zech's poem 'Das schwarze Revier' ('The Black Quarter'; 1913).

Kokoschka's drawings to *Mörder, Hoffnung der Frauen* mark the beginning of Expressionist literary illustration, in so far as it was printed and made accessible to the public. From the point of view of the history of ideas, the drama, a variation on the Strindbergian theme of isolation in sexual relations, presupposes the existence of Sigmund Freud's psycho-analytical studies. It was written in 1907 and the first drawings were presumably made in 1908.[6] Kokoschka's drawings to *Mörder, Hoffnung der Frauen* are already an Expressionist 'classic' and an early masterpiece of Expressionist illustration as a whole: the angles, spikes, sharp edges, dislocations, drawn in vehement contours with a vigorous internal script seem to express disturbance and unrest, to signal the approach of a period of collapse.

Another highly important work of Expressionist illustration made its appearance in *Der Sturm*. This was a woodcut by Franz Marc, the plate 'Versöhnung' ('Reconciliation'), dating from 1912,[7] to a poem of the same title by Else Lasker-Schüler. The woodcut (on the title-page of the journal) and the poem (on the verso, top of the left-hand column) were published in Vol. III, No. 125/126, September 1912. The poem begins and ends with the line: 'Es wird ein großer Stern in meinen Schoß fallen' ('A great star will fall into my lap'). Marc, who had recently come into full possession of his formative means, transposed this verbal image into a visual image, celebrating the beauty of the poet's words in a vibrating rhythm of forms. His poetic language matches the spirit of the verse; it does not re-create the text, does not straightforwardly illustrate it; it is a new work, a self-sufficient visual creation that springs from shared convictions. The vibrating, arching curves of the woodcut wordlessly recompose the dynamic flow of emotion in Lasker-Schüler's work. Quite apart from this Marc had a great affection for her, as the precious postcards he sent her ('Botschaften an den Prinzen Jussuff') ('Messages to Prince Jussuff')[8] show most clearly.

Sadly enough, Franz Marc was never given an opportunity of illustrating a literary work. He would have been the ideal illustrator for Else Lasker-Schüler, for they drew their inspiration from the same principle, a passionate pantheism that embraced man and all creatures. So, as a document of Expressionist illustration, Marc's woodcut stands as a solitary masterpiece, but his art was never seen between the covers of a book.

There were, of course, also journals which preferred to devote themselves to the art of illustration in the true and specific sense of the word. The most important are the luxurious publications of the late Expressionist period: *Marsyas*, *Menschen*, *EOS* and *Kündung*.

Marsyas was edited by Theodor Tagger (pseudonym of Ferdinand Bruckner) at the Verlag Heinrich Hochstim in Berlin; it appeared from 1917 until 1919. Printed in a semibold roman on fine strong hand-made paper in an edition limited to 235 numbered copies, the journal – in complete contrast to *Der Sturm* and *Die Aktion* – was one of the most expensive of the Expressionist period. The annual subscription for the edition on handmade paper was 600 marks, that for the edition on Japon 1,500 marks. The journal published literary texts which were illustrated as a matter of course – by full-page lithographs, tipped-in etchings and

Woodcut by Conrad Felixmüller
on the title-page of the weekly *Die Aktion* (Vol. X, Nos. 21/22), Berlin, 29 May 1920. 280 × 215 mm.

mounted woodcuts. The plates are not, indeed, always Expressionist: Robert Genin, Hans Meid and Adolf Schinnerer were far removed from the movement; Ines Wetzel marked a transition, her fine woodcuts to sonnets by Max Pulver represent a folkloric variant in late Expressionism. The case of Edwin Scharff, Max Pechstein, Georg Tappert, Rudolf Grossmann, Willi Geiger and Walter Gramatté is different: they either belonged to the Expressionist movement or, like Grossmann, were momentarily subject to its

influence. The sculptor Edwin Scharff and Max Pechstein, one of the artists of Die Brücke, made the most important contributions to the Expressionist illustration of this journal. Scharff contributed an Expressionist cycle *Sintflut* (*Flood*), also etchings to Theodor Tagger's *Marsyas und Apoll* (No. 1, July/August 1917). With their delight in sharp edges, in intersecting lines and planes, revealing the sculptor's desire for expressively disciplined exaggeration, these etchings and the lithographs to Wedekind's *Herakles* (Munich, Georg Müller, 1920) form a slight but highly cultivated contribution to Expressionist illustration.

Max Pechstein did four etchings each to *Heidenstam* by Carl Sternheim (Vol. 1, No. 4, January/February 1918) and to Hermann Stehr's story *Der Schatten* (*The Shadow*; Vol. 1, No. 5, summer 1918). The etchings – etchings represent a small proportion of this artist's total output of graphic art (some 100 etchings, 200 lithographs and 160 woodcuts) – were done at the same time as his illustrations to Lautensack's *Die Samländische Ode* (*Samland Ode*) and are among the masterpieces of Expressionist illustration. The plates to the story of Heidenstam the war-profiteer contain within themselves the whole of Pechstein's art. Like his etchings to Stehr's brooding tale of Johannes Teuber, they follow the text closely and are in this respect illustrations of the literary scene: they are a visual gloss on the writer's message. And yet at the same time these plates are entirely independent, visually self-contained pieces. The etching 'Heidenstam betritt das Café, in dem die Warenbörse tagt' ('Heidenstam enters the Café in which the Commodity Exchange is Meeting'), uttering social criticism in every detail, reveals in the toned structure of the lines Pechstein's characteristic slanting of the compositional framework, which, through the rhythm of many angles, locks all the spatial planes together and, in this plate, produces a sense of danger and morbidity. The same goes for the etching – which depicts a tall, slim Johannes Teuber in a sunlit landscape – except that the plate has a quiet beauty in which lurks a foreboding of the man's tragedy.

EOS, a 'quarterly of poetry and art', was another luxuriously printed journal. It was edited by Emil Pirchan at the Verlag Die Wende in Berlin. The type chosen for this esoteric publication was an old Schwabacher in a large size; hand-coloured initials heightened its aristocratic appearance. *EOS* was also a product of late Expressionism and published not only Expressionist illustrations but also sheets in the tradition of Klinger and others of a more symbolist character. Plates by Josef Eberz, Carl Rabus and Will Wanzer are notable works of art. Eberz and Rabus, with their vital and powerfully expressive etchings, pro-

Drawing by Oskar Kokoschka to his drama *Mörder, Hoffnung der Frauen*, first published in *Der Sturm* (Vol. 1, No. 20), Berlin and Vienna, 14 July 1910. 410 × 300 mm.

duced many book illustrations; not so Will Wanzer, who contributed lithographs to sketches by Anton Gourby ('Welten'). Wanzer's prints consist of four rectangular sections on each plate, each section illustrating a different story from the sketches. They should be noted as examples of an epigonal style of Expressionist illustration. The influence of Grosz and Beckmann is not difficult to recognize here.

Wilhelm Niemeyer's *Die Kündung*, hand-printed in Johannes Schulz's workshop in Hamburg, was another aristocratically exclusive journal. It appeared in eleven issues (13 numbers) during the year 1924. The noble typography (the typefaces employed were Genzsch Roman and Leibniz Fraktur) was seriously at variance with the Expressionist decoration provided by Karl Schmidt-Rottluff's woodcut initials; nor did the free prints form any kind of unity with the typography. However, the covers and the verses cut in wood that adorned the first page of each number of the periodical were important examples of design. The verse woodcuts combine woodcut text and a woodcut illustration to create an entity that is rich in contrasts and well within the scope of the medium. Woodcut lettering by Karl Schmidt-Rottluff was printed on the covers, each number being distinguished by the use of ink of a different colour.

Writing retrospectively in 1930, the editor of *Die Kündung* stated that the journal had set itself the task of 'enabling the graphic style of Expressionism to make its effect in a book'.[9] However, *Die Kündung* failed to achieve the desired integration of plate and typography. Niemeyer himself concluded in the same context: 'A conflict existed between the ordered pattern of historically evolved type and the intellectual audacity and uniqueness of painterly black-and-white planes, between the sober, austere nobility of the letter forms serving the word without fuss, and the visual drama of the deep, gloomy, seething fields of darkness and spasmodic flashes of light on the woodcut pages; and this conflict stood in the way of any pure artistic effect. As an Expressionist periodical, *Die Kündung* ought to have been cut in wood throughout, for Expressionist lettering is possible only as decoration and not as a medium for reading.'[10] It was not, however, impossible to resolve the disharmony of lettering and image within Expressionism. The designer of Heym's *Umbra vitae*, Ernst Ludwig Kirchner, had proved that concord between type area and Expressionist print is not only attainable but may be the basis of an excellent art – as is the case with that book.

The periodicals discussed above were designed for collectors; small editions were printed, so they did not circulate widely and are now very rare. They ignored politics. The same cannot be said of *Menschen*, a monthly of modern art, which appeared in Dresden between 1918 and 1921 (though its exact sequence is difficult to ascertain) under the editorship of Heinar Schilling, Walter Hasenclever and at the end Yvan Goll. This journal is characteristic of the anti-capitalist activism of post-Brücke Expressionism in Dresden, which based its ideas on the Utopia of a new universal brotherhood of man and criticized the existing so-

Franz Marc: Versöhnung
Originalholzschnitt für ein Gedicht von Else Lasker-Schüler

Woodcut 'Versöhnung' ('Reconciliation') by Franz Marc to the poem by Else Lasker-Schüler, published in *Der Sturm* (Vol. 3, Nos. 125/126), Berlin, September 1912. 410 × 300 mm.

cial and moral order. Felix Stiemer, who published the journal, wrote in the third number: 'The monthly *Menschen* is a broadsheet, an organ for poets, writers, painters and musicians for whom art is a way of changing humanity and of calling for unity and collectivism.' And in Vol. 2, No. 1, Walter Rheiner announces its programme in more detail: 'The journal *Menschen* represents in literature, painting, criticism, music and politics the rising generation of intellectually active men and women (drawn from all age-groups) who resolutely oppose the still influential and active leftovers and legacies of the generation which led mankind by a thousand paths to the state of collapse in which it finds itself today. In place of materialism and its variations, masked and unmasked, it offers in artistic, political and practi-

cal action its principles of idealism – principles that have been strengthened and intensified by the bloodbath that lasted for over four years and was caused by that materialism, principles which it is convinced will prevail in the end. In literature, painting, music and criticism this idealism is called Expressionism. Expressionism therefore is no purely technical or formal problem, but is primarily an intellectual (epistemological, metaphysical, ethical) attitude which emerged, not today, not yesterday, but thousands of years ago in the history of mankind. In politics this idealism is called anti-national socialism; we need it, radically and absolutely, not in the mind alone, but in action!' A logical consequence of these declarations was the journal's championship of the Bavarian Soviet Republic and its printing of texts by Marx and Lenin. On 7 April 1919 *Menschen* – which was published for a short time during the second quarter of 1919 by the socialist group of intellectual workers in Dresden as *Dresdner Monatszeitung, früher Menschen* ('Dresden Monthly, formerly Menschen') – printed Lenin's speech on world revolution addressed to the St Petersburg Soviet.

The most important of the illustrators of this journal was Conrad Felixmüller. He designed the title-page, which is one of the most characteristic of all the Expressionist periodicals, and published numerous graphic plates. He produced illustrations to Walter Rheiner's *Kokain* (*Cocaine*) in No. 3, 1 February 1919, and to Heinar Schilling's *Die Sklaven* (*The Slaves*) in No. 6, 20 March 1919, which occasionally betray a lingering influence of Kokoschka.

Another journal with a similar political involvement was *Der Weg*, which appeared in Munich under the direction of Eduard Trautner and Fritz Schaefler and was modelled on *Die Aktion* of Berlin. During the period of the Soviet Republic in Munich (7 April – 2 May 1919) it wholeheartedly supported a socialist order of society and published writers and artists who professed revolution and socialism. The literary contributors included Johannes R. Becher, Oskar Maria Graf, Ernst Toller, Alfred Wolfenstein, the artists Felixmüller, Grosz, Kaus, Klee, Nerlinger, Schaefler and Schmidt-Rottluff.

The journals we have examined were extremely influential, not so much on account of the size of the editions (*Der Sturm* was the only one to achieve a 'mass' circulation with its 30,000 copies) as because of the suggestive power of their design which has summed up the spontaneous urgency of the woodcuts. The aim of those journals that were not specifically designed for collectors was to make an appeal; they were not interested in providing entertainment. The external appearance of many periodicals of those

Woodcut lettering by Karl Schmidt-Rottluff for the journal *Kündung*, 1920. 323 × 257 mm.

years that had nothing to do with art were also strongly influenced by them.

1 For full details see P. Raabe, *Die Zeitschriften und Sammlungen des literarischen Expressionismus. Repertorium der Zeitschriften, Jahrbücher, Anthologien, Sammelwerke, Schriftenreihen und Almanache 1910–1921*, Stuttgart, 1964.

2 Paul Westheim in *Kunstblatt*, vol. II, (1918), p. 228.

3 See Lothar Lang, '"Die Schaffenden" 1918–1932, eine Zeitschrift für Sammler', in *Marginalien, Zeitschrift für Buchkunst und Bibliophilie*, no. 33, Berlin, 1969, pp. 7–15.

4 Swift reactions were characteristic of Pfemfert and he was able for years to keep his journal right up to date. Felixmüller writes '... I usually did my cuts without time for proofs, because Pfemfert was always in a hurry' (letter to the author, 9 November 1967).

5 Cited from *Expressionistische Literatur und Kunst. 1910–1923*, Marbach 1960, p. 144 (temporary exhibition at the Schiller Nationalmuseum, no. 7).

6 See *Oskar Kokoschka. Illustrationen, Mappenwerke, Plakate, Graphische Beiträge zu Zeitschriften und Büchern* ..., Hamburg 1965, p. 14 (Catalogue of the Museum für Kunst und Gewerbe, no. 37).

7 See Alois J. Schardt, *Franz Marc*, Berlin, 1936, VII. 1912/4; and *Franz Marc – das grafische Werk*, Berne, Kunstmuseum, 1967, no. 28.

8 See the little volume with the same title, Munich, 1954.

9 W. Niemeyer, 'Die Hamburger Handdrucke der Werkstatt Lerchenfeld', in *Imprimatur. Jahrbuch für Bücherfreunde*, Hamburg, 1930, p. 133.

10 Op. cit., p. 136.

WILHELM NIEMEYER · VERZÜCKTE LANDSCHAFTEN

STURMEICHE

aldeinsame Eiche ◆ Windhorst ◆ Windharfe! ◆ In Blitzaststrängen ◆ Stürme stauend ◆ Hallst du sausend ◆ Hehren Sang ◆ Sang Sangsein ◆ Horchlied Sein Herzlied Sein ◆ Sang Sangsein! ◆ Gebüsche der Zweige ◆ Brülle Waldzorne! ◆ Dröhne Borken ◆ Drohsteinscharr Boote! ◆ Strömend gellt ◆ Sturmgeige ◆ Windwut ◆ Getöse der Heere ◆ Toben der Hasse ◆ Tausend Tode ◆ Trunkene Trauer ◆ Weltsiedendes Leid ◆ Lied Sein ◆ Gramgroß ◆ Sturmstarr ◆ Sang Sangsein ◆ Horchangsthall ◆ Sang Sangsein!

ABEND IM AUTO

ahrt furcht ◆ Land Luft! ◆ Rollen Raum ◆ Rasen ◆ Rauchende Reife! ◆ Flirre Fluren ◆ Beizen Blick! ◆ Schrecke Scholle ◆ Bellt Bilder ◆ Zornzuck ◆ An reiße Räder! ◆ Stämme stieben ◆ Hecken huschen ◆ Dörfer ducken ◆ Brücke bleckt! ◆ Flüge Felder ◆ Kreisen kahl ◆ Wölbe Wiesen ◆ Wallen Wurf ◆ Fahre Forste ◆ Schlingen Schlucht! ◆

Page with initials by Karl Schmidt-Rottluff from the journal *Kündung* (Nos. IV–VI), April-June 1921. Typographer: Johannes Schulz. 461 × 342 mm.

VII. Publishers and series

The publishing history of Expressionism has still to be written. Although basic, publicly accessible material is available in volumes of letters, memoirs and publishers' biographies, there were after all 108 publishing houses that can be shown to have issued books with Expressionist illustrations. Of these, however, only seventeen did very much for Expressionist book illustration; their interest in the Expressionist movement was policy and deliberate involvement, not – as was to a greater or lesser degree the case with all the others – lip-service paid to fashion. Of these highly commendable presses some were relatively shortlived, emerging with the art of their day, supporting it ardently and vanishing at its demise. Among them were the Verlag Paul Steegemann in Hanover, Die Dachstube in Darmstadt, and the Dresdner Verlag von 1917. Like the editors of the periodicals, the publishers of Expressionist literature were usually either artists themselves or at least moved in artistic circles; we think in this connection of the poet-publisher Alfred Richard Meyer and Heinrich F.S. Bachmair, associate of Johannes R. Becher. In the main, however, it was the new publishers who took the Expressionists under their wings out of preference. The most important publisher of literary Expressionism was Kurt Wolff. His press grew (15 February 1913) out of Ernst Rowohlt's first publishing venture; this dated from 1907/08 and Kurt Wolff had joined it as a partner in 1908. Wolff then purchased Rowohlt's share in the business and gave his name to the press; its office was in Leipzig, moving in September 1919 to Munich. From 1913 onwards for many years the Kurt Wolff Verlag became the focal point of Expressionist literature. This state of affairs was due in large part to the series 'Der jüngste Tag' ('Judgment Day'), which published the best-known Expressionist writers, although it did not restrict its programme to them. The series was inaugurated in the early part of 1913; the final volume appeared in 1921; in all seventy-three small volumes (86 numbers) were issued, and from Number 34 (October 1916) onwards were normally published in sober black jackets bearing a small coloured stuck-on label. In a letter of 28 April 1913 to Georg Trakl, Kurt Wolff wrote of this series: 'In a few weeks' time I am bringing out a series of books by young authors at a very cheap price (0.80 M) ... whose works have a quality in common – that they are an independent and powerful expression, of whatever kind, of the times in which we live.'[1] A press prospectus further states: '"Der jüngste Tag" does not confine

itself to any clique, to any friendship or enmity, to any city, to any country. Faithfully reflecting its title, therefore, it will endeavour to collect every item of importance from the multitude of ephemeral things that seems to it to promise everlasting life.' 'Der jüngste Tag' includes many first appearances in print of previously unknown writers, most of them lyric poets. Its authors include Franz Werfel, Walter Hasenclever, Franz Kafka, Carl Ehrenstein, Georg Trakl, Carl Sternheim, Kasimir Edschmid, René Schickele, Johannes R. Becher, Albert Ehrenstein, Mynona, Ludwig Rubiner, Rudolf Leonhard, Oskar Kokoschka, Max Herrmann-Neiße, Alfred Wolfenstein, Yvan Goll and Ernst Toller. The series was highly successful and some of the titles went into second editions. Not many, however, contain Expressionist illustrations. Oskar Kokoschka, Ludwig Meidner and Lyonel Feininger did a few cover designs and other decorations; Ottomar Starke contributed far more in the way of graphic decoration, but his work was not Expressionist.[2]

Kurt Wolff was an extremely cultivated and perceptive man whose interests included the fine illustrated book. His mind was continually occupied with problems of graphic decoration and typography. Letters show that on 4 September 1912 he asked Franz Kafka[3] whether he wished his *Betrachtung* (*Contemplation*), published in 1913, to be set in roman or Fraktur (i.e. gothic) type. In April 1913 Georg Trakl requests that his poems be printed 'in Fraktur or a fairly early roman', and that 'in choosing the format the greatest possible consideration should be given to the poems' own structure'; the press subsequently sent proofs to Trakl for his consideration and the poet decided on a roman face because it would create a 'calm type area' suited to the character of the poems.

These exacting typographical demands necessitated close collaboration with the author and with the printers, Drugulin of Leipzig, who printed many of Wolff's books; the result was that Kurt Wolff succeeded in creating many typographically excellent editions, among which, setting aside Masereel's illustrations, were a few masterpieces of Expressionist book illustration. These include Karl Kraus's *Die chinesische Mauer* (*The Great Wall of China*) with eight original lithographs by Kokoschka (1914); Victor Dirsztay's *Der Unentrinnbare* (*The one from whom you cannot escape*) with eight drawings by Oskar Kokoschka (1923); Ludwig Meidner's *Im Nacken das Sternemeer* (*Behind one the Sea of Stars*) with twelve drawings by the author (1918); Voltaire's

Kandide with twenty-six pen-and-ink drawings by Paul Klee (1920); and finally the most consistent and most finished example of Expressionist book design, Georg Heym's *Umbra vitae* (1924) with forty-seven woodcuts by Ernst Ludwig Kirchner.

Another early publisher of Expressionist literature was the writer Alfred Richard Meyer, who occasionally used the pseudonym Munkepunke. His most important editor-

O du Weithingewölbter, enthirne doch
stillflügelnd über Fluch und Gram
des Werdens und Geschehens
mein Auge.

('O thou distantly-vaulted, silently winging over curse and grief of becoming and happening, unbrain my eye'.)

Part of Benn's poem describes in poetic terms the 'un-

Publishers' colophons:
Die Dachstube, Darmstadt – probably by Joseph Würth; Kiepenheuer-Verlag – by Lyonel Feininger; Verlag R. Piper & Co. – by Paul Renner; Verlag Kurt Wolff – variant form by Emil Preetorius; Verlag Fritz Gurlitt – by E. R. Weiß; Verlag Ernst Rowohlt – by Walter Tiemann; Der Zweemann Verlag – designer not known.

ial work was the series of 'Lyrische Flugblätter' ('Lyrical Broadsheets'), of which he published 105 in Berlin-Wilmersdorf between 1907 and 1923. The little books usually contained sixteen pages and, mainly after 1912, were in large part devoted to Expressionist writing. Authors included Paul Zech, Gottfried Benn, Else Lasker-Schüler, Alfred Lichtenstein, Rudolf Leonhard, Max Herrmann-Neiße, Ernst Wilhelm Lotz, Alfred Döblin and Georg Heym. About half of the 'Flugblätter' have a design on the title and a few of the volumes are illustrated. The title decorations emphasized their broadsheet-like character. The decorative pieces were not all, however, the work of Expressionist artists; others contributed, among them Georg Walter Rößner and Richard Scheibe, as well as numerous artists who stood right outside the Expressionist movement. Max Odoy, Magnus Zeller, Ludwig Kainer, Ernst Ludwig Kirchner and especially Ludwig Meidner, who was responsible for the title-pages, were the ones whose style is unmistakeably Expressionist. Meidner's title decorations to Paul Zech's *Das schwarze Revier* (*The Black Quarter*) of February 1913, and Gottfried Benn's *Söhne* (*Sons*; 1913) are famous. The title to Benn's poems is a salutation to the poet formulated in an image of ecstatic emotion. Benn had written:

braining' of man – his release from rationality; it is the expression of an intellectual capitulation in the face of a capitalist reality that ceased to be controllable or intelligible. Meidner transposes this into a vital, quivering figure of a man, brother of all men, who feels himself at one with mountains, water and stars.

One of the masterpieces of Expressionist illustration appeared in the series 'Lyrische Flugblätter'. This is Ernst Ludwig Kirchner's set of five woodcuts to Alfred Döblin's novella *Das Stiftsfräulein und der Tod* (*The Canoness and Death*) of December 1913. The title-page is a compelling example of Kirchner's mastery, integrating type and image into a totally consistent whole.

Thanks to Kirchner's work and to the many title decorations, Alfred Richard Meyer's publishing enterprise played an important part in the genesis of Expressionist illustration.[4]

After 'Der jüngste Tag' and the 'Lyrische Flugblätter' the best-known and most successful series of Expressionist writings was 'Die Silbergäule' ('The Silver Nags'). Altogether sixty volumes (153 numbers) were issued between 1919 and 1922. The series was started by Paul Steegemann and was the principal business of the press that he had founded in Hanover in 1919. This 'radical series' published texts by late Expressionist authors, volumes containing contemporary graphic work, essays on art, politics and philosophy. The Steegemann Verlag became famous, however, as the result of publishing Dadaist works in its series 'Die Silbergäule' (by, for example, Hans Arp, Richard Huelsenbeck, Kurt Schwitters, Serner and Vischer), and especially works by Schwitters, whose poem 'Anna Blume' ('Die Silbergäule', no. 39/40) was first published in 1919 and by 1922 had run to 13,000 copies. The volume in which the poem appeared included a total of twenty-one poems in 'classic' Dada vein; apart from Schwitters's 'Kathedrale' of 1920 ('Die Silbergäule', no. 41/42), it was the most famous number in the series, other notable contributors to which were the writers Rudolf Leonhard, Heinrich Mann, Kurt Hiller, Kasimir Edschmid, Heinrich Vogeler, Berta Lask, Carl Hauptmann, Kurt Schwitters, Richard Huelsenbeck, Hans Arp, Mynona, Kla-

bund, Victor Curt Habicht and Heinar Schilling. The inventive designs on the jackets of these small volumes in the series were its special contribution to Expressionist book illustration.

A characteristic example of these decorated jackets, most of which were done in a radical, ecstatic idiom, is Viktor Joseph Kuron's pictorial title to Friedrich Wilhelm Wagner's volume of poems *Jungfrauen platzen männertoll* (*Virgins burst out, Crazy for Men*). Most of them were done by Walter O. Grimm, Karl Jakob Hirsch, Ernst Schütte, Otto Hohlt, Ernst Krantz and Kuron himself.

Another volume in the series (no. 43/44, published in 1919) with illustrations that are entirely Expressionist is *Die Dämonen* (*The Possessed*), consisting of eight lithographs by Max Burchartz to Dostoyevsky's novel.

The publishing houses of Piper, Paul Cassirer, Kiepenheuer and Georg Müller are still remembered and some are still active. Their lists too included books illustrated by Expressionist artists. Reinhard Piper of Munich was associated in particular with Der Blaue Reiter and with Max Beckmann. Established in 1904, the firm published in 1912 the almanac *Der Blaue Reiter* edited by Wassily Kandinsky and Franz Marc. An important document in the history of Expressionism, the almanac contains reproductions of works by the major modern painters, texts by Burljuk, Kandinsky, Macke, Marc and Schönberg and others, also musical compositions by Alban Berg, Arnold Schönberg and Anton von Webern. The disharmony between type area and decoration is seriously disturbing, yet the animal initials and vignettes and the initials by Hans Arp showed what Expressionist book decoration might become. Like Kandinsky's coloured cover designs, they represent the Expressionist art of the book in its infancy. The only other illustrations dating from 1912 that are still remembered are Kokoschka's etchings to Ehrenstein's *Tubutsch*, F. H. E. Schneidler's plates to Heine's *Atta Troll* and Kandinsky's ten original woodcuts to his own book *Über das Geistige in der Kunst* (*Concerning the Spiritual in Art*). In 1913 Reinhard Piper published Kandinsky's *Klänge* (*Sounds*), a volume of verse and prose, which, with some fifty woodcuts, including twelve in colour, is one of the earliest, fullest and most imposing of the illustrated books of the Expressionist period. Piper's contacts with the Expressionist artists had many facets. For instance, his desire for close and fruitful collaboration with Franz Marc in particular was clear to see and, had Marc not lost his life so early, would presumably have resulted in much important work. For example, Marc made decorations for the binding of Piper's *Das Tier in der Kunst* (*Animals in Art*) and for Meier-Graefe's mono-

S Ö H N E
Neue Gedichte von GOTTFRIED BENN, dem Verfasser der Morgue
A. R. MEYER VERLAG BERLIN - WILMERSDORF

Drawing by Ludwig Meidner on jacket of *Söhne* by Gottfried Benn, in the series 'Lyrische Flugblätter'. Berlin: A. R. Meyer, 1913. 180 × 140 mm. [225]

graph on Cézanne. Both pieces are drawings, one after a watercolour by Delacroix and the other after Cézanne's painting *Women Bathers before a Tent*. There is no reference in either book, neither of which appeared until some years after the artist's death in the war, to the fact that these were copies by Marc; the information is taken from Piper's memoirs.[5]

Shortly before war broke out Marc had discussed with Piper a plan for an extensive series of Bible illustrations.[6] A team effort, including Klee, Heckel, Kubin and Kokoschka, was proposed. Klee had taken in hand the Psalms, Kubin the Book of Daniel – this was published in Munich in 1918 – while Franz Marc chose Genesis. However, only the two woodcuts 'Schöpfungsgeschichte' I and II ('The Story of Creation') of 1914 – one of them in three colours – were executed.[7] The outbreak of war and Marc's death put an end to the great project of a Bible illustrated by Expressionist artists. Piper later became interested in Max Beckmann. The celebrated Beckmann portfolios *Gesichter* (*Faces*) of 1919 and *Jahrmarkt* (*Annual Fair*) of 1922 appeared as publications 13 and 36 of the Marées-Gesellschaft. The Marées-Gesellschaft had been founded in 1916 by the distinguished writer on art Julius Meier-Graefe in association with Piper, and its publications (known as 'Drucke der Marées-Gesellschaft') were issued by the Piper Verlag. The programme of the publications was very catholic and was not Expressionist in character. In 1921 Piper published Lili von Braunbehrens's volume of poems *Stadtnacht* (*City Night*) with illustrations by Max Beckmann.

Compared with Piper, the other publishers who are either still remembered or still in existence contributed less to the Expressionist art of the book. Nevertheless Paul Cassirer, the Berlin art-dealer and publisher, brought out many volumes illustrated by Barlach, editions of Else Lasker-Schüler illustrated by herself, and Kokoschka's collection of previously published pieces with a cover design by himself. In a prospectus of 1919, Paul Cassirer declared that he desired to 'serve fine literature through books fine in craftsmanship'. In 1920 he published Ludwig Meidner's *Septemberschrei. Hymnen, Gebete und Lästerungen* (*September Cry. Hymns, Prayers and Blasphemies*), for which the author made fourteen drawings; the book is an important example of Expressionist illustration. In addition, Paul Cassirer and his cousin Bruno Cassirer performed a valuable service in publishing many celebrated illustrated works by Max Slevogt – but his work cannot be classified as Expressionist illustration.

Gustav Kiepenheuer started his firm in 1910 in Weimar and later moved to Potsdam. For Paul Westheim he published *Das Kunstblatt*, and soon afterwards the periodical portfolios for collectors, *Die Schaffenden*. Kiepenheuer instigated the series 'Graphische Bücher' with which he sought

Title woodcut by Conrad Felixmüller for the Dresden journal *Menschen*, Vol. 1, 1918. Dresden: Felix Stiemer Verlag. Woodcut 450 × 155 mm.

Jacket designs for volumes in the series 'Die Silbergäule', published by the Paul Steegemann Verlag, Hanover. Each 214 × 138 mm.
Viktor Joseph Kuron. 1920. [208]   Otto Hohlt. 1919. [127]

to break through the exclusiveness of so many Expressionist illustrated books, the result of very small editions and high prices. At all events the volumes of this collection – which included Gogol's *Der Mantel* (*The Overcoat*) of 1920 with illustrations by Walter Gramatté – ran into impressions of 1,100 copies.

Publication of Expressionist literature represented only a small part of the business of the Verlag Georg Müller in Munich, although its authors did include Ehrenstein and Döblin. The most important work of Expressionist illus-

tration issued by this publisher came from Klee, who made ten lithographs to the book *Potsdamer Platz* by Curt Corrinth (1920).

The Rowohlt Verlag, still widely known today, was founded in 1911 by Ernst Rowohlt, who published the poems of Georg Heym, one of the first books of Expressionist writing. And after it was re-founded in 1919 it again took an interest in Expressionism, in particular through its series 'Umsturz und Aufbau' ('Ruin and Rebuilding') and a collected edition of the most important Expressionist

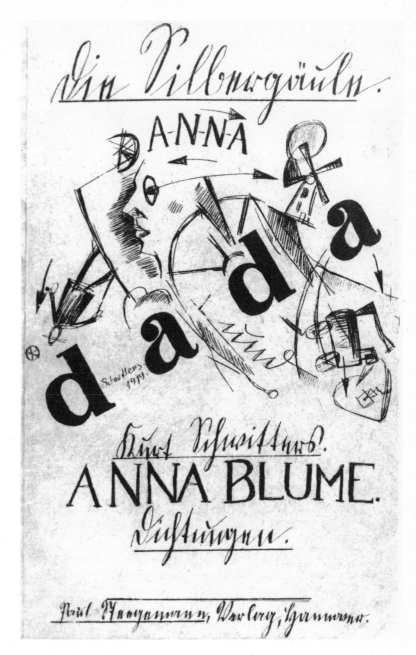

Ernst Schütte. 1919. [314]

Kurt Schwitters. 1919.

poems edited by Kurt Pinthus in 1920 under the title *Menschheitsdämmerung* (*Twilight of Mankind*).

The series appeared during 1919 and 1920 and continued through eight small volumes. A programmatic announcement contained the words: 'We have lived through the most outrageous catastrophe that has ever struck a nation. Through anguish and death, through blood and tears, only one weapon has remained to us, but that a powerful one: the spirit. The aim of the series 'Umsturz und Aufbau' is to fertilize the spirit for the renewal of our nation-

hood. The series will bring together documents that will soar above our despairing present like lights signalling a better future.' The pamphlets were written by Georg Büchner, Georg Herwegh, Karl Marx, George Herron, Walter Hasenclever, Rudolf Leonhard, Stefan Grossmann and Johannes R. Becher and Wilhelm Plünnecke, Karl Jakob Hirsch and Ludwig Meidner provided Expressionist cover designs. Meidner's pictorial titles can best be described as a graphic parallel to the programme. For Hasenclever's poems and speeches – *Der politische Dichter* (*The Political*

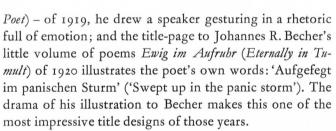

Jacket designs by Ludwig Meidner for volumes in the series 'Umsturz und Aufbau',
published by the Ernst Rowohlt Verlag, Berlin, 1919 and 1920. 233 × 153 mm. [233, 231]

Poet) – of 1919, he drew a speaker gesturing in a rhetoric full of emotion; and the title-page to Johannes R. Becher's little volume of poems *Ewig im Aufruhr* (*Eternally in Tumult*) of 1920 illustrates the poet's own words: 'Aufgefegt im panischen Sturm' ('Swept up in the panic storm'). The drama of his illustration to Becher makes this one of the most impressive title designs of those years.

Franz Pfemfert, in his Verlag der Wochenschrift Die Aktion (the press of the weekly *Die Aktion*) of 1917–25, was another who issued books in series. This one was called 'Der rote Hahn' ('The Red Cock'). It flourished through forty-one volumes (59 numbers) and published authors such as Johannes R. Becher, Gottfried Benn, Yvan Goll, Max Herrmann-Neiße, Jakob van Hoddis, Karl Otten, Pfem-

fert himself and Carl Sternheim, as well as numerous political writings, including some by Franz Mehring, Lenin, Lunacharsky and Marx. The volumes appeared in red jackets and, with one exception, were unillustrated. The exception, Alfred Brust's *Das Spiel Christa vom Schmerz der Schönheit des Weibes* (*The Play Christa of the Pain of the Beauty of Woman*) with nine woodcuts by Karl Schmidt-Rottluff (no. 29/30, 1918), was, however, an important example of Expressionist book illustration.

During the late Expressionist period a few small publishing houses did a great deal for book illustration. These include Adolf Harms's Die schöne Rarität (The Fine Rarity) in Kiel, the Dresdner Verlag von 1917, and Die Dachstube (The Garret) in Darmstadt. Adolf Harms directed the series of 'Drucke der schönen Rarität', which included a few pieces illustrated by Josef Eberz. The Dresden firm was, however, by far the more important and more influential. Established in 1917, it had grown out of a circle of Expressionist artists who had begun to hold literary soirées in September of the same year. The group included Heinar Schilling, Walter Rheiner, Raoul Hausmann, Felix Stiemer, Bess Brenck Kalischer, Conrad Felixmüller, Richard Fischer, A. Rudolf Leinert and – these might almost be called corresponding members – Oskar Maria Graf, Gerhard Ausleger, Georg Tappert and Walter O. Grimm.[8] Together with the publishing houses of Felix Stiemer, Robert Kaemmerer, the Sibyllen-Verlag, the Verlag der Neuen Schaubühne and of the art-dealer Emil Richter, the Dresdner Verlag von 1917 reflected the extraordinarily brisk literary and artistic activity which Dresden enjoyed at the time. In addition to the journal *Menschen*, the Dresdner Verlag von 1917 published books in two series: 'Die Dichtung der Jüngsten' ('Poetry of the Very Young') – nine volumes (13 numbers), 1917–19; and 'Das neueste Gedicht' ('The Latest Poetry') – twenty-seven volumes (35 numbers), 1918–20. Most of the works in the series were written by Dresden Expressionists. The series 'Das neueste Gedicht' is notable for its important late Expressionist cover designs, for which Georg Schrimpf, Walter O. Grimm, Eugen Ludwig Gattermann, Georg Tappert, Peter August Böckstiegel, Heinar Schilling, Georg Kind and Conrad Felixmüller, among others, were responsible. Felixmüller also designed the one illustrated volume of the series, Schilling's epic verse drama *Die Sklaven* (*The Slaves*). The covers fully live up to the intention expressed in one of the firm's advertising slogans 'Holzschnitt auf buntem Umschlag schreit in die Zeit' ('The woodcut on the coloured wrapper cries out into time'). A politically progressive note characteristic of late Expressionism in Dresden is sounded in a number of books published by this firm.

That engaging press Die Dachstube in Darmstadt grew out of the enthusiasm of a fifteen-year-old schoolboy. In 1915 Joseph Würth and a few friends founded a school magazine called *Die Dachstube* which continued in existence until 1918, ran to sixty-five numbers and became the germ of a publishing house which survived into the 1930s. Die Dachstube published texts by Carlo Mierendorff, Theodor Haubach, Kasimir Edschmid, Heinar Schilling, Hans Schiebelhuth, Fritz Usinger and Max Krell among others; its illustrators included Carl Gunschmann, Ludwig Breitwieser, Josef Eberz, Walter O. Grimm and Victor Joseph Kuron. The firm inaugurated two series: 'Bücher der Dachstube' – in which eight volumes appeared between 1917

and 1923; and 'Die kleine Republik. Eine Flugschriftenreihe' ('The Little Republic. A Series of Pamphlets'), with fifteen volumes outstanding for their typographic design – published between 1918 and 1924. Nearly all these volumes contain several original prints, not all of which can be considered illustrations, which form – during the late Expressionist period! – a compelling example of that harmony of text and plate that is characteristic of Expressionism as a whole. The two Dachstube series are impressive instances of a premeditated and very deliberate plan to integrate text and plate and they carry it through with a single-mindedness that is found in no other Expressionist series. The consistency and unity of their programme constitute the importance of Die Dachstube's publications.

Among other publishers who promoted Expressionist illustration were Robert Kaemmerer (Dresden), Hans Heinrich Tillgner (Potsdam), Erich Reiss (Berlin), Euphorion-Verlag (Berlin) and Hesperos Verlag (Munich). Reiss, whose special protégé was Willy Jaeckel, also published the series directed by Kasimir Edschmid, 'Tribüne der Kunst und Zeit' ('Tribunes of Art and Time'), in which new artistic problems were treated as generalized theory, Edschmid himself writing on literary questions, Wilhelm Hausenstein on painting, Paul Bekker on music and Willi Wolfradt on sculpture. Some of the first monographs on the visual artists of the time – and this includes many illustrators – appeared in the series 'Junge Kunst' published by the Verlag Klinkhardt und Biermann in Leipzig. This firm also published the *Jahrbuch der neuen Kunst* (1920–22).

Certain publishing enterprises that served Expressionist illustration well fall into a different category. These are the art-dealers who affiliated themselves for short periods with a publishing house. They include the Alfred Flechtheim and Hans Goltz galleries, and most notably Fritz Gurlitt. The Gurlitt-Verlag published not only two unusually illuminating almanacs and annuals but also several illustrated series. The almanacs appeared in 1919 and 1920, with cover designs by César Klein and Max Pechstein, who also drew the calendar. Both volumes contained original graphics. The graphic annuals (1921 and 1923) contained many illustrations, but the presentation is modest. The central editorial concern of the Gurlitt-Verlag was, however, four luxurious series issued in very small editions designed entirely to please the collector and amateur. They did not in fact press Expressionist illustration on their readers but catered for the taste of countless private collectors at a period when the collecting of prints and illustrated books had returned to fashion. The four series are the 'Drucke der Gurlitt-Presse' (portfolios), 'Das geschriebene Buch' ('The Writ-

Woodcut by Max Pechstein on cover of the *Almanach auf das Jahr 1920*, issued by the Fritz Gurlitt Verlag, Berlin

ka, Max Pechstein and Richard Seewald, including Kokoschka's Bach cantata and Pechstein's illustrations to Seidel's *Yali und sein weißes Weib* (*Yali and his White Woman*) and to Lautensack's *Die Samländische Ode* (*Samland Ode*) – three crucial events in Expressionist illustration.

Twenty-nine Expressionist illustrated books can be attributed to Fritz Gurlitt and – as far as numbers are concerned – his press takes first place among publishers of Expressionist illustrated books.

Very many Expressionist illustrated books contain original graphic illustrations; the favourite techniques were woodcut and etching, though lithography was not unusual. Books illustrated by original prints were bound of necessity to be issued in small editions. Technical considerations were therefore responsible for the exclusive character of the Expressionist art of the book. The smallest edition of an important book is Max Beckmann's four-act comedy *Ebbi* issued in thirty-three copies. *Ebbi* was printed at the Johannes-Presse in Vienna in the autumn of 1924 for the Gesellschaft der 33 (Society of 33) and contains six etchings by the artist. Most of the editions comprised between 125 and 350 copies, though larger editions were printed of certain important works. Edschmid's *Die Fürstin* (*The Princess*) with etchings by Beckmann was limited to 500 copies; Braunbehrens's *Stadtnacht* (*City Night*) with lithographs by Beckmann – 600 copies; Heym's *Umbra vitae* with woodcuts by Kirchner – 510 copies; and *Robinson Crusoe* illustrated by Janthur – 800 copies. Some publishers, Kiepenheuer in particular, issued editions of 1,100 copies. The little Dresdner Verlag von 1917 produced books in editions of up to 3,000 copies. In fact the only major work of the Expressionist art of the book to have been issued in a very large edition was Paul Klee's illustrated *Kandide* (*Candide*) by Voltaire, though in this case the line-etchings are after the artist's drawings and for this reason are not original graphics.

The fact that the size of the editions was generally small was due, however, not only to the technical difficulties and limitations involved in printing originals. Another equally important cause lay in the timidity of many publishers and booksellers and a large section of their readership when faced with the Expressionists' highly individual interpretations. The new world of images expressed by these artists in their illustrations, as in their paintings, flouted visual

ten Book'), 'Die Neuen Bilderbücher' ('The New Picture Books') and the 'Privatdrucke der Gurlitt-Presse: Der Venuswagen' ('Private Publications of the Gurlitt-Presse: The Chariot of Venus') edited by Alfred Richard Meyer. All appeared after the war, the earliest began publication in 1918; the first volume of the series 'Das geschriebene Buch' did not appear until the autumn of 1921. Not all the illustrations in the series, however, are Expressionist: they include works by Lovis Corinth, Heinrich Zille, Hans Meid, Paul Scheurich, Max Slevogt, Hugo Steiner-Prag, George Grosz, Charlotte Berend, Wilhelm Wagner and Georg Walter Rößner. Meanwhile, the texts were written by a calligrapher on the stone, and contain a few important Expressionist illustrations by Richard Janthur and Ludwig Meidner. 'Die Neuen Bilderbücher'[9] were conceived as examples of a new book illustration and contained influential works by Willi Geiger, Willy Jaeckel, Oskar Kokosch-

Herm Dienz: woodcut to *Meier Helmbrecht* by Wernher der Gärtner. Cut in 1922. Published as 'Seldwyla-Druck' No. 6 by Verlag Seldwyla, Zürich, in 1924. The book, containing twelve woodcuts, appeared in an edition of 200 copies. 247 × 200 mm.

convention altogether too flagrantly. Publishers who decided nevertheless to commission Expressionists to illustrate their authors' works risked not selling their books or finding difficulty in doing so. It is therefore all the more remarkable that publishing houses did exist – and they were usually small and often impecunious ones, most of them new and lacking name and reputation – which were prepared to assist the Expressionist art of the book to gain acceptance.

No wonder, then, that Expressionist illustrated books are uncommon in the antiquarian book trade today and that the works of the masters are rarities of the very first order. Few in number from the first, the scarcity of these books was increased by the shameful burning of books by the Nazis. The Expressionist artists were on the Index and as a result many public collections had valuable works expropriated. For this reason Expressionist books in museums, collections, public and private libraries have become precious and protected rarities.

1 Kurt Wolff, *Briefwechsel eines Verlegers 1911–1963*, ed. B. Zeller and E. Otten, Frankfurt am Main, 1966, p. 80.

2 For 'Der jüngste Tag' see Raabe ,op. cit., no. 145. Also Ludwig Dietz, 'Kurt Wolffs Bücherei "Der jüngste Tag". Seine Geschichte und Bibliografie', in *Philobiblon*, vol. 7, Hamburg, 1963, p. 96ff.

3 All letters are cited from Kurt Wolff, op. cit.; see pp. 25, 77, 86.

4 For the 'Lyrische Flugblätter' see in particular A. R. Meyer, *die maer von der musa expressionistica*, Düsseldorf, 1948.

5 Reinhard Piper, *Mein Leben als Verleger*, Munich, 1964, p. 295f.

6 Piper, op. cit., p. 299.

7 Alois J. Schardt, *Franz Marc*, Berlin 1936; VII, 1914/1 and 2; also *Franz Marc – das grafische Werk*, Berne, Kunstmuseum 1967, nos. 44, 45.

8 According to H. Schilling in the journal *Menschen*, vol. 2, no. X, 1919.

9 A. Thurandt, 'Die Neuen Bilderbücher' in *Almanach auf das Jahr 1920*, Verlag Fritz Gurlitt, Berlin, p. 206.

The Plates

Oskar Kokoschka: illustration to *Tubutsch* by Albert Ehrenstein.
Vienna and Leipzig: Jahoda & Siegel [1912].
The book, containing twelve line etchings after drawings,
also has an illustration on the cover. 180×118 mm. [187]

Pages 96–99 Oskar Kokoschka: lithographs to *Die chinesische
Mauer* by Karl Kraus. Leipzig: Kurt Wolff Verlag, 1914.
The book, containing eight original lithographs, appeared in
an edition limited to 200 copies. 334×277 mm; 280×278 mm;
313×250 mm; 285×276 mm. [188]

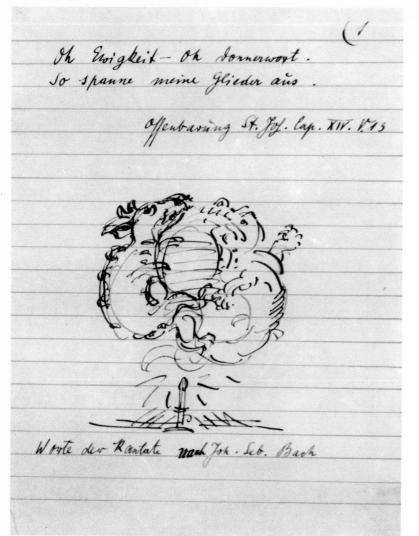

Oh Ewigkeit — Oh Donnerwort.
So spanne meine Glieder aus.

Offenbarung St. Joh. Cap. XIV. V. 13

Worte der Kantate nach Joh. Seb. Bach

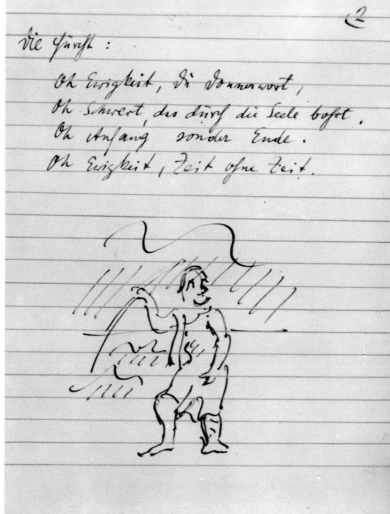

die Furcht :

Oh Ewigkeit, du Donnerwort,
Oh Schwert, das durch die Seele bohrt.
Oh Anfang sonder Ende.
Oh Ewigkeit, Zeit ohne Zeit.

Pages 100–104   Oskar Kokoschka: *O Ewigkeit – Du Donnerwort.*
Pen-and-ink sketches and manuscript text to the cantata by
Johann Sebastian Bach, probably 1913/14. The original leaves
are in the Staatliche Galerie Moritzburg, Halle. 200 × 160 mm.

100

Die Hoffnung:

1.

Herr, ich warte auf dein Heil,
Ich warte auf dein Heil, ich warte auf dein Heil.
Dein Heil! Herr, ich warte auf dein Heil.

Ich weiß vor großer Traurigkeit nicht,
wo ich mich hin wende; mein ganz er-
schrocknes Herze bebt
daß mir die Zung am Gaumen klebt.

Die Hoffnung und die Furcht:

Ein schwerer Gang zum letzten Kampf und Streite,
Mein Beistand ist schon da.
Mein Heiland steht mir ja mit Trost zur Seite.
Die Todesangst, der letzte Schmerz
ereilt und überfällt mein Herz
und martert diese Glieder.

Die Furcht und die Hoffnung:

Ich lege diesen Leib vor Gott zum Opfer nieder.
Ist gleich der Trübsal Feuer heiß,
Genug, es reinigt auch zu Gottes Preis.
Doch mir wird nicht der Sünden große Schuld vor
                    mein Gesichte stellen!
Gott wird deswegen doch kein Todesurtheil fällen,
Es giebt ein Ende der Versuchungsplagen,
    daß man sie kann ertragen.

Die Furcht:
    Mein letztes Lager will mich schrecken.
Die Hoffnung:
    Mich wird des Heiland Hand bedecken.
Beide:
    Des Glaubens Schwachheit sinket fast.
Die Hoffnung:
    Mein Jesus trägt mit mir die Last.

!!!!
(Gehört zu Seite 7)
← Achtung!

Die Furcht:
   Das offne Grab sieht gräulich aus.

Die Hoffnung:
   Es wird mir doch ein Friedenshaus.

Die Furcht:
   Der Tod bleibt doch der menschlichen Natur
   verhaßt und reißet fast die Hoffnung ganz
      zu Boden.

Heiliger Geist:
   Selig sind die Toten, selig sind die Toten,
   die Toten, selig sind die Toten,

Die Hoffnung:
   Ach! aber ach! wie viel Gefahr
   stellt sich der Seele dar,
   den Sterbeweg zu gehen.
   Vielleicht wird ihr der Todesrachen den Tod
      erschrecklich machen,
   wenn er sich zu verschlingen sucht,
   Vielleicht ist sie bereits verflucht zum ewigen Ver-
      derben.

← (gehört zu Seite 6)
Achtung!

Heiliger Geist:
   Selig sind die Toten, selig sind die Toten,
   die Toten, die Toten,
   die in dem Herrn sterben.

Die Hoffnung:
   Wenn ich im Herrn sterbe,
   ist dann die Seligkeit mein Teil und Erbe?
   Der Leib wird ja der Würmer Speise.
   Ja, werden meine Glieder zu Staub und Erde
   da ich ein Kind des Todes heiße — wieder, —
   so schein ich ja im Grabe zu verderben.

Heiliger Geist:
   Selig sind die Toten, die Toten.
   Die in dem Herrn sterben; von nun an —
   Selig sind die Toten, die im Herrn sterben.

Die Furcht:
Wohlan! Soll ich von nun an selig sein,
so stelle Dir es Hoffnung wieder ein:
Mein Leib mag ohne Furcht im Schlafe ruhen,
der Geist kann einen Blick in jene Freude thun.

Beide:
Es ist genug: Herr, wenn es dir gefällt,
so spanne mich doch aus.
Mein Jesus kommt: nun gute Nacht,
Oh Welt! Ich fahr ins Himmelshaus,
ich fahre ein mit Frieden,
mein großer Jammer bleibt darnieden.
Es ist genug, es ist genug.

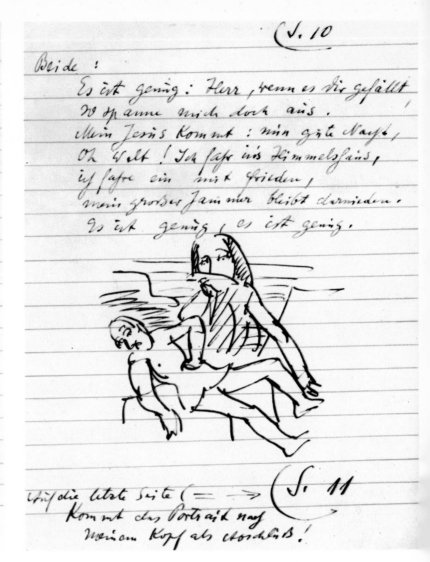

Auf die letzte Seite (= —>) S. 11
Kommt das Portrait nach
meinem Kopf als Abschluß!

Pages 105–111 Oskar Kokoschka: *O Ewigkeit – Du Donnerwort.*
Lithographs to the words of Bach's cantata. Berlin: Fritz Gurlitt,
1914. The eleven lithographs were published in a portfolio
edition limited to 125 copies. In 1918 the same press issued an
edition in book form, also limited to 125 copies, forming part
of its collectors' series 'Die Neuen Bilderbücher'. Sheet size
546 × 420 mm. [189]

Oskar Kokoschka: Drawing for the novel Der *Unentrinnbare* by
Victor Dirsztay. Munich: Kurt Wolff, 1923. 191 × 142 mm. [199]

Pages 113–115 Oskar Kokoschka: lithographs to his dramatic
poem *Der gefesselte Kolumbus*. Berlin: Fritz Gurlitt, 1916. The
twelve lithographs were published in a portfolio edition limited
to 200 copies. In 1920/21 Gurlitt issued an edition in book form
limited to 120 copies. Portfolio leaf size 490 × 387 mm. [190]

116

Erich Heckel: woodcuts to *Die Ballade vom Zuchthaus zu Reading*
(*The Ballad of Reading Gaol*) by Oscar Wilde. Although dating
from 1907, the twelve woodcuts were first published in book
form only in 1963, in an edition of 600 copies, by Ernest Rathenau, New York. 200×150 mm.; 200×150 mm.; 200×150 mm.;
203×147 mm. [113]

Ernst Ludwig Kirchner: woodcuts to the novella *Das Stiftsfräulein und der Tod* by Alfred Döblin, published in the series of
'Lyrische Flugblätter'. Berlin: Alfred Richard Meyer, 1913.
116 × 80 mm.; 115 × 78 mm.; 117 × 80 mm.; 118 × 79 mm. [171]

I

Der Lindenwirt, Metzgermeister und Jäger Andreas Erdinger in Gündlach hatte die Augen geschlossen. Er war noch kein alter Mann. Das den Wirten verhängnisvolle Alter liegt um fünfzig. Seine zwei Söhne beerdigten ihn, wie's Brauch ist, die Tochter, die in Freienstein verheiratet war, hatte ihren Mann geschickt. Sie lag im Wochenbett.

Nach dem Leichenmahl, als sich die Verwandten auf den Heimweg begeben hatten,

Ernst Ludwig Kirchner: woodcut illustrations in
Neben der Heerstraße by Jakob Boßhart. The book contains
24 original woodcuts. Zürich and Leipzig: Grethlein & Co.,
1923. 79 × 72 mm.; 91 × 88 mm.; 60 × 78 mm. [174]

verflucht! — — —" bis er erschöpft in sich zu-
sammensank. Auf dem kleinen Steinaltar hatte
er das Geld verflucht. Briggel hörte die erste
Haustüre im Dorfe knarren, die erste Kuh brül-
len, eine Lerche jubelte aus einem Acker auf.
Fern über dem Säntis brodelte der Tag empor,
immer greller und blendender, bis die lange
Nadel des ersten Sonnenstrahls unter dem Himmel durchschoß und das Häufchen Geldfluch auf
dem Granitaltar gierig traf. Der Briggel sah,

sprechen in wilder Verzückung an. Sie streckte
ihm das Büchlein entgegen und stieß mit über-
höhter Stimme hervor: „Du bist Naboth! Alle
sollen sterben, die uns an das Gut wollen. Will's
Gott!"

„Wer es angreifen will, soll kein Glied
rühren können!" rief er milder, aber ebenso über-
höht.

„Es ist vielleicht Sünde, was wir tun," fuhr
sie fort, „aber wer Sünde sät, soll keinen Segen
ernten!"

„Wenn uns kein Gesetz hilft, müssen wir uns
selber helfen," beschwichtigte er seine und ihre
Unruhe. „Wer Gerechtigkeit sucht, sündigt nicht!"
Beide glaubten in diesem Augenblick fest an die
Wirkung des Bannspruches, so erregt waren sie.

„Das Werk ist getan, nun wollen wir, so Gott

Pages 122–126 Ernst Ludwig Kirchner: title-page and text
pages with woodcuts from *Umbra vitae* by Georg Heym. The
book was designed in its entirety by Kirchner, the type being
set in Grotesque bold. It contained forty-seven original woodcuts and was published in an edition limited to 510 numbered
copies. Munich: Kurt Wolff Verlag, 1924. 230×157 mm. [175]

GEORG HEYM
UMBRA VITAE
NACHGELASSENE
GEDICHTE

MIT 47 ORIGINALHOLZSCHNITTEN
VON
ERNST LUDWIG KIRCHNER

KURT WOLFF VERLAG MÜNCHEN
1924

DER KRIEG

Aufgestanden ist er, welcher lange schlief,
Aufgestanden unten aus Gewölben tief.
In der Dämmrung steht er, groß und unbekannt,
Und den Mond zerdrückt er in der schwarzen Hand.

In den Abendlärm der Städte fällt er weit,
Frost und Schatten einer fremden Dunkelheit.
Und der Märkte runder Wirbel stockt zu Eis.
Es wird still. Sie sehn sich um. Und keiner weiß.

In den Gassen faßt es ihre Schulter leicht.
Eine Frage. Keine Antwort. Ein Gesicht erbleicht.
In der Ferne zittert ein Geläute dünn,
Und die Bärte zittern um ihr spitzes Kinn.

Auf den Bergen hebt er schon zu tanzen an,
Und er schreit: Ihr Krieger alle, auf und an!
Und es schallet, wenn das schwarze Haupt er schwenkt,
Drum von tausend Schädeln laute Kette hängt.

DIE STADT DER QUAL

Ich bin in Wüsten eine große Stadt
Hinter der Nacht und toten Meeren weit.
In meinen Gassen herrscht stets wilder Zank
Geraufter Bärte. Ewig Dunkelheit

Hängt über mir wie eines Tieres Haut.
Ein roter Turm nur flackert in den Raum.
Ein Feuer braust und wirft den Schein von Blut
Wie einen Keil auf schwarzer Köpfe Schaum.

DIE IRREN

I.

Papierne Kronen zieren sie. Sie tragen
Holzstöcke aufrecht auf den spitzen Knien
Wie Szepter. Ihre langen Hemden schlagen
Um ihren Bauch wie Königshermelin.

DAS INFERNALISCHE ABENDMAHL

Ihr, denen ward das Blut vor Trauer bleich,
Ihr, die der Sturm der Qualen stets durchrast,
Ihr, deren Stirn der Lasten weites Reich,
Ihr, deren Auge Kummer schon verglast,

Ihr, denen auf der jungen Schläfe brennt
Wie Aussatz schon das große Totenmal,
Tretet heran, empfangt das Sakrament
Verfluchter Hostien in dem Haus der Qual.

Pages 127, 128   Ernst Ludwig Kirchner: designs for front
and back covers of *Neben der Heerstraße* by Jakob Boßhart.
192 × 127 mm. [174]

Pages 129, 130   Ernst Ludwig Kirchner: woodcut on front cover
and frontispiece of *Umbra vitae* by Georg Heym. 234 × 160 mm;
147 × 91 mm. [175]

129

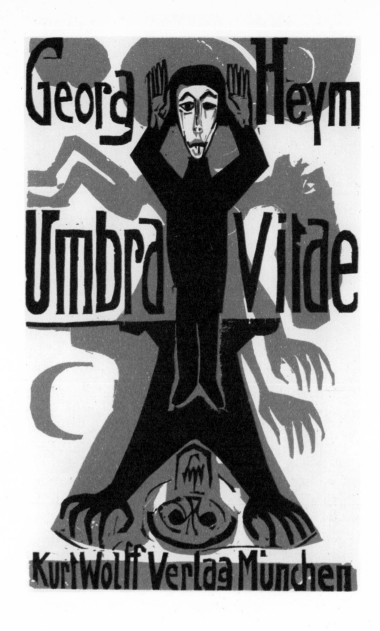

Georg Heym

Umbra Vitae

Kurt Wolff Verlag München

Pages 131, 132   Max Pechstein: etchings to *Heidenstam* by Carl
Sternheim, published in the bi-monthly *Marsyas* (Vol. 1, No. 4),
Berlin, January/February 1918. 226 × 170 mm.; 202 × 155 mm.
[263]

Max Pechstein: etching to *Der Schatten* by Hermann Stehr, published, together with three other etchings, in the bi-monthly *Marsyas* (Vol. 1, No. 5), Berlin, summer 1918. 202 × 155 mm. [264]

Max Pechstein: lithograph to *Die Samländische Ode* by Heinrich Lautensack. The book, which contained twenty-two lithographs, was published in an edition limited to 130 copies. Berlin: Fritz Gurlitt, 1918. 320 × 280 mm. [262]

Pages 135–137   Max Pechstein: page of text and etchings from *Yali und sein weißes Weib* by Willy Seidel. The book, which contained eight original etchings, was published in 1924 in an edition limited to 220 copies. 350 × 280 mm. [269]

s war zu jener Zeit / als noch lange Jahrzehnte verdämmerten / ohne daß ein Schiff die Magellanstraße passierte / da warf ein großer Wirbelsturm den Dreimaster „Swallow" einer englischen Handelslinie gegenüber von Kap Virgenes an die küste. Ein etwa zwölfköpfiger Trupp Ona / der mit Fisch= und Seehundsfang beschäftigt in der Nähe war / bemächtigte sich des Wracks / tötete die Besatzung / soweit sie noch lebte / und einer der Wilden / den sie Yali nannten / fand ein einjähriges kind weiblichen Geschlechts und nahm es an sich. Es bewegte sich wie eine krake / war schneeweiß und schrie scharf. Irgend etwas an ihm fesselte Yali und hielt ihn ab / dem kinde den kopf zu zerschellen / vielleicht war es das durchaus Neue / Flaumzarte / Blendende / was den ratlosen Gliederchen anhaftete. „Man muß es wachsen lassen" / dachte Yali. „Wenn es groß wird / kann man es ja erschlagen."

Dies dachte er / weil er unbefangen aus dem Morgenzwielicht der Schöpfung trat und noch an keinem Wesen / das ihm glich / eine andere Farbe als schmutziges kupferbraun wahrgenommen hatte. Er war ein großer Mann

H M Pechstein

Pages 138, 139   Karl Schmidt-Rottluff: four woodcuts from
Das Spiel Christa vom Schmerz der Schönheit des Weibes
by Alfred Brust, published in the series 'Der rote Hahn', ed.
Franz Pfemfert. Berlin: Die Aktion, 1918. 205×130 mm. [300]

Pages 140–143 Paul Klee: drawings to *Kandide* by Voltaire,
executed in 1911. The book contains twenty-six pen-and-ink
drawings. Type: Unger-Fraktur. Munich: Kurt Wolff Verlag,
1920. 85 × 132 mm.; 85 × 132 mm.; 90 × 132 mm. [176]

Zweites Kapitel

Wie's Kandiden unter den Bulgaren geht

Vertrieben aus seinem irdischen Paradiese wanderte Kandide mit weinendem Auge fort,
ohne zu wissen wohin. Mit leerem Magen legte er sich mitten im Felde hin, zwischen
zwei Furchen. Es schneite die Nacht durch heftig; ganz erstarrt schlich Kandide mit dämmern-
dem Morgen nach einer benachbarten Stadt. Sterbensmatt vor Hunger und Strapazen, nicht
einen Heller Geld bei sich, machte er vor der Türe eines Wirtshauses höchst betrübt halt.
Zwei Blauröcke wurden ihn gewahr. „Ha! ein hübscher Kerl, Herr Bruder!" sagte der
eine. „Wie'n Rohr gewachsen! Just so groß, wie wir'n brauchen!" Sie gingen auf Kan-
diden los und baten ihn sehr höflich, zu Mittag mit ihnen zu speisen. „Ich finde mich
ungemein durch Ihre Einladung beehrt, meine Herren," sagte Kandide mit einem be-
scheidenen Ton, der gleich seine Nation verriet, „allein ich habe kein Geld, kann meine

8

Sechstes Kapitel

Probates Mittel der hochehrwürdigen Inquisition fürs Erdbeben, bestehend in einem schönen Autodafé, wobei Kandide den Staubbesen bekommt

Nachdem das Erdbeben drei Viertel von Lissabon verwüstet hatte, war im Rate der Wächter und Weisen des Landes beschlossen worden, dem Pöbel ein gar stattliches Autodafé zu geben. Ein kräftigeres Mittel, dem gänzlichen Untergange der Stadt vorzubauen, hatten sie nicht können ausfindig machen.

Sonach hatte man einen Biskajer eingezogen, der überführt war, seine Gevatterin geheiratet zu haben, und zwei Portugiesen, die den Speck aus einem Huhn geschnitten hatten, ehe sie's gegessen. Nach dem Essen ward Magister Panglos samt seinem Jünger Kandide in Ketten und Banden gelegt; jener wegen seiner Reden, dieser wegen der Miene des Beifalls, mit der er zugehört hatte.

Zehntes Kapitel

Kandide, Kunegunde und die Alte kommen in einer gar schlimmen Lage
in Cadix an und schiffen sich ein

Kunegunde (schluchzend): „All mein Geld und meine Diamanten sind fort! Wer muß
mir die gestohlen haben! Wovon wollen wir nun leben? Wo Inquisitoren und
Juden finden, die mir andere geben?"

Die Alte: „Ich denke, der ehrwürdige Pater Graurock, der mit uns zu Badajos sein
Nachtquartier hatte, hat sie mitgenommen. Der Barfüßermönch hätte uns wenigstens
so viel Geld lassen sollen, um unsere Reise bestreiten zu können. Haben Sie denn gar
nichts behalten, gnädige Baroneß?"

Kunegunde: „Nichts."

Kandide: „Was nun zu tun?"

26

Siebentes Kapitel

Kandide wird von der Alten wohl gepflegt und findet unverhofft seine Geliebte

Getrost und unverzagt ward Kandide nun zwar nicht, aber mit ging er. Sein Führer brachte ihn in ein altes, ganz verfallenes Gebäude, gab ihm ein Krügelchen Pomade, sich damit zu salben, setzte ihm zu essen und zu trinken hin, zeigte ihm ein ganz sauberes Bettchen und daneben einen ganz vollständigen Anzug. „So wünsche ich Ihnen denn gesegnete Mahlzeit und auch angenehme Ruh. Morgen früh mache ich Ihnen wieder meine Aufwartung."

Kandide, in die heftigste Rührung versetzt, ergriff mit Wärme ihre Hand und wollte sie zum Munde führen. „Ne, das wollt ich mir sehr verbeten haben; das gebührt mir nicht. Na, morgen bin ich wieder da. Brauchen Sie nur die Pomade recht hübsch, lieber junger Herr, und speisen Sie und ruhen Sie fein wohl."

Das tat denn Kandide; aß und schlief recht gut, so hart ihn auch so vielerlei Ungemach zu Boden drückte. Am folgenden Morgen brachte ihm die Matrone zu frühstücken, besichtigte

19

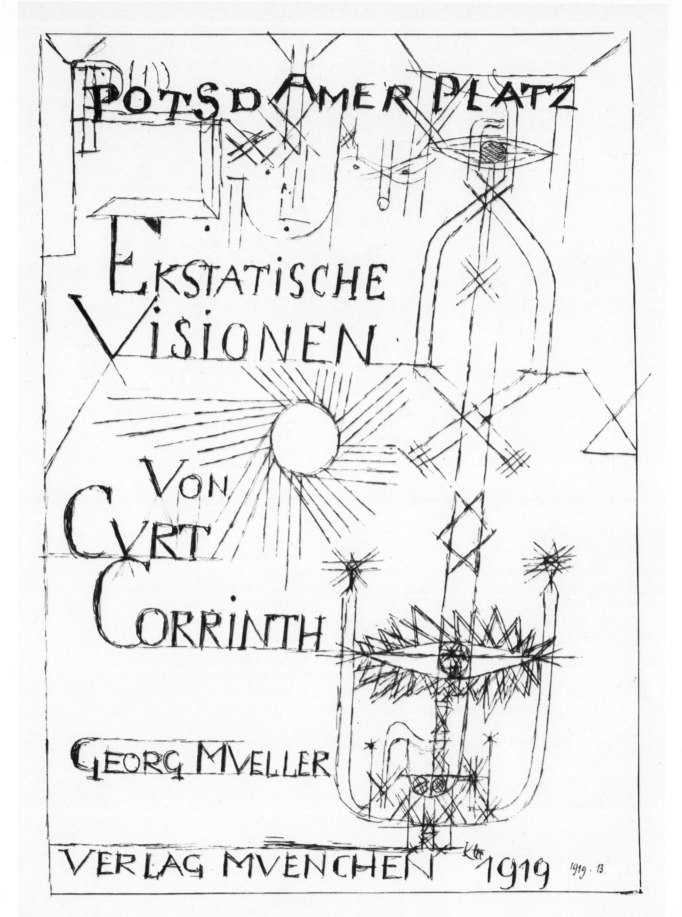

Paul Klee: title-page and drawings for *Potsdamer Platz.*
Ekstatische Visionen by Curt Corrinth. Munich: Georg Müller,
1920. Reproductions from ten drawings. 322 × 250 mm.;
122/152 × 220 mm.; 289 × 220 mm. [177]

Max Beckmann: three etchings for *Die Fürstin* by Kasimir Edschmid.
The book, which contains six original etchings, was published
in an edition limited to 500 copies. Weimar: Gustav Kiepenheuer,
1918. 293 × 225 mm.; 189 × 126 mm.; 180 × 136 mm. [12]

147

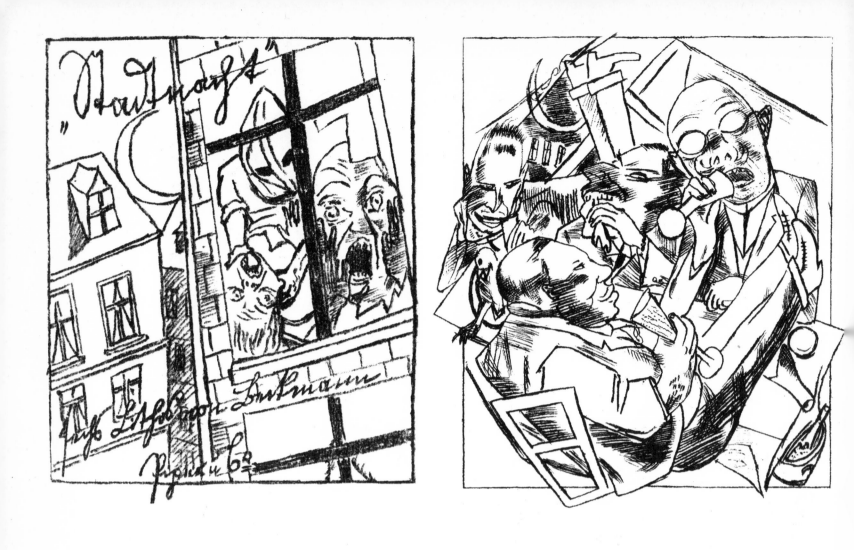

Pages 148–150   Max Beckmann: lithographs to the volume of
poems *Stadtnacht* by Lili von Braunbehrens. The book, which
contains seven original lithographs, was published in an edition
of 600 copies. Munich: R. Piper & Co., 1921. The following are
reproduced here: title-page (270 × 225 mm.); 'Trinklied'
('Drinking Song'; 180 × 165 mm.); 'Verbitterung' ('Embitterment'; 185 × 150 mm.); 'Vorstadtmorgen' ('Suburb Morning';
195 × 150 mm.); 'Möbliert' ('Furnished'; 210 × 155 mm.);
'Die Kranke' ('The Sick Woman'; 190 × 155 mm.). [13]

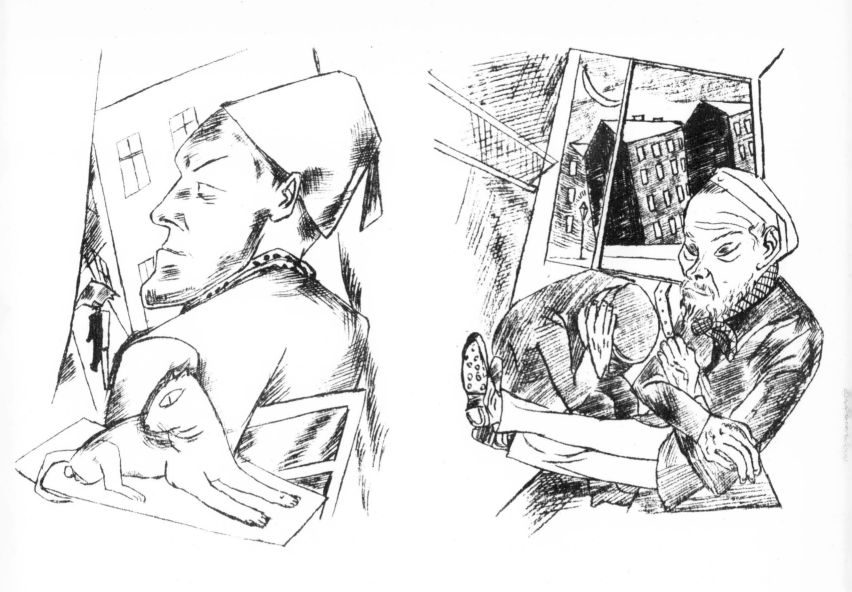

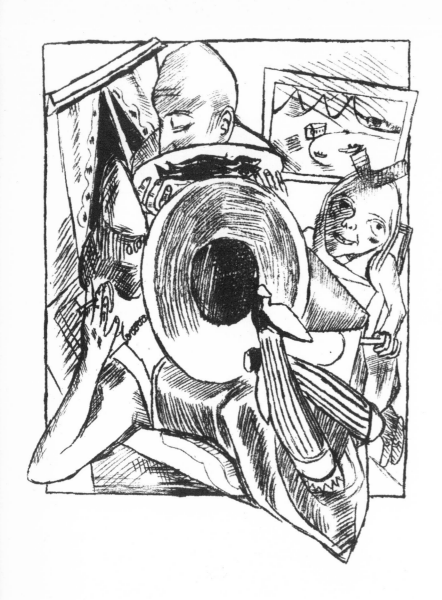

Page 151   Wassily Kandinsky: cover design for the almanac
Der Blaue Reiter. Munich: R. Piper & Co., 1912. 288 × 213 mm.

Pages 152, 153   Wassily Kandinsky: double-page spread from
his volume of poems *Klänge*, which contains fifty-five woodcuts
(twelve in colour), published in an edition limited to 300 copies.
Munich: R. Piper & Co., 1913. Page size 282 × 273 mm. [164]

DAS

Ihr kennt alle diese Riesenwolke, die dem Carviol gleicht. Sie läßt sich schneeweißhart kauen. Und die Zunge bleibt trocken. Also lastete sie auf der tiefblauen Luft.
Und unten, unter ihr auf der Erde, auf der Erde stand ein brennendes Haus. Es war aus dunkelroten Ziegelsteinen fest, oh, fest gebaut.
Und es stand in festen gelben Flammen.
Und vor diesem Haus auf der Erde . . .

Wassily Kandinsky: colour woodcut 'Lyrisches' ('Lyrical') from
his volume of poems *Klänge*. 147 × 218 mm. [164]

154

Pages 155, 156   Max Beckmann: three etchings to *Fanferlieschen*
by Clemens von Brentano:
'Der Koch' ('The Cook'; 193×143 mm.); 'Die fliegende Kirche'
('The Flying Church'; 193×143 mm.); 'Das Begräbnis'
('The Burial'; 193×145 mm.).
A total of eight etchings were issued in a portfolio edition
limited to 220 copies. Berlin: Fritz Gurlitt, 1924. [14]

Ludwig Meidner: one of fourteen lithographs to his volume
of poems *Septemberschrei*. Berlin: Paul Cassirer, 1920.
204 × 147 mm. [234]

Ludwig Meidner: drawings to his book *Im Nacken das Sterne-meer*. Leipzig: Kurt Wolff, 1918. 246 × 185 mm. [230]

Walter Becker: lithograph for *Rede des toten Christus vom Welt-gebäude herab, daß kein Gott sei* by Jean Paul. The little book, which contains sixteen lithographs, was issued in an edition limited to 225 copies. Heidelberg: Richard Weissbach, 1921. 140 × 120 mm. [9]

Hans Arp: illustration for his book *der vogel selbdritt*. The book, which contains 60 woodcuts, was issued in an edition limited to 150 copies. Berlin: privately printed by Otto von Holten, 1920. 190 × 140 mm. [2]

AUSGABE DER GALERIE ALFRED FLECHTHEIM
ZWEITES WERK

RASKOLNIKOFF

10 STEINZEICHNUNGEN VON MAX BURCHARTZ
MIT EINEM VORWORT VON P·E·KÜPPERS

Max Burchartz: lithograph title to *Raskolnikoff* by Feodor
Dostoyevsky issued in a portfolio edition limited to 100 copies.
Düsseldorf: Galerie Flechtheim, 1919. 690 × 505 mm. [26]

Max Burchartz: lithograph title to *Die Dämonen* by Feodor
Dostoyevsky. The book, containing eight lithographs,
was published in the series 'Die Silbergäule'. Hanover:
Paul Steegemann Verlag, 1919. 214 × 183 mm. [27]

Karl Caspar: one of eight lithographs to *Die cumäische Sibylle* by Konrad Weiß. Edition limited to 500 copies. Munich: Georg Müller, 1921. 200 × 155 mm. [28]

Josef Eberz: etching to *Der Sprung in den Tag* by Otto Zarek, published in the quarterly *EOS* (Vol. 1, No. 2), Berlin, 1918. 235 × 146 mm. [35]

Page 166   Heinrich Ehmsen: drawings for *Der Narr in Christo Emanuel Quint* by Gerhart Hauptmann, Drawings for a portfolio of thirty etchings issued in an edition limited to 90 copies. Gerhart-Hauptmann-Stiftung 1927. 205 × 240 mm.; 200 × 250 mm. [46]

Right   Lutz Ehrenberger: jacket design for the *Deutscher Revolutions-Almanach* for 1919. 154 × 116 mm.

Below   Lyonel Feininger: woodcut from *Dada* by Adolf Knoblauch, published in the series 'Der jüngste Tag' (nos. 73/74). Leipzig: Kurt Wolff, 1919. 120 × 85 mm. [52]

Conrad Felixmüller: three pen-and-ink drawings to Walter
Rheiner's novella *Kokain*. The book, which contains seven draw-
ings, was issued in an edition limited to 300 copies. Dresden:
Dresdner Verlag von 1917, 1918. 302 × 225 mm. [58]

Willi Geiger: one of nine etchings to *Carmen* by Prosper Mérimée. Edition limited to 125 copies. Berlin: Fritz Gurlitt, 1920. 235 × 166 mm. [72]

Willi Geiger: one of twelve lithographs to *Frühlingserwachen*, Frank Wedekind's tragedy of adolescence. Edition limited to 330 numbered copies. Munich: Georg Müller, 1920. 176 × 136 mm. [71]

Otto Gleichmann: lithograph from the portfolio *Chimären*.
Düsseldorf: Galerie Flechtheim, 1921. 270 × 208 mm. [84]

Rochus Gliese: lithograph to *Der Sohn*, a play by Walter Hasenclever, the first privately printed publication for the members of the society *Das junge Deutschland*, Berlin, 1918. 205 × 177 mm. [85]

Walter Gramatté: etching to *Der Rebell* by Manfred Georg,
published in the bi-monthly *Marsyas* (Vol. 1, No. 5), Berlin, 1918.
170 × 125 mm. [89]

Walter Gramatté: copper-plate to *Il Pantegan* by Victor
Hadwiger. Edition limited to 500 copies. Berlin: Axel Juncker,
1919. 179 × 170 mm. [91]

Page 176   Albert Paris Gütersloh: lithograph for jacket of *Der bestrafte Wollüstling* by Franz Blei. Vienna and Leipzig: Avalun Verlag, 1921. 252 × 176 mm. [110]

Pages 177, 178   Richard Janthur: page of text and a hand-coloured lithograph from *Die Gazelle*, a collection of African fairy-tales. The book, which contains ten lithographs, was published in an edition limited to 200 copies. Berlin, Leipzig and Vienna: Franz Schneider, n.d. 287 × 225 mm. [156]

Walter Gramatté: lithographs to *Der Mantel* by Nikolai Gogol. The book, which contains twelve lithographs, was issued in an edition of 1,100 copies. Potsdam: Gustav Kiepenheuer, 1920. 166 × 135 mm.; 165 × 132 mm. [92]

Franz Blei.

DER BESTRAFTE WOLLVSTLING.

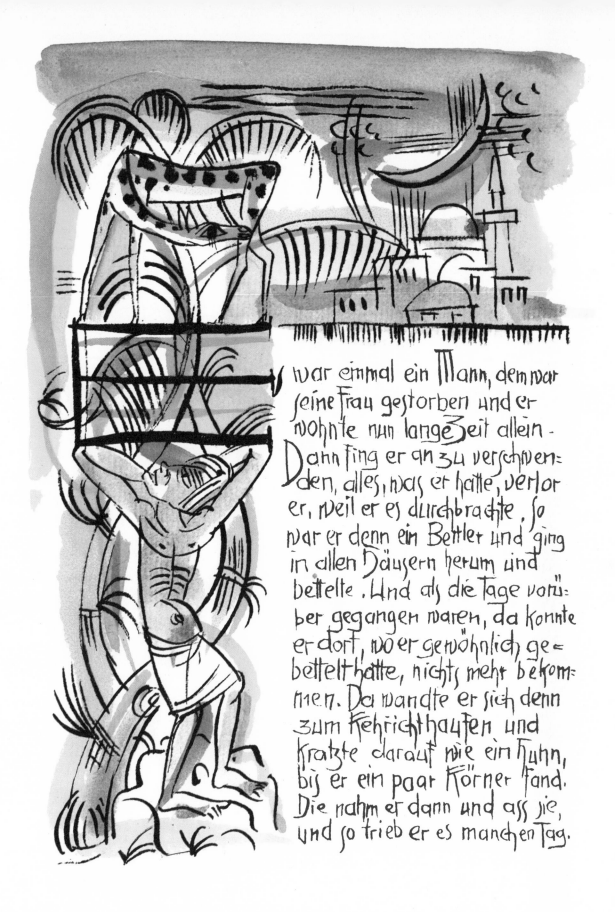

war einmal ein Mann, dem war
seine Frau gestorben und er
wohnte nun lange Zeit allein.
Dann fing er an zu verschwen=
den, alles, was er hatte, verlor
er, weil er es durchbrachte. So
war er denn ein Bettler und ging
in allen Häusern herum und
bettelte. Und als die Tage vorü=
ber gegangen waren, da konnte
er dort, wo er gewöhnlich ge=
bettelt hatte, nichts mehr bekom=
men. Da wandte er sich denn
zum Kehrichthaufen und
kratzte darauf wie ein Huhn,
bis er ein paar Körner fand.
Die nahm er dann und ass sie,
und so trieb er es manchen Tag.

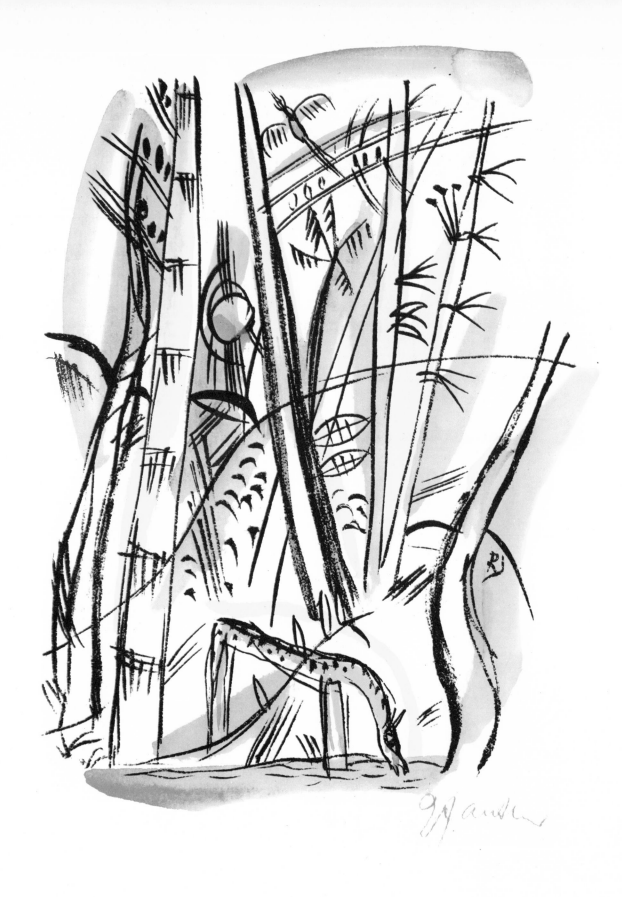

178

Richard Janthur: colour lithograph to *Robinson Crusoe* by
Daniel Defoe. The book, which contains thirty-one lithographs,
was published in an edition limited to 800 copies. Leipzig:
Insel-Verlag, 1922. 205 × 140 mm. [154]

Constantin von Mitschke-Collande: colour woodcut from the
portfolio to *Montezuma* by Klabund. Four woodcuts were issued
in an edition limited to 30 copies. Dresden: Dresdner Verlag
von 1917, February 1922. 195 × 165 mm. [244]

Carl Hofer: one of ten lithographs to *Liebesgedichte* by Adolf
von Hatzfeld, published in an edition limited to 125 copies.
Berlin: Verlag der Galerie Flechtheim, 1922. 182×160 mm.
[124]

Franz Maria Jansen: etching to *Der chiliastische Pilgerzug* by
Josef Winckler. Berlin and Leipzig: Deutsche Verlagsanstalt,
1923. 150 × 110 mm. [143]

Above Hermann Keil: woodcut to *Der Abenteurer* by Anton Schnack, published in an edition limited to 250 copies. Darmstadt: Die Dachstube, 1919. 115×141 mm. [166]

Hermann Keil: woodcut to *Rede an einen Dichter* by Kasimir Edschmid. The book, which contains four woodcuts (three by Keil and one by Masereel), was published in an edition limited to 200 copies. Hamburg: Adolf Harms, 1922 ('Die Drucke der schönen Rarität', No. 5). Page size 338×235 mm. [167]

Above   Willy Jaeckel: one of thirteen lithographs to *Grashalme*
by Walt Whitman. Edition limited to 265 numbered copies.
Berlin: Erich Reiß, 1920. 194×194 mm. [135]

Right   Richard Janthur: one of eleven original etchings to
Gilgamesch. Edition limited to 125 copies. Berlin: Fritz Gurlitt,
1919. 246×167 mm. [145]

184

Above Richard Janthur: lithograph to *Das Dschungelbuch* (*The Jungle Book*) by Rudyard Kipling. Edition limited to 250 copies. Berlin: Fritz Gurlitt, 1921. 290 × 230 mm. [148]

Left Richard Janthur: one of twelve original etchings to *Der goldene Esel* by Apuleius. Edition limited to 200 copies. Berlin, Leipzig and Vienna: Franz Schneider, 1924. [155]

Right   César Klein: cover design for 'Almanac for the year 1920'. Berlin: Fritz Gurlitt. 201 × 142 mm.

Below   Max Kaus: one of twelve original lithographs to *Die Sage von Sankt Julian dem Gastfreien* by Gustave Flaubert. Weimar: Gustav Kiepenheuer, 1918. 180 × 130 mm. [165]

Alexander Mohr: cover design (lithograph) for *Der ekstatische Fluß* by Carl Maria Weber. Edition limited to 150 copies. Düsseldorf: A. Bagel, 1919. 240×185 mm. [246]

Below   Constantin von Mitschke-Collande: one of six woodcuts to the poem *Der begeisterte Weg* by Walter Georg Hartmann. Dresden: Robert Kaemmerer, 1919. 190×164 mm. [241]

Right   Heinrich Nauen: one of ten etchings to *Die Judenbuche*
by Annette von Droste-Hülshoff. Edition limited to 250 copies
('Flechtheim Druck', No. 25). Frankfurt am Main: Querschnitt-
Verlag, 1923. 72 × 80 mm. [248]

Below   Otto Nückel: woodcut to *Solnemann der Unsichtbare*
by A. M. Frey. Munich: Delphin-Verlag, 1914. 175 × 138 mm.
[251]

Otto Pankok: etchings to *Die Ballade des Zuchthauses zu Reading*
by Oscar Wilde. Edition limited to 300 numbered copies.
Berlin: Axel Juncker, 1923. Each 198×142 mm. [261]

Carl Rabus: etching to *Kreisende Schatten* by Elsa Maria Bud, published in Book 4 of the journal *EOS*, Munich, 1921. 299 × 218 mm. [284]

Carl Rabus: one of eighteen original etchings to *Oberon* by Christoph Martin Wieland. Edition limited to 350 numbered copies. Munich: Hesperos Verlag, 1920. 208 × 147 mm. [280]

Carl Rabus: etching from *Das öde Haus* by E. T. A. Hoffmann.
Edition limited to 500 numbered copies. Munich: Hesperos
Verlag, 1920. 112 × 63 mm. [281]

Carl Rabus: lithograph from *Blaubart und Miß Ilsebill*
by Alfred Döblin. Berlin: Hans Heinrich Tillgner, 1923.
170 × 124 mm. [285]

Wilhelm Plünnecke: one of five original lithographs to
Die Prophezeiung by Rudolf Leonhard. Edition limited to
30 copies. Berlin: Verlag der Gesellschaft von Freunden neuer
deutscher Kunst, 1922. 198×150 mm. [277]

Left Karl Rössing: one of thirty woodcuts to *Taras Bulba* by
Nikolai Gogol. Edition limited to 150 copies. Vienna, Leipzig
and Munich: Rikola Verlag, 1922. 166 × 113 mm. [289]

Above Georg Schrimpf: woodcut for title-page of *Amen und
Anfang* by Oskar Maria Graf. Munich: Bachmair & Co., 1919.
259 × 194 mm. [306]

Above   Edwin Scharff: etching from the cycle *Sintflut*,
published in the bi-monthly *Marsyas* (Vol. 1, No. 2), Berlin,
September/October 1917. 230 × 170 mm. [296]

Right   Edwin Scharff: one of twenty lithographs to the
dramatic poem *Herakles* by Frank Wedekind. Edition limited to
330 copies. Munich: Georg Müller, 1920. 160 × 110 mm. [297]

Rudolf Schlichter: lithographs from *Auszug aus Lucians Nach-richten vom Tode des Peregrinus* by Christoph Martin Wieland. Edition limited to 150 copies. Heidelberg: Richard Weissbach, 1920. 182 × 150 mm.; 195 × 155 mm. [299]

Kaput 24

In dem Tal von Ronceval,
Auf demselben Platz, wo weiland
Des Caroli Magni Neffe
Seine Seele ausgeröchelt,

Dorten fiel auch Atta Troll,
Fiel durch Hinterhalt, wie jener,
Den der ritterliche Judas,
Ganelon von Mainz, verraten.

F. H. E. Schneidler: illustration to *Atta Troll* by Heinrich Heine.
Berlin: Morawe & Scheffelt, 1912. Page size 214 × 176 mm. [301]

Otto Schubert: one of six original lithographs to the tale *Die
lilienweiße Stute* by Carl Hauptmann. Edition limited to 400
copies. Dresden: R. Kaemmerer, 1920. 190 × 160 mm. [309]

20/30   Max Schwimmer

Max Schwimmer: title-leaf and three dry-point etchings
from the portfolio *Abenteurer*, for which Johannes R. Becher
wrote a prefatory note. Leipzig: Friedrich Dehne, c. 1918.
Sheet sizes 322 × 247 mm.; 185 × 142 mm.; 185 × 142 mm.;
187 × 143 mm. [322]

20/30   Max Beckmann

20/30   Max Beckmann

199

Richard Seewald: colour woodcut to *Fabeln* by Christian
Fürchtegott Gellert. Editions limited to 125 and 50 copies.
Berlin: Fritz Gurlitt, 1920. 207 × 159 mm. [325]

Max Unold: woodcut for the cover of *Altbayrische Bilderbogen*
by Heinrich Lautensack. Berlin: Fritz Gurlitt, 1920.
234 × 148 mm. [352]

Jakob Steinhardt: woodcut title-page for
Der Flügelmann by Alfred Wolfenstein. Dessau: Karl Rauch,
1924. 227 × 158 mm. [341]

Page 203   Curt Stoermer: four of six woodcuts to *Der Verworfene* by Charles Baudelaire, published in 1,000 copies.
Hanover: Der Zweemann-Verlag, 1920. 106 × 81 mm. [343]

Page 204   Jakob Steinhardt: one of five original lithographs
to *Musikalische Novellen* by Jizchok-Leib Perez. Berlin: Fritz
Gurlitt, 1920. 227 × 163 mm. [340]

Aloys Wach: one of four woodcuts to *Große Elegie* by Fritz
Usinger. Edition limited to 100 copies (20 coloured). Darmstadt:
Die Dachstube, 1920. 191 × 122 mm. [357]

Page 206   Will Wanzer: illustration (shallow lithograph) to the
poem *Welten* by Anton Gourby, published in the journal *EOS*
(Book 4), Munich, 1920. 255 × 166 mm. [360]

Page 207   Ines Wetzel: lithograph to *Biblische Gedichte* by
Theodor Tagger, published in the bi-monthly *Marsyas* (Vol. 1,
No. 3), Berlin, November-December 1917. 120 × 170 mm. [365]

206

Biblische Gedichte

Eva und Susanne

I.

Strahlt deine Keuschheit Schuschan durch das geläuterte Glas erhaben
In das betörte sündenflammende Babel
leicht mit dem Geruch des jungfräulichen Knaben,
der aus dem getöteten Abel
noch heute duftend strömt. Tausend Wege schäumender Verführung miedest du
in der Stadt lauten Versündens sanft wie ein Gruß
des Herzens. Die Wasser der Wollust schiedest du
und gingst, eine himmlische Wolke mit unbeflecktem Fuß.

191

208

Page 208   Magnus Zeller: lithograph 'Betrunkener unter einer Laterne' ('Drunk under a street-lamp') from the portfolio *Entrückung und Aufruhr*, which also contains poems written by Arnold Zweig. Executed 1917. Edition limited to 105 copies. Privately printed 1920. 250 × 165 mm. [371]

Pages 209, 210   Magnus Zeller: etchings to *Das rote Lachen* by Leonid Andreyev. The book, which contains seven etchings, was published in an edition limited to 320 numbered copies. Berlin: Euphorion Verlag, 1922. Each 137 × 98 mm. [374]

Bibliographies

Illustrated works: a provisional bibliography

After many years spent in searching I have ventured to define the works listed in the following pages as Expressionist illustrated books. In establishing the list I have used as my yardstick the characteristic features as described in chapter I, 'Expressionist illustration: characteristics, major works, chronology'. Many of these criteria, however, came to mind for the first time as work proceeded. There was no preliminary research to refer to: Expressionist book illustration is a largely unstudied field. In order to avoid any narrowness of interpretation, works have also been included that show mere Expressionist influence.

The search has in principle been for illustrations in books. Portfolios have been included only exceptionally and only when they relate to literary works. Cover designs have been considered, though only of literary works; artists' designs for the covers of catalogues of their exhibitions have only been mentioned by way of example. Suites of separate sheets (both drawings and prints), even when they occur in portfolios, have been omitted from the bibliography, although the occasional example is reproduced in the plates section.

Certain adverse circumstances have prevented me from handling every book, although I have been fortunate enough to do so in the vast majority of cases under consideration; in other instances I have had to rely on kind helpers and on copies. This also explains why in the main the bibliography reproduces the wording of the main title of the works. The aim has been to give the following information in this order: place of publication, publisher (in shortened form) and date, series title (where appropriate), number of pages, number of copies printed, indication of illustrations. Bibliophiles and collectors will sometimes note the absence of one or other of these indications: I ask them to accept the large quantity of new material as my excuse.

Periodicals have not been included in the bibliography. This part of the work had already been done by Paul Raabe, to whose book *Die Zeitschriften und Sammlungen des literarischen Expressionismus* (Stuttgart, 1964), the reader is referred. Intensive though the search has been, there can be no certainty that the whole field of Expressionist book illustration has been covered. Any bibliographical references will be gratefully received.

Achmann, Josef

Painter and graphic artist. Born 1885. Co-editor with Georg Britting 1919–21 of *Die Sichel* (Regensburg).

1 Britting, Georg: *Das Storchennest*

Hamburg: Adolf Harms, 1921 (3rd publication in the series 'Die Drucke der Tafelrunde', ed. Karl Lorenz). 14 pp. 200 numbered copies. 1 original woodcut.

Arp, Hans

Sculptor, painter, graphic artist and poet. 1887–1966. One of the founders of Dadaism, Zürich, 1916–19.

2 Arp, Hans: *der vogel selbdritt*

Berlin: Otto von Holten (privately printed), 1920. 150 numbered copies. 60 woodcuts. Set in Flinsch-Mediäval. An example of Abstract Expressionism. All his other book illustrations are either Dadaist or Abstract. Bibliography by Hans Bolliger in *Hans Arp. Graphik 1912–1959*, Basle, Kunstmuseum 1959.

Barlach, Ernst

Sculptor, graphic artist and poet. 1870–1938. Lived from 1910 at Güstrow. Not pronouncedly Expressionist as an illustrator. See chapter V, 'Excursus on Kubin, Barlach and Masereel'. Bibliography of his illustrated works: Lautz-Oppermann, Gisela, *Ernst Barlach der Illustrator*, Wolfshagen-Scharbeutz, 1952. Catalogue of prints and illustrated works: Schult, Friedrich, *Ernst Barlach. Das graphische Werk*, Hamburg, 1958. More references of the illustrated books in: *Ernst Barlach. Das druckgraphische Werk, Dore and Kurt Reutti Foundation*, Catalogue of an exhibition at the Kunsthalle, Bremen, 1968.

Bató, Jósef

Hungarian painter and graphic artist. Born 1888. Lived for a long time in Berlin.

3 Ferenczi, Sári: *Madame Flamingos Schatten*

Berlin: Fritz Gurlitt, 1921. 31 pp. 100 numbered copies. Many graphic illustrations.

Baumberger, Otto

Painter and graphic artist. Born 1889. Lives in Zürich.

4 Kesser, H.: *Die Peitsche. Erzählende Dichtung*

Leipzig: Freifeld, 1918. 66 pp. 300 copies. Lithographs.

Becker, Walter

Painter, graphic artist and illustrator. Born 1893. Last known living at Tutzing on the Starnberger See.
Becker's work, obviously influenced by Kokoschka, is not pure Expressionism. In varying degrees, his illustrations merely draw their forms from the new movement.

5 Hoffmann, E.T.A.: *Der Puppenspieler*

Heidelberg: Richard Weissbach, 1919. 50 copies. In portfolio, half vellum. Title-page and 10 original lithographs.

6 Hoffmann, E.T.A.: *Die Königsbraut*

No place [Potsdam]: Gustav Kiepenheuer, n.d. [before 1920], ('Graphische Bücher', no. 4). 89 pp. 1st–3rd thousand. Binding, title and 49 original lithographs in the text.

7 Gogol, Nikolai: *Der Unhold*

Heidelberg: Richard Weissbach, 1920 ('Die Drucke des Argonauten-Kreises', no. 4). 61 pp. 225 copies. 74 lithographs.

8 Hauff, Wilhelm: *Phantasien im Bremer Ratskeller Ein Herbstgeschenk für Freunde des Weines*

Potsdam: Gustav Kiepenheuer, 1920 ('Graphische Bücher', no. 5). 117 pp. 1st–3rd thousand. Many original lithographs and vignettes.

9 Paul, Jean (i.e. J.P.Richter): *Rede des toten Christus vom Weltgebäude herab, daß kein Gott sei*

Heidelberg: Richard Weissbach, 1921. 20 pp. 225 copies issued for the Friends of the Argonauten-Kreis. 16 lithographs.

10 Balzac, Honoré de: *Die derbdrolligen Geschichten*

Bad Rothenfelde: Holzwarth, 1924. 149 pp. Many drawings.

11 Dostoyevsky, Feodor: *Aufzeichnungen aus dem Kellerloch*

Munich: R.Piper & Co., 1927. 148 pp. 50 woodcuts by A.Fellscheer, after Becker's pen-and-ink drawings.

Beckmann, Max

Painter and graphic artist. 1884–1950. Adolf Jannasch ('Max Beckmann als Illustrator', in *Imprimatur. Ein Jahrbuch für Bücherfreunde*, New Series, Vol. III, Frankfurt am Main, 1962, pp. 23 ff.) lists eleven books illustrated by Beckmann. Beckmann's prints in portfolio have not been listed here. See Gallwitz, Klaus, 'Werkverzeichnis der Druckgraphik', in *Max Beckmann. Die Druckgraphik*, catalogue of an exhibition at Karlsruhe 1962.

12 Edschmid, Kasimir: *Die Fürstin*

Weimar: Gustav Kiepenheuer, 1918. 81 pp. 500 copies. 6 original etchings. (35 copies on Japon issued as a portfolio, 465 copies in book form on hand-made paper.)

13 Braunbehrens, Lili von: *Stadtnacht*

Munich: R.Piper & Co., 1921. 47 pp. 600 copies (of which 500 are in book form). 7 original lithographs.

14 Brentano, Clemens von: *Fanferlieschen*

Berlin: Fritz Gurlitt, 1924. 220 copies. 8 etchings to Brentano's fairy-tale, in portfolio. No edition in book form has been traced.

15 Beckmann, Max: *Ebbi. Komödie in vier Akten*

Vienna: Johannes-Presse, 1924. 33 copies. Printed in the autumn of 1914 for the Gesellschaft der 33. 6 etchings.

Beeh, René

Painter, graphic artist and illustrator. 1886–1922. After 1918 he devoted himself almost exclusively to drawing and illustrating. Strongly influenced by Kokoschka. His works have only a tangential connection with Expressionism. The two books cited here are examples.

16 Gotthelf, Jeremias: *Die schwarze Spinne*

Munich: Delphin, n.d. 1,200 copies. 30 drawings and a cover design.

17 *Gottfried-Keller-Bilderbuch*

Erlenbach-Zürich. Eugen Rentsch, n.d. 10 lithographs.

Berlit, Rüdiger

Painter and graphic artist. 1883–1939. Lived in Leipzig.

18 Vogel, Bruno: *Es lebe der Krieg!*

Leipzig: Die Wölfe, 1925. 71 pp. Jacket design and illustrations.

Blau, Friedrich

Painter and woodcut artist. Born 1883 in Berlin.

19 *Die Geißelungen Sant Elisabeths
   nach den alten Chroniken*

   Berlin: A. R. Meyer (privately printed), August 1919.
   300 copies. 4 original woodcuts.

Böckstiegel, Peter August

Painter and graphic artist. 1889–1951. Lived in Dresden
until 1945.

20 Fischer, Richard: *Du heilige Erde!*

   Dresden: Dresdner Verlag von 1917, 1918 ('Das
   Neueste Gedicht', no. 10). 16 pp. Jacket design.

Brass, Hans

Painter. 1885–1959. Lived latterly at Ahrenshoop.

21 Hasenclever, Walter: *Die Menschen*

   Berlin: Ackermannscher Verlag, 1922 ('Drucke der
   Zwei'). 25 copies. 8 etchings and title-page, drawn on
   the stone, in portfolio.

Breeger, Egon

No biographical details ascertainable.

22 Omanowski, Willibald: *Der Fackelträger*

   Wolfach: Ferdinand Acker, 1925 ('Els-Druck', no. 8).
   175 copies. Frontispiece.

Breitwieser, Ludwig

No biographical details ascertainable.

23 Mierendorff, Carlo: *Lothringer Herbst*

   Darmstadt: Die Dachstube, 1918 ('Die kleine Republik. Eine Flugschriftenreihe', no. 1). 15 pp. Binding
   and illustrations.

24 Haubach, Theodor: *Jacques Prince*

   Darmstadt: Die Dachstube, 1918 ('Bücher der Dachstube', no. 2). 20 pp. Original woodcuts.

Bruiez-Mavromati, Fortuna

Romanian painter and graphic artist. She lived from 1920
in Hamburg.

25 Stuckenschmidt, H. H.: *Neue Musik*

   Hamburg: Adolf Harms, 1921 ('Die Drucke der Ta-

felrunde', ed. Karl Lorenz, no. 6). 14 pp. 200 numbered copies. 1 original woodcut.

Burchartz, Max

Painter and graphic artist; later industrial designer. 1887–
1961. Also noted for his theoretical writings on art.

26 Dostoyevsky, Feodor: *Raskolnikoff*

   Düsseldorf: [May-June 1919], 'Ausgabe der Galerie
   A. Flechtheim', no. 2. 11 leaves. With a foreword by
   Paul E. Küppers. 100 copies. 10 lithographs.

27 Dostoyevsky, Feodor: *Die Dämonen*

   Hanover: Paul Steegemann, 1919 ('Die Silbergäule',
   no. 43/44). 10 leaves. 8 lithographs and cover design.

Caspar, Karl

Principally a painter. 1879–1956.

28 Weiß, Konrad: *Die cumäische Sibylle*

   Munich: Georg Müller, 1921. 100 pp. 500 numbered
   copies. 8 lithographs.
   Important work, recalling Kokoschka's style.

Dietrich, Rudolf Adrian

Late Expressionist poet, known as 'der Gotiker' (the Gothic one). Born 1894. Lived for a time in Dresden, then in
Constance and lastly in Hamburg.

29 *Dietrich*, R. A.: *Der Selbstmörder. Die Mutter*

   Dresden: Dresdner Verlag von 1917, 1919 ('Das
   Neueste Gedicht'). Author's own jacket design.

Dollerschell, Eduard

Painter and graphic artist. 1887–1948.

30 Schmidt, Carl Robert: *Moloch. Gesichte*

   Leipzig: Friedrich Dehne, 1919. Etchings, in portfolio.

Dungert, Max

Painter and graphic artist. 1896–1945. Was a member of
the Novembergruppe and of the 'Kugel', a group of
artists in Magdeburg.

31 Gellhorn, Alfred: *Sehnen. Gedichte*

   Berlin: Leon Hirsch, 1922. Original lithographs.

Eberz, Josef

Painter and graphic artist; also did stained glass and mosaic. 1880–1942. Member of the Novembergruppe. Eberz's illustrations are by no means thoroughly Expressionist; many are modish and shallow.

32 Brock, Stephan: *Die Fackel loht!*
Die ausgewählten Gedichte 1908–1918
Wolgast: Kentaur-Verlag, Hermann Kruse, 1918. Lithograph.

33 Edschmid, Kasimir: *Die Karlsreis*
Darmstadt: Die Dachstube, 1918 ('Die kleine Republik. Eine Flugschriftenreihe', no. 3). 27 pp. 7 original lithographs. (250 numbered copies of this book were printed by hand on the press of Die Dachstube by J. Würth in the second month of the Republik.)

34 Hiller, Kurt: *Unnennbar Brudertum.*
Verse. 1904–1917
Wolgast: Kentaur-Verlag, Hermann Kruse, 1918 ('Kentaur-Druck', no. 1). 36 pp. 350 copies. 6 lithographs.

35 Zarek, Otto: *Der Sprung in den Tag*
In *EOS, Eine Dreimonatsschrift für Dichtung und Kunst,* ed. Emil Pirchan, Vol. 1, No. 2. Berlin: Wende-Verlag, n.d. [1918]. 3 etchings.

36 Moreck, Curt (i.e. Konrad Haemmerling):
Der strahlende Mensch
Munich: Wende-Verlag, 1920. 167 pp. 15 illustrations.

37 Eichendorff, Joseph von: *Ahnung und Gegenwart*
Stuttgart: (publisher not known), 1920. 33 etchings.

38 Heine, Heinrich: *Vitzliputzli*
Munich: Die Serapionsbrüder, 1922 (third publication). 23 pp. 150 copies. Many illustrations.

39 Goethe, J. W. von: *Hymne an die Natur*
Hamburg: Adolf Harms, 1922 ('Die Drucke der schönen Rarität', ed. Niels Hoyer). 200 copies. 3 original etchings.

40 Shakespeare, W.: *Sonette an den geliebten Knaben*
Hamburg: Adolf Harms, 1922 ('Die Drucke der schönen Rarität'). 200 copies. 4 original etchings.

41 Hoyer, Niels: *Nachtlied*
Hamburg: Adolf Harms, December 1921 ('Die Drukke der schönen Rarität'). 200 copies. 3 original etchings.

42 Heine, Heinrich: *Buch der Lieder*
Munich: O.C. Recht, 1923. 507 pp. 1,000 numbered copies. 15 etchings, some coloured.

43 Moreck, Curt (i.e. Konrad Haemmerling):
Die Pole des Lebens
Hanover: (publisher not known), n.d. 85 pp. 180 copies. 7 original lithographs.

Edzard, Dietz

Painter and graphic artist. Born 1893. Last known living in Canada.

44 Gogol, N.: *Wij. Eine Volkslegende*
Munich: Pflüger, 1924. Text and 6 etchings in portfolio.

Eggeler, Stefan

Etcher, woodcut artist and lithographer. Born 1894. Last known living in Austria.

45 Villiers de l'Isle-Adam, P.-A.:
Novellen der Grausamkeit
Vienna: Artur Wolf, 1923. 120 pp. 900 copies. 8 original lithographs.

Ehmsen, Heinrich

Painter and graphic artist. 1886–1964.

46 *30 Radierungen zu dem Roman Gerhart Hauptmanns 'Der Narr in Christo Emanuel Quint'*
Berlin: Gerhart-Hauptmann-Stiftung (through Wasservogel Verlag), 1927. 90 copies. Portfolio.

Elert, Konrad

No biographical details ascertainable.

47 Hesse, Otto Ernst: *Kämpfe mit Gott.*
Biblische Köpfe
Berlin-Wilmersdorf: Alfred Richard Meyer, 1920. Illustrated.

Ell, Michel

No biographical details ascertainable.

48 Andersen, H.: *Des Kaisers neue Kleider. Ein Märchen*

Berlin: 1923. Specially printed on the press of the Kunstgewerbe- und Handwerkerschule Charlottenburg. 5 original woodcuts.

Engelhorn, Charlotte Christine

No biographical details ascertainable.

49 Wilde, Oscar: *Der junge König*

Weimar: Gustav Kiepenheuer, 1918 ('Graphische Bücher', no. 2). 66 pp. 1,100 copies. Many lithographs.

50 Hoffmann, E. T. A.: *Das Gelübde*

Munich: Hesperos, n. d. [1920]. 63 pp. 500 numbered copies. Cover design and original etchings.

Feininger, Lyonel

German-American painter and graphic artist. 1871–1956. Taught at the Bauhaus.

51 *Ja! Stimmen des Arbeitsrates für Kunst in Berlin*

Charlottenburg: Photographische Gesellschaft, 1919. Woodcut and 41 plates (by other artists). Feininger's woodcut ('Rathaus') in original impressions was bound in as frontispiece to 55 copies.

52 Knoblauch, Adolf: *Dada (Kleine Prosa)*

Leipzig: Kurt Wolff, 1919 ('Der jüngste Tag', no. 73/74). 77 pp. 1 woodcut.

Felixmüller, Conrad

Painter and graphic artist. Born 1897. Was in Dresden during the Expressionist period. Worked on many journals, including *Menschen* and *Die Aktion*. Lives in West Berlin. Felixmüller did many illustrative pieces that date from the Expressionist period. Some appeared in periodicals and some as free prints. An example is his woodcut *Für Däublers 'mit silberner Sichel'* which appeared in the journal *Die Sichel*, Vol. 1, No. 1, Regensburg [July 1919].

53 *Lieder des Pierrot Lunaire, Gedichte von Albert Giraud, Melodramen von Arnold Schönberg, op. 21*

Dresden: published by the artist, 1913. Suite of woodcuts on 10 leaves. Very few suites printed.

54 *Hebräische Balladen. Zu Gedichten von Else Lasker-Schüler*

Dresden: published by the artist, 1914. Suite of woodcuts on 8 leaves. Very few suites printed.

55 *Das Aktionsbuch*

Berlin-Wilmersdorf: Die Aktion Verlag (ed. Franz Pfemfert), 1917. Design for cover.

56 *Der Hahn. Übertragungen aus dem Französischen von Theodor Däubler*

Berlin-Wilmersdorf: Die Aktion Verlag (Franz Pfemfert), 1917 ('Die Aktions-Lyrik', no. 5). 64 pp. Jacket design.

57 Rheiner, Walter: *Insel der Seligen. Ein Abendlied*

Dresden: Dresdner Verlag von 1917, 1918. Inset illustration.

58 Rheiner, Walter: *Kokain. Novelle*

Dresden: Dresdner Verlag von 1917, 1918. 43 pp. 300 numbered copies. 7 pen-and-ink drawings. (Four of the drawings reprinted in the journal *Menschen*, Vol. II, No. 3 [1919].)

59 Schilling, Heinar: *Die Sklaven. Episch-dramatisches Gedicht*

Dresden: Dresdner Verlag von 1917, 1919 ('Das Neueste Gedicht', no. 11/13). 44 pp. 2nd and 3rd thousand. 4 drawings. (The drawings also appeared in the journal *Menschen*, Vol. II, No. 6 [1919].)

60 Schilling, Heinar: *Mensch, Mond, Sterne – Gedicht*

Dresden: Dresdner Verlag von 1917, 1918 ('Das Neueste Gedicht', no. 1). 16 pp. Woodcut on jacket.

61 Rheiner, Walter: *Der inbrünstige Musikant. Eine lyrische Szene*

Kiel: 'Die schöne Rarität', 1918. 4 drawings.

62 Hoffmann, E. T. A.: *Aus dem Leben dreier Freunde. Ein Fragment*

Berlin: Axel Juncker, 1920. 1st–3rd thousand. Pen-and-ink drawing.

Fingesten, Michel

Painter and graphic artist. Born 1884. Executed many illustrations and portfolios. The following illustrations and many others by Fingesten (e. g. A. Holz's *Blechschmiede* and A. Kerr and R. Strauss's *Krämerspiegel*) are in the main examples of an Expressionism that has become modish and superficial.

63 Sternheim, Carl: *Vier Novellen. Neue Folge der Chronik vom Beginn des zwanzigsten Jahrhunderts*

Berlin: Heinrich Hochstim, 1918. 125 pp. 12 original lithographs.

64 Weissmann, Adolf: *Der klingende Garten. Impressionen über das Erotische in der Musik*

Berlin: Verlag Neue Kunsthandlung, 1920. 62 pp. 10 plates hors-texte. Edition de luxe limited to 200 copies with original etchings. The book was also published by Paul Graupe (also Berlin, 1920). 67 pp. 10 original etchings.

65 Leonhard, Rudolf: *Mütter*

Berlin: Verlag Neue Kunsthandlung, 1920. 10 etchings.

66 Przybyszewski, Stanislaw: *De Profundis*

Berlin: Alfred Hoemicke, 1921 (manuscript for friends). 50 copies.

67 König, Melita: *Der Topf voll Mäuse. Rhythmische Reimraketen*

Berlin-Frohnau: J.J.Ottens, 1927. 46 pp. 500 copies. 7 original etchings.

Gangolf, Paul

Graphic artist and writer. 1879–1939.
Gangolf's lithographs in portfolio, *Metropolis*, were published by the Malik-Verlag in 1922.

68 Wowes, Fritz: *Großstadt*

Constance: (no publisher), 1922. 1,200 copies. 6 lithographs.

Gattermann, Eugen Ludwig

No biographical details ascertainable.

69 Bock, Kurt: *Verse vor Tag*

Dresden: Dresdner Verlag von 1917, 1918. Jacket design.

Geiger, Willi

Painter and graphic artist. 1878–1971. Lived in Munich. Geiger illustrated numerous works. Many are not Expressionist, even when they date from the period of the books described here.

70 Huysmans, J.-K.: *Gilles de Rais*

Berlin: Fritz Gurlitt, 1919/20 ('Der Venuswagen', private publications of the Gurlitt-Presse, Series I, ed. A.R. Meyer). 15 lithographs.

71 Wedekind, Frank: *Frühlingserwachen. Eine Kindertragödie*

Munich: Georg Müller, 1920 ('Welttheater. Meisterdramen mit Originalgraphik', Vol. 3). 154 pp. 330 numbered copies. 12 lithographs.

72 Mérimée, Prosper: *Carmen*

Berlin: Fritz Gurlitt, 1920 ('Drucke der Gurlitt-Presse. Die Neuen Bilderbücher', New Series, Vol. 6). 64 pp. 125 copies. 9 etchings.

73 Dostoyevsky, Feodor: *Der Gatte*

Berlin: Euphorion, 1923. 100 copies. 12 etchings, in portfolio.

74 Balzac, Honoré de: *Eine Leidenschaft in der Wüste*

Berlin: Fritz Gurlitt, 1924 ('Die Neuen Bilderbücher', series 5, Vol. 4). 40 pp. 220 copies. 8 etchings.

75 Dostoyevsky, Feodor: *Nasser Schnee*

Berlin: Franz Schneider, n.d. [1924], ('Luxus-Graphik Schneider'). 94 pp. 200 copies. Several etchings.

76 Kleist, Heinrich von: *Die Verlobung in San Domingo*

Berlin: Euphorion, 1924. 60 pp. 150 numbered copies. 8 original etchings.

77 Dostoyevsky, Feodor: *Das junge Weib. Eine Novelle*

Leipzig: E.A. Seemann, n.d. [1924]. 89 pp. 200 numbered copies. 12 etchings.

78 Wedekind, Frank: *Lulu*

Munich: Othmar Kern & Co., n.d. 9 lithographs in portfolio.

Gelbke, Georg

Painter and graphic artist. 1882–1947. Lived in Dresden.

79 Gebhardt, A.F.: *Das fühlende Schweigen. 6 Dichtungen*

Dresden: E. Richter, n.d. [1919]. 48 pp. 100 copies. Bound in Japon and batik cloth. 6 initials and 7 lithographs.

Georgi, Hermann

No biographical details ascertainable.

80 Ed Schmid (i.e. Kasimir Edschmid):
Bilder. Lyrische Projektionen

Darmstadt: H. Hohmann, 1913. 210 numbered copies.
6 woodcuts.

81 Schüler, Leonhard: *Das Band. Fragmente*

Darmstadt: Die Dachstube, 1919 ('Die kleine Republik. Eine Flugschriftenreihe', no. 4). 18 pp. Cover design and 2 original lithographs.

Gleichmann, Otto

Painter and graphic artist. 1887–1963. Worked mainly in Hanover.

82 *Judas Makkabäus*

Berlin: Paul Cassirer, 1919. Few copies printed.
10 lithographs in portfolio.

83 *Antiochus*

Berlin: Paul Cassirer, 1919. Few copies printed.
10 lithographs in portfolio.

84 *Chimären*

Düsseldorf: Galerie Flechtheim, 1921 ('Ausgaben der Galerie Flechtheim', Portfolio X). 100 copies. 8 lithographs. With an introduction by Hans Koch.

Gliese, Rochus

Stage-designer, mainly in Berlin. Born 1891.

85 Hasenclever, Walter: *Der Sohn*

In *Das junge Deutschland. Phantasien über die Aufführungen des Jahres 1917/18.* Published by the society Das junge Deutschland, Berlin. First privately printed publication for the members of the society. 9 lithographs by E. Büttner, R. Gliese (2) and E. Stern.

Godal, Erich

Painter and draughtsman. For many years draughtsman on the *Berliner 8-Uhr-Abendblatt*. No other details known.

86 Lieber, Alfred von: *Orphische Küste*

Potsdam: Hans Heinrich Tillgner, 1920. 42 pp. 30 copies on papier de Hollande. Original lithographs.

Goesch, Paul

Painter and architect. 1885–1940.

87 *Isaac bekommt Rebecca zum Weibe.*
Eine Geschichte aus der Heiligen Schrift

Potsdam: Hadern, 1923. 275 copies. Woodcuts.

Goldschmitt, Bruno

Painter and graphic artist; also designed tapestries and furniture. Born 1881. Last known living in Munich.

88 *Die Nachtwachen des Bonaventura*

Munich: Der Bücherwinkel, October 1923 ('Der Bücherwinkel', no. 3). 150 pp. 275 numbered copies. 17 original etchings.

Gramatté, Walter

Painter and graphic artist. 1897–1929.

89 Georg, Manfred: *Der Rebell*

In *Marsyas. Eine Zweimonatsschrift*, ed. T. Tagger, Vol. I, No. 5. Berlin: Verlag H. Hochstim, n.d. [1918]. 4 original etchings.

90 Tolstoy, Leo: *Der lebende Leichnam*

Darmstadt: Karl Lang, 1919. 5 lithographs.

91 Hadwiger, Victor: *Il Pantegan*

Berlin: Axel Juncker, 1919. 75 pp. 500 copies. 6 copper-plates after drawings.

92 Gogol, Nikolai: *Der Mantel*

Potsdam-Berlin: Gustav Kiepenheuer, 1920. 39 pp. ('Graphische Bücher', no. 3). 1,100 copies. 12 lithographs.

93 Kasack, Hermann: *Tragische Sendung*
Berlin: Rowohlt, 1920. 10 woodcuts.

94 *Joseph wird aus Neid von seinen Brüdern verkauft*

Potsdam: Hadern, 1923. 10 pp. 275 copies. 2 etchings.

95 Büchner, Georg: *Lenz*

Hamburg: Buchbund Hamburg, 1924 ('Hamburger Handdrucke der Werkstatt Lerchenfeld', 7th book). 54 pp. 150 numbered copies. 12 etchings.

96 Büchner, Georg: *Wozzeck*

1925. 12 etchings. Single leaves. Did not appear in book form.

97 Ssadowsky, Boris: *Der Apfelkönig*

Berlin: Axel Juncker, n.d. Reproductions after drawings.

Grimm, Walter O.

Painter and graphic artist. Died 1919. Was associated with the Expressionists of Darmstadt and Dresden.

98 Jaquemar, Hans: *Weg in Feuer. Dichtung*

Kiel: November Verlag, 1918. 38 pp. Title design.

99 Leinert, Rudolf A.: *Gott – Mensch Geburt (Gedichte)*

Dresden: Dresdner Verlag von 1917, 1918 ('Das Neueste Gedicht', no. 5). 19 pp. Jacket design.

100 Schilling, Heinar: *Die Richtung.*

Dialog mit einer Sphinx

Dresden: Dresdner Verlag von 1917, 1918 ('Das Neueste Gedicht', no. 7/8). Jacket design.

101 Schilling, Heinar: *Zwölf Gedichte*

Darmstadt: Die Dachstube, 1919 ('Die kleine Republik. Eine Flugschriftenreihe', no. 6). 24 pp. 250 numbered copies. 4 drawings.

102 Harbeck, Hans: *Revolution: Gedichte*

Dresden: Dresdner Verlag von 1917, 1919 ('Das Neueste Gedicht', no. 16). 19 pp. Jacket design.

103 Voigt, Carl Rolf: *Geballte Fäuste*

Dresden: Dresdner Verlag von 1917, 1919 ('Das Neueste Gedicht', no. 18). 14 pp. Jacket design.

104 Fischer, Richard: *Schrei in die Welt*

Dresden: Dresdner Verlag von 1917, 1919 ('Das Neueste Gedicht', no. 20). 23 pp. Jacket design.

105 Schilling, Heinar: *Freundschaft. Gedichte 1914–19*

Hanover: Paul Steegemann, 1921 ('Die Silbergäule', no. 128/131). 80 pp. Jacket design.

Gunschmann, Carl

Painter and graphic artist. Born 1895. Last known living in Darmstadt.

106 Usinger, Fritz: *Der ewige Kampf*

Darmstadt: Die Dachstube, 1918 (4th book issued by Die Dachstube). 37 pp. 125 copies. 4 original lithographs.

107 Merck, Wilhelm: *Verse*

Darmstadt: Die Dachstube, 1918 ('Die kleine Republik. Eine Flugschriftenreihe'). 200 copies. 5 lithographs.

108 Krell, Max: *Entführung*

Darmstadt: Die Dachstube, 1920 ('Die kleine Republik. Eine Flugschriftenreihe', no. 8). 34 pp. 250 numbered copies. 4 original lithographs.

109 Usinger, Fritz: *Irdisches Gedicht*

Darmstadt: Die Dachstube, 1927. 150 copies. 4 original etchings.

Gütersloh, Albert Paris (pseudonym)

Painter and writer; real name Albert Konrad Kiehtreiber. Born 1887. Lives in Vienna. He is regarded as the founder of the 'Vienna School'.

110 Blei, Franz: *Der bestrafte Wollüstling.*

Eine Arabeske

Vienna/Leipzig: Avalun, 1921 ('Avalun-Tausenddrucke', no. 4). 87 pp. Lithograph on jacket.

Hasler, Bernhard

Painter and graphic artist. 1884–1945. Lived latterly in Berlin.

111 Shakespeare, William: *Romeo und Julia*

Berlin: Erich Reiß, 1920 ('Prospero-Drucke', no. 10). 400 numbered copies. 10 original lithographs.

112 Grimm, Jakob, and Wilhelm Grimm: *Frau Holle und anderes*

Berlin: Bruno Cassirer, n.d. 83 drawings.

Heckel, Erich

Painter and graphic artist. 1883–1970. Co-founder of Die Brücke. Lived latterly at Hemmenhofen.

113 Wilde, Oscar: *Die Ballade vom Zuchthaus zu Reading*

New York: Ernest Rathenau (formerly Euphorion Verlag, Berlin), 1963. (English title: 'The Ballad of Reading Gaol'.) 52 pp. 600 numbered copies. Reproductions in the same size as the originals of the 12 (previously unpublished) woodcuts of 1907. The earliest known Expressionist illustrations and the last work of this character to have been published.

Henseler, Franz

Painter and graphic artist. 1885–1918.

114 Otten, Karl: *Die Reise durch Albanien*

Munich: Heinrich F. Bachmair, 1913. 71 pp. 7 drawings.

115 Jung, Franz: *Das Trottelbuch*

Berlin: Verlag der Wochenschrift Die Aktion, 1918 (Franz Pfemfert). 122 pp. Coloured cover design.

Herricht, Walter

No biographical details ascertainable.

116 Dostoyevsky, Feodor: *Petersburger Träume*

Dortmund: Dortmunder Bibliophilen Vereinigung, 1921. 17 pp. 100 copies. Several lithographs.

Heuser, Heinrich

Painter and graphic artist. Born 1887. Last known living in Berlin.

117 Kleist, Heinrich von: *Die Marquise von O...*

Leipzig: Friedrich Dehne, 1919. 61 pp. 300 copies. 6 etchings.

Heuser, Werner

Painter and graphic artist. 1880–1964. Lived latterly at Büderich near Düsseldorf.

118 Petzet, Wolfgang: *Der Vorläufer, Gedichte*

Darmstadt: Die Dachstube, 1924 ('Die kleine Republik. Eine Flugschriftenreihe', no. 14). 20 pp. 150 copies. 4 original lithographs.

Hirsch, Karl Jakob

Painter, graphic artist, writer and stage-designer. 1892–1952. Worked on the journals *Die schöne Rarität* (Kiel) and *Die Aktion* (Berlin).
A very versatile artist. Was responsible for other illustrations and title-pages, but less in Expressionist vein.

119 Bäumer, Ludwig: *Das Wesen des Kommunismus*

Hanover: Paul Steegemann, 1919 ('Die Silbergäule', no. 25/26). 27 pp. 1st–3rd thousand. Drawing on jacket.

120 *Ja! Stimmen des Arbeitsrates für Kunst in Berlin*

Charlottenburg: Photographische Gesellschaft, 1919. Title-page.

121 Herwegh, Georg: *Reißt die Kreuze aus der Erden!*

Berlin: Rowohlt, 1920 ('Umsturz und Aufbau. Eine Folge von Flugschriften', no. 6). 46 pp. Drawing on jacket.

122 *Acht Radierungen zu Liedern Gustav Mahlers*

Dresden: Dresdner Verlag von 1917, autumn 1921 ('Graphische Reihe', portfolio IV). Foreword by H. H. Stuckenschmidt. 40 copies. Dating from 1915.

Hoerle, Heinrich

Painter and graphic artist. 1895–1935. Hoerle's contact with Expressionism was very brief. His work in the main belongs to the social criticism of Die Neue Sachlichkeit.

123 Rodionoff, Tarasoff: *Schokolade*

Berlin: Die Aktion Verlag, 1924 (ed. Franz Pfemfert). 166 pp. Drawing on jacket.

Hofer, Carl

Painter and graphic artist. 1878–1955.

124 Hatzfeld, Adolf von: *Liebesgedichte*

Berlin: Galerie Flechtheim, 1922 ('Ausgaben der Galerie Flechtheim', no. 21). 16 pp. 125 copies. 10 lithographs.

125 *Zenana*

Munich: Verlag der Marées-Gesellschaft R. Piper & Co., 1923 ('Drucke der Marées-Gesellschaft', no. 41). 200 copies. 10 original lithographs in portfolio.

Hohlt, Otto

No biographical details ascertainable.

126 Hauptmann, Carl: *Lesseps Legendarisches Porträt*

Hanover: Paul Steegemann, 1919 ('Die Silbergäule', no. 20). 15 pp. Design for title.

127 Hauptmann, Carl: *Der schwingende Felsen von Tandil. Legende*

Hanover: Paul Steegemann, 1919 ('Die Silbergäule', no. 23/24). 20 pp. Drawing on jacket.

Holthoff, Hermann, and Adolf Rademacher

No biographical details ascertainable.

128 *Doctor Eisenbart*

Munich: Dreimaskenverlag, 1923. Bound in the style of a block book. Linocuts. Example of a fairy-tale book decorated in a graphic style influenced by Expressionism.

Homeyer, Lothar

Graphic artist in Berlin. Born 1883.

129 Mynona (i.e. S.Friedländer). *Graue Magie*

Dresden: Kaemmerer, 1922. Illustrations.

130 Mynona (i.e. S.Friedländer). *Ich möchte bellen und andere Grotesken*

Berlin: Seeigel, 1924. 33 pp. Drawing on jacket.

Jacob, Walter

Painter and lithographer. 1893–1965.

131 Klabund (i.e. Alfred Henschke): *Der Neger*

Dresden: R.Kaemmerer, 1920. 22 pp. Drawing on jacket.

132 Wolfenstein, Alfred: *Der gute Kampf. Eine Dichtung*

Dresden: R.Kaemmerer, 1920. 22 pp. 5 original lithographs.

Jaeckel, Willy

Painter and graphic artist. 1888–1944. Jaeckel's work is rarely pure Expressionism, though many of his illustrations are influenced by the movement.

133 *Das Buch Hiob*

Berlin: Erich Reiß, 1917 ('Prospero-Druck', no.1). 200 copies. 13 original lithographs.

134 Lautensack, Heinrich: *Erotische Votivtafeln*

Berlin: Fritz Gurlitt, 1919/20 ('Der Venuswagen', private publications of the Gurlitt-Presse, Series 1, Vol.6, ed. A.R.Meyer). Several original lithographs.

135 Whitman, Walt: *Grashalme*

Berlin: Erich Reiß, 1920 ('Prospero-Druck', no.9). 81 pp. 265 numbered copies. 13 original lithographs.

136 Dehmel, Richard: *Aber die Liebe. Gedichte*

Berlin: Erich Steinthal, 1921. 144 pp. 340 copies. 30 original etchings and numerous initials.

137 *Daniel*

Berlin: August Kuhn, 1922. 48 pp. 20 copies for sale. 15 original lithographs. (Initials by Doris Homann.)

138 Dante Alighieri: *Die Hölle*

Berlin: Hans Heinrich Tillgner, 1923. 96 pp. 200 copies. 35 etchings.

139 Louÿs, Pierre: *Lieder der Bilitis*

Berlin: Fritz Gurlitt, 1924 ('Die Neuen Bilderbücher', 5th series). 12 or (in edition B) 10 etchings.

140 Molo, Walter von: *Fugen des Seins*

Berlin: Eigenbrödler, 1924 (edited by Künstlerdank). 70 pp. 550 numbered copies. 8 etchings.

141 Goethe, J.W.von: *Faust. Eine Tragödie*

Berlin: Erich Reiß, 1925. 212 pp. 150 copies. 26 etchings.

142 Georg, Eugen: *Die Götter der Tolteken. Ein Mythos*

Berlin/Leipzig/Hamburg: Morawe & Scheffelt, 1927. 177 pp. 500 copies. 60 etchings.

Jansen, Franz Maria

Painter and graphic artist. 1885–1953.

143 Winckler, Josef: *Der chiliastische Pilgerzug. Die Sendung eines Menschheitsapostels*

Berlin/Leipzig: Deutsche Verlagsanstalt, 1923. 300 pp. 14 copper-plate engravings after etchings.

Janthur, Richard

Painter and graphic artist; also industrial artist. 1883–1956.

144 *Pantscha Tantra. Fabeln aus dem indischen Liebesleben*

Berlin: Fritz Gurlitt, 1919 ('Der Venuswagen', private publications of the Gurlitt-Presse, Series I, edited by A.R.Meyer). Coloured lithographs.

145 *Gilgamesch. Eine Erzählung aus dem alten Orient*

Berlin: Fritz Gurlitt, 1919 ('Die Neuen Bilderbücher', Series II). 50 pp. 125 copies. 11 original etchings.

146 Tagore, Rabindranath: *Vierzehn Gedichte*

Berlin: Karl Schnabel, 1920 ('Cid Drucke', ed. Const. I. David, no.1). 400 numbered copies. Etchings on stone (nos. 1–25 coloured by hand).

147 Swift, Jonathan: *Gullivers Reise …*

Berlin: Fritz Gurlitt, 1921 ('Die Neuen Bilderbücher', Series 2). 12 original lithographs.

148 Kipling, Rudyard: *Das Dschungelbuch*

Berlin: Fritz Gurlitt, 1921 ('Die Neuen Bilderbücher', Series 4). 74 pp. 250 copies. Original lithographs (copies I–X coloured by hand).

149 *Der indische Frühling. Sanskrit-Strophen des Ritusanhara des Kalidasa*

Berlin: Fritz Gurlitt, 1921 ('Das geschriebene Buch', no.1). 100 copies. 11 original lithographs.

150 *Die Rosen von Schiras. Persische Liebesgedichte*

Berlin: Fritz Gurlitt, 1921 ('Das geschriebene Buch', no. 4). 100 copies. 11 original lithographs.

151 *Das Blumenboot der Nacht.*
Chinesische Liebesgedichte

Berlin: Fritz Gurlitt, 1921 ('Das geschriebene Buch', no. 6). 100 copies. 11 original lithographs.

152 Kalischer, Bess Brenck: *Die Mühle. Eine Kosmee*

Berlin: Leon Hirsch, 1922. 48 pp. Several decorations.

153 Mérimée, Prosper: *Tamango*

Berlin: Franz Schneider, 1922 ('Luxusgraphik Schneider', no. 1). 200 copies. With initials and illustrations.

154 Defoe, Daniel: *Das Leben und die ganz ungemeinen Begebenheiten des weltberühmten Engelländers Robinson Crusoe*

Leipzig: Insel, 1922. 800 copies. 31 lithographs (coloured).

155 Apuleius: *Der Goldene Esel*

Berlin/Leipzig/Vienna: Franz Schneider, n.d. [1924], ('Luxusgraphik Schneider'). 87 pp. 200 copies. 12 original etchings.

156 *Die Gazelle. Aus einer Sammlung Afrikanischer Märchen*

Berlin/Leipzig/Vienna: Franz Schneider, n.d. ('Luxusgraphik Schneider'). 200 copies. Drawn and written on the stone; 10 lithographs coloured by hand.

157 Chamisso, Adelbert von: *Peter Schlemihl*

Berlin: Graphisches Kabinett I. B. Neumann, n.d. Lithographs in portfolio.

Kahn, Jakob

Painter in Darmstadt. 1899–1923.

158 Müller, Ernst: *Das Bacchanal*

Darmstadt: Die Dachstube, 1923. 21 pp. 6 illustrations.

Kainer, Ludwig

Painter, graphic artist and stage-designer. Born 1885. Last known living in Berlin. Examples of modishly watered-down Expressionism.

159 Scher, Peter: *Holzbock im Sommer und andere aktuelle Lyrik*

Berlin: Alfred Richard Meyer, n.d. [1913] ('Lyrisches Flugblatt'). Design for title.

160 Vallentin, Antonina: *Die purpurne Flut. Märchen und Grotesken*

Berlin: Reuss & Pollack, 1920. 86 pp. Several illustrations.

161 Goetz, Adolf: *Die Blaue Stunde*

Hamburg: Konrad Hanf, n.d. [1920]. 64 pp. 220 copies. 3 original lithographs.

Kampmann, Walter

Painter, graphic artist and book artist. 1887–1945. Lived latterly in Berlin.

162 Pollack, Heinz: *Die Revolution des Gesellschaftstanzes*

Dresden: Sibyllen-Verlag, 1922. 124 pp. Edition de luxe limited to 200 copies on papier Ingres. 8 original lithographs.

Kandinsky, Wassily

Painter, graphic artist, writer on art, poet. 1866–1944. Founder of Der Blaue Reiter.
Kandinsky did many designs for covers and jackets to catalogues, art books and almanacs, including the celebrated almanac *Der Blaue Reiter* (Munich; R. Piper), 1912.

163 Kandinsky, W.: *Über das Geistige in der Kunst, insbesondere in der Malerei*

Munich: R. Piper, 1913. Cover design and 10 original woodcuts.

164 Kandinsky, W.: *Klänge*

Munich: R. Piper, 1913. 300 numbered copies. Cover design, 12 coloured and 43 black-and-white woodcuts.

Kaus, Max

Painter and graphic artist. Born 1891. Lives in Berlin.

165 Flaubert, Gustave: *Die Sage von Sankt Julian dem Gastfreien*

Weimar: Gustav Kiepenheuer, 1918 ('Graphische Bücher', no. 1). 50 pp. 12 original lithographs.

Keil, Hermann

Graphic artist and architect. Born 1889. A member of the Dachstube circle.

166 Schnack, Anton: *Der Abenteurer*

Darmstadt: Die Dachstube, 1919 ('Die kleine Republik. Eine Flugschriftenreihe', no.7). 18 pp. 250 numbered copies. 2 original woodcuts.

167 Edschmid, Kasimir: *Rede an einen Dichter*

Hamburg: Adolf Harms, March 1922 ('Die schöne Rarität', no.5, ed. Niels Hoyer). 200 copies. 4 woodcuts (3 by Keil and one by Frans Masereel).

168 Krell, Max: *Der Henker*

Darmstadt: Die Dachstube, summer 1924 ('Die kleine Republik. Eine Flugschriftenreihe', no.15). 20 pp. 150 numbered copies. 6 original lithographs.

Kern, Walter

Painter, graphic artist and poet. Born 1898. Lives at Winterthur. Illustrated his own poems.

169 *Credo, Gedichte und Lithos*

Thun: Verlag für neue Graphik W.P. Krebser, n.d. 50 copies.

Kind, Georg

Sculptor, painter and graphic artist. 1897–1945. Lived in Dresden.

170 Schnack, Anton: *Strophen der Gier*

Dresden: Dresdner Verlag von 1917, 1919 ('Das Neueste Gedicht', no.22). 15 pp. Drawing on jacket.

Kirchner, Ernst Ludwig

Painter and graphic artist. 1880–1938. Co-founder of Die Brücke. Kirchner executed woodcuts for many monographs on his work; also for catalogues and Die Brücke documents. His œuvre includes a considerable number of graphic illustrations of literary texts, not all of which appeared in book form. I have cited the colour woodcuts to *Peter Schlemihl* as the most important example.

171 Döblin, Alfred: *Das Stiftsfräulein und der Tod. Eine Novelle*

Berlin: Alfred Richard Meyer, November 1913 ('Lyrisches Flugblatt'). Woodcut on title and 4 full-page woodcuts.

172 Chamisso, Adelbert von: *Peter Schlemihls wundersame Geschichte*

Hand-printed by Kirchner 1915/16. 7 colour woodcuts. The suite of woodcuts did not appear in book form. Edition in book form with reproductions published by Reclam, Leipzig, 1974.

173 Corrinth, Curt: *Die Leichenschändung. Ein Spiel vom wollüstigen Tod*

Berlin-Wilmersdorf: Alfred Richard Meyer, 1920 ('Lyrisches Flugblatt'). 8 unnumbered leaves. Woodcut on title.

174 Boßhart, Jakob: *Neben der Heerstraße. Erzählungen*

Zürich/Leipzig: Grethlein & Co., 1923. 436 pp. Edition de luxe limited to 120 copies. Illustration on cover, 24 original woodcuts.

175 Heym, Georg: *Umbra vitae. Nachgelassene Gedichte*

Munich: Kurt Wolff, 1924. 64 pp. 510 numbered copies. 47 original woodcuts. Illustration on cover. Book designed by Kirchner.
A rejected binding also exists (colour woodcut).

Klee, Paul

Painter, graphic artist and writer on art. 1897–1940.

176 Voltaire: *Kandide oder Die beste Welt. Eine Erzählung*

Munich: Kurt Wolff, 1920. 92 pp. 26 pen-and-ink drawings (the drawings were done in 1911).

177 Corrinth, Curt: *Potsdamer Platz. Ekstatische Visionen*

Munich: Georg Müller, 1920. 90 pp. 10 lithographs.

Klein, César

Painter, graphic artist, industrial artist. 1876–1954. In addition to the two items listed, Klein was also responsible for the jacket design for the Gurlitt 'Almanac for the year 1920'.

178 Corrinth, Curt: *Bordell. Ein infernalischer Roman in fünf Sprüngen*

Berlin: (publisher not known), 1920. 250 pp. Coloured drawing on cover.

179 Hauptmann, Carl: *Die Heilige. Oper in drei Aufzügen. Musik von Manfred Gurlitt*

Berlin: Fritz Gurlitt, autumn 1921. 5 colour lithographs.

Kleinschmidt, Paul

Painter and graphic artist. 1883–1949.

180 *Acht Radierungen zu Don Quixote*

Berlin: I. B. Neumann, 1919. 50 copies. Portfolio of 8 etchings.

181 Mendoza, Diego Hurtado di:
Die Abenteuer des Lazarillo von Tormes

Berlin: Hans Heinrich Tillgner, 1923 ('Das Prisma', no. 6). 67 pp. Several lithographs.

Klemm, Wilhelm

Lyric poet. 1881–1968. A member of the *Die Aktion* group.

182 Klemm, W.: *Aufforderung. Gesammelte Verse*

Berlin-Wilmersdorf: Die Aktion Verlag, 1917 (Franz Pfemfert), ('Die Aktionslyrik', vol. 4). Design on jacket and 1 illustration.

183 Klemm, W.: *Traumschutt, Gedichte*

Hanover/Leipzig/Vienna/Zürich: Paul Steegemann, 1920. Title design by the author.

Kohlhoff, Wilhelm

Painter and graphic artist. 1893–1971. Lived latterly in Schweinfurth.

184 Coster, Charles de: *Herr Halewijn.*
Eine vlämische Märe

Berlin: Erich Reiß, 1920 ('Prospero-Druck', no. 12). 250 numbered copies. 16 original lithographs.

185 Hesse, Otto Ernst: *Großstadtballaden*

Berlin: Fritz Gurlitt, 1923 ('Das geschriebene Buch', no. 8). 20 copies. Several lithographs. Kohlhoff also wrote the text on the stone.

Kokoschka, Oskar

Painter, graphic artist and poet. Born 1886. Lives at Villeneuve.

186 Kokoschka, Oskar: *Mörder, Hoffnung der Frauen*

The drama first appeared, with drawings, in *Der Sturm*, Vol. 1, No. 20, 1910, pp. 155 ff.
Edition de luxe in book form. Berlin: Der Sturm, 1916. 100 copies, with 5 line etchings after drawings.

187 Ehrenstein, Albert: *Tubutsch*

Vienna/Leipzig: Jahoda & Siegel, n.d. [1912]. 67 pp. Illustration on binding and 12 line etchings after drawings. 2nd edition Leipzig: Insel, 1918 ('Insel-Bücherei', no. 261). The first volume of the Insel-Bücherei to contain illustrations by a contemporary artist.

188 Kraus, Karl: *Die chinesische Mauer*

Leipzig: Kurt Wolff, 1914. 44 pp. 200 numbered copies. 8 original lithographs.

189 *O Ewigkeit – Du Donnerwort,*
so spanne meine Glieder aus

Berlin: Fritz Gurlitt, 1914. 125 copies in portfolio. 11 lithographs. Edition in book form, Berlin: Fritz Gurlitt, 1918 ('Die Neuen Bilderbücher', Series 1, Vol. 4). 125 copies. Design for title and 11 lithographs illustrating the text of the cantata by J. S. Bach.

190 Kokoschka, Oskar: *Der gefesselte Kolumbus*

Berlin: Fritz Gurlitt, 1916. 200 copies. 12 lithographs in portfolio. Edition in book form, Berlin: Fritz Gurlitt, 1920/21 ('Die Neuen Bilderbücher', Series 3, Vol. 6). 120 copies. Written on the stone by E. R. Weiß. So-called 'popular editions', reproduced by photolithography in a smaller size, exist of this and other works by Kokoschka; these have not been listed separately.

191 Kokoschka, Oskar: *Allos Makar*

In *Zeit-Echo. Ein Kriegstagebuch der Künstler*, Vol. 1 [1915], No. 20, pp. 297 ff. 5 original lithographs. (Allos Makar is an anagram of Alma Oskar.)

192 *Die Passion*

Berlin: Fritz Gurlitt, 1916. 6 lithographs in portfolio.

193 Walden, Herwarth: *Die Judentochter*

Berlin: Der Sturm, 1916. 8 pp. Jacket design. Setting for voice and piano of a poem from *Des Knaben Wunderhorn*. Kokoschka did not design the text appearing on the jacket. First edition of Walden's composition and only edition to have the jacket design.

194 Ehrenstein, Albert: *Nicht da, nicht dort*

Leipzig: Kurt Wolff, 1917 ('Der jüngste Tag', no. 27/28). 76 pp. Design on jacket for part of the edition.

195 Kokoschka, Oskar: *Hiob*

Berlin: Paul Cassirer, 1917. 100 copies. 7 lithographs printed in red and black.

196 Dirsztay, Victor: *Lob des hohen Verstandes*

Leipzig: Kurt Wolff, 1917. 6 lithographs and vignette on title.

197 Kokoschka, Oskar: *Vier Dramen*

Berlin: Paul Cassirer, 1919. Cover design.

198 Kokoschka, Bohuslav: *Adelina oder Der Abschied vom neunzehnten Lebensjahr. Aufzeichnungen*

Munich: Kurt Wolff, n.d. [1920], ('Der jüngste Tag', no. 76/77). 85 pp. 1 drawing.

199 Dirsztay, Victor: *Der Unentrinnbare. Roman*

Munich: Kurt Wolff, 1923. 128 pp. 7 drawings and design on jacket.

200 Kokoschka, Bohuslav: *Geh, mach die Tür zu, es zieht!*

Vienna: Johannes-Presse, 1926 (seventh publication). 57 pp. 33 copies. 2 original etchings.

Körber, Helmuth

Painter and graphic artist. Born 1890. Last known living in Berlin.

201 Balzac, Honoré de: *Eine Leidenschaft in der Wüste*

Potsdam: Müller & Co., 1920 ('Sanssouci-Bücher', no. 6, ed. F. Blei). 53 pp. 6 etchings.

Krantz, Ernst

Painter and graphic artist. 1889–1954.

202 Mynona (i.e. S. Friedländer): *Unterm Leichentuch. Eine tolle Spukgeschichte*

Hanover: Paul Steegemann, 1920 ('Die Silbergäule', no. 45/47). 27 pp. 1st–3rd thousand. Design on jacket.

Krauskopf, Bruno

Painter, graphic artist and stage-designer. 1892–1960. Lived latterly in New York.
Krauskopf did many illustrations, of which only a few are Expressionist.

203 Dauthendey, Max: *Zwölf Gedichte*

Berlin: Fritz Gurlitt, 1920 ('Das geschriebene Buch', Vol. 3). 100 copies. 12 original lithographs.

204 Dostoyevsky, Feodor: *Die Sanfte*

Berlin: Erich Weiß, 1920 ('Prospero Druck', no. 8). 50 pp. 300 copies. 10 lithographs.

205 Reisiger, Hans: *Santa Caterina da Siena. Novelle*

Berlin: S. Fischer, 1921. 53 pp. Edition de luxe, 300 copies. 7 drawings.

Kubin, Alfred

Painter, illustrator and writer. 1877–1959. Not an Expressionist. See chapter V, 'Excursus on Kubin, Barlach and Masereel'.
For a bibliography of his work as illustrator, see Raabe, Paul: *Alfred Kubin, Leben, Werk, Wirkung*, Hamburg, 1957.

Kuron, Viktor Joseph

No biographical details ascertainable.

206 Habicht, Victor Curt: *Die letzte Lust. Ein Roman*

Hanover: Paul Steegemann, 1920 ('Die Silbergäule', no. 69/75). 129 pp. 1st–3rd thousand. Design on jacket.

207 Michel, Wilhelm: *Essays über Gustav Landauer, Romain Rolland. Die Metaphysik des Bürgers*

Hanover: Paul Steegemann, 1920 ('Die Silbergäule', no. 33/33 a). 21 pp. 1st–3rd thousand. Design on jacket.

208 Wagner, Friedrich Wilhelm: *Jungfrauen platzen männertoll. Grotesken*

Hanover: Paul Steegemann, 1920 ('Die Silbergäule', no. 48/49). 17 pp. 1st–3rd thousand. Design on jacket.

209 Schiebelhuth, Hans: *Der Hakenkreuzzug. Neo-dadaistische Ungedichte*

Darmstadt: Die Dachstube, 1920 ('Die kleine Republik. Eine Flugschriftenreihe', no. 9). 500 numbered copies (nos. 1–100 coloured by hand). 4 original woodcuts.

Lange, Otto

Painter and graphic artist. 1879–1944. Lived in Dresden.

210 *Van Zantens glückliche Zeit*

Dresden: Galerie Arnold, 1920. Colour woodcuts. Foreword by Hans F. Secker. The Deutsche Bücherei Leipzig possesses copy no. 28.

Lasker-Schüler, Else

Poet. 1869–1945. Illustrated many of her own books. The reader is referred to 'Bibliographie der Buchveröffentlichung Else Lasker-Schülers' in *Nachrichten aus dem Kösel-Verlag. Sonderheft für Else Lasker-Schüler*, Munich, December 1965, pp. 19 ff.

211 Lasker-Schüler, E.: *Die Nächte Tino von Bagdads*

Berlin/Stuttgart/Leipzig: Axel Juncker, 1907. 86 pp. Frontispiece (drawing).
Second edition. Berlin: Paul Cassirer, 1919. Design on cover.

212 Lasker-Schüler, E.: *Mein Herz. Ein Liebesroman mit Bildern und wirklichlebenden Menschen*

Munich and Berlin: Heinrich F.S. Bachmair, 1912. 167 pp. 20 full-page drawings (and portrait drawing by Karl Schmidt-Rottluff). Design on cover.
Second edition. Berlin: Paul Cassirer, 1920. 13 drawings. Design on cover.

213 Lasker-Schüler, E.: *Hebräische Balladen*

Berlin-Wilmersdorf: Alfred Richard Meyer, 1913 ('Lyrisches Flugblatt'). Drawing on title-page.

214 Lasker-Schüler, E.: *Der Prinz von Theben. Ein Geschichtenbuch*

Leipzig: Verlag der weißen Bücher, 1914. 98 pp. Design on cover. 25 illustrations after drawings by the author and 3 coloured illustrations by Franz Marc.
Second edition. Berlin: Paul Cassirer, 1920. 13 drawings.

215 Lasker-Schüler, E.: *Der Malik. Eine Kaisergeschichte mit Bildern und Zeichnungen*

Berlin: Paul Cassirer, 1919. 102 pp. Designs on cover and 4 crayon drawings by the author, also drawings by other artists, including a coloured reproduction of a watercolour by Franz Marc.

216 Lasker-Schüler, E.: *Die Wupper. Schauspiel in 5 Aufzügen*

Berlin: Paul Cassirer, 1919. 102 pp.
Second edition with design on cover by the author (self-portrait).

217 Lasker-Schüler, E.: *Theben. Gedichte und 10 Lithografien*

Frankfurt am Main/Berlin: Querschnitt, 1923 ('Flechtheim-Druck', no. 24). 13 leaves. 250 copies written and drawn on the stone by the author (nos. 1–50 coloured by hand). Cover illustration impressed and gilt.

Lismann, Hermann

Painter and art scholar. Born 1878. Died in Maidanek concentration camp after 1943.

218 Flaubert, Gustave: *Die Versuchung des Heiligen Antonius*

Munich/Berlin/Leipzig: Verlag für praktische Kunstwissenschaft F. Schmidt, 1921. 170 pp. 14 woodcuts. Lismann also translated the text.

Mahlau, Alfred

Painter, graphic artist, stage-designer, illustrator. 1894–1967. Lived latterly in Hamburg.

219 Harich, Walther: *Der Turmbau zu Babel*

Berlin: Erich Reiß, 1920. 57 pp. 830 copies. 7 original lithographs.

Marc, Franz

Painter and graphic artist. 1860–1916. One of the founders of Der Blaue Reiter.
There are no books with illustrations by Marc. *Stella peregrina, 18 Faksimile-Nachbildungen nach Marcschen Arbeiten* (published in Munich in 1917 by Hanfstaengl), with drawings to various poems, dates from before Expressionism: the drawings were done between 1904 and 1907. There are various (few) binding designs, including one for H. Walden, *Einblick in Kunst*, Berlin, 1924, eighth impression. Marc's most important illustrative work is his woodcut 'Versöhnung' (to a poem by Else Lasker-Schüler) published in *Der Sturm*, Vol. 3, no. 125/126 [1912].

Marcks, Gerhard

Sculptor, draughtsman and woodcut artist. Born 1889. Lives near Cologne.

220 *Das Wielandslied der älteren Edda*

Munich and Weimar: Bauhaus Verlag, 1923. 110 numbered copies. 10 woodcuts in portfolio. Bound by Otto Dorfner, woodcuts printed at the Bauhaus.

Masereel, Frans

Woodcut artist. 1889–1972. Lived latterly in Nice. Not an Expressionist in the true sense. See chapter, 'Excursus on Kubin, Barlach and Masereel'. Bibliography of portfolios and books illustrated by Masereel, by Hanns-Conon von der Gabelentz, in *Frans Masereel. Mit Beiträgen von S. Zweig, P. Vorms, G. Pommeranz-Liedtke*, Dresden, 1959.

Mathey, Georg Alexander

Graphic artist and book artist. 1884–1968. Lived latterly in Offenbach.

The greater part of Mathey's work consists of examples of a tasteful manipulation of Expressionist formative principles.

221 *Zehn Holzschnitte zur Bibel*

Leipzig: Insel, 1921, 150 copies. Portfolio. With a foreword by Theodor Däubler.

222 Bethge, Hans: *Satuila oder vom Zauber der Südsee*

Berlin: Morawe & Scheffelt, 1921. 40 pp. 250 numbered copies. Many illustrations.

223 Bethge, Hans: *Pfirsichblüten aus China*

Berlin: Ernst Rowohlt, 1922. 100 numbered copies. 6 original lithographs, lithograph on cover and drawing on title-page. Bound in Chinese tussore silk, in slip-case.

224 *Das Hohe Lied in der Nachdichtung Goethes*

Berlin: Dietrich Reimer & Ernst Vohsen, 1924 ('Daedalus-Druck', no. 2). 1,050 copies including fifty numbered copies on hand-made paper, with the full-page plates signed by the artist. Also an edition of 350 copies in Latin.

Mehring, Walter

Writer. Born 1896. One of the founders of Berlin Dada. Illustrated a few of his books with his own drawings. See chapter IV, 'Writers as illustrators'.

Meidner, Ludwig

Painter, graphic artist and writer. 1884–1966.

225 Benn, Gottfried: *Söhne. Neue Gedichte*

Berlin: Alfred Richard Meyer, 1913 ('Lyrisches Flugblatt'). Design on title-page.

226 Zech, Paul: *Das schwarze Revier*

Berlin: Alfred Richard Meyer, 1913 ('Lyrisches Flugblatt'). 1st–4th thousand. Design on title-page.

227 Leonhard, Rudolf: *Barabaren. Balladen*

Berlin: Alfred Richard Meyer, 1914 ('Lyrisches Flugblatt'). Design on jacket.

228 Meyer, Alfred Richard: *Und ich sabe das Tier*

Berlin: Alfred Richard Meyer, 1915 ('Lyrisches Flugblatt'). Design on title-page.

229 Mynona (i.e. S. Friedländer): *Schwarz-Weiß-Rot. Grotesken*

Leipzig: Kurt Wolff, 1916 ('Der jüngste Tag, no. 31). 45 pp. 2 drawings.

230 Meidner, Ludwig: *Im Nacken das Sternemeer*

Leipzig: Kurt Wolff, 1918. 82 pp. 12 drawings and cover illustration.

231 Hasenclever, Walter: *Der politische Dichter. Gedichte und Reden*

Berlin: Ernst Rowohlt, 1919 ('Umsturz und Aufbau. Eine Folge von Flugschriften', no. 2). 36 pp. Design on jacket.

232 Nadel, Arno: *Der Sündenfall. Sieben biblische Szenen*

Berlin: Jüdischer Verlag, 1920. Design on title-page.

233 Becher, Johannes R.: *Ewig in Aufruhr. Gedichte*

Berlin: Ernst Rowohlt, 1920 ('Umsturz und Aufbau. Eine Folge von Flugschriften', no. 7). 46 pp. Design on jacket.

234 Meidner, Ludwig: *Septemberschrei. Hymnen, Gebete, Lästerungen*

Berlin: Paul Cassirer, 1920. 82 pp. 14 lithographs.

235 Weiß, Ernst: *Die Feuerprobe*

Berlin: Die Schmiede, 1923 (Offizina Fabri, first and only publication). 114 pp. 675 copies. 5 original etchings.

236 *Der Knecht des Herrn im tiefsten Leid. Ein Psalm Davids*

Potsdam: Hadern, 1923. 8 pp. 250 copies. 2 etchings.

237 Klopstock, F. G.: *Der Tod Adams. Ein Trauerspiel*

Freiburg im Breisgau: Pentos, 1924. Facsimile reprint of the edition of 1757. 5 original etchings.

Meier-Thur, Hugo

No biographical details ascertainable.

238 Stramm, August: *Welt-Wehe. Ein Schwarz-Weiß-Spiel in Marmorätzungen*

Meseck, Felix

Painter and illustrator. 1883–1955.
Meseck did many illustrations. His contact with Expressionism was no more than tangential.

239 Novalis (i. e. F. von Hardenberg):
Hymnen an die Nacht

Berlin: Fritz Gurlitt, 1919 ('Drucke der Gurlitt-Presse. Die Neuen Bilderbücher', Series 2, Vol. 3). 125 copies. 11 original etchings.

240 *Das Jahr. Ein Zyklus deutscher Gedichte*

Selected by Max Krell. Berlin: Fritz Gurlitt, 1920 ('Die Neuen Bilderbücher', Series 3). 125 copies. 15 etchings.

Mitschke-Collande, Constantin von

Painter and graphic artist. 1884–1956. Was a member of the Dresden group of late Expressionists.

241 Hartmann, Walter Georg: *Der begeisterte Weg*

Dresden: R. Kaemmerer, 1919 ('Europäische Bücherei', Vol. 1). 47 pp. 6 woodcuts.

242 Reymer, Rudolf: *Doktor Stumm.*
Schauspiel in drei Akten

Dresden: R. Kaemmerer, 1920. Design on title-page.

243 Harden, Sylvia von: *Verworrene Städte*

Dresden: R. Kaemmerer, 1920. Design on title page.

244 Klabund (i. e. Alfred Henschke): *Montezuma*

Dresden: Dresdner Verlag von 1917, February 1922 ('Graphische Reihe', Portfolio XIV). 30 copies. 4 woodcuts.

245 Hartmann, Walter Georg: *Die Tiere der Insel*

Dresden: Sibyllen-Verlag, 1922. 77 pp. 11 original woodcuts, coloured.

Mohr, Alexander

Painter and illustrator. After the First World War lived in Stuttgart, and in the 1930s in Trier and Paris.

246 Weber, Carl Maria: *Der ekstatische Fluß.*
Rheinklänge ohne Romantik

Düsseldorf: A. Bagel, 1919. 39 pp. 150 numbered copies. Lithographs by F. M. Jansen, A. Mohr, O. Raber and W. Schmetz.
Design on cover by A. Mohr.

Müller-Worpswede, Walter

Graphic artist and artist-craftsman. Born 1901.

247 Schiebelhuth, Hans: *Hymne des Maropampa*

Worpswede: Hollander-Presse, 1921. (First and only work printed on this hand-press.) 20 pp. 200 copies. 12 woodcuts coloured by hand.

Nauen, Heinrich

Painter and graphic artist. 1880–1941.

248 Droste-Hülshoff, Annette von: *Die Judenbuche*

Frankfurt am Main: Querschnitt, 1923 ('Flechtheim-Drucke', no. 25). 114 pp. 250 copies. 10 etchings.

Neher, Caspar

Stage-designer. 1897–1962.

249 Brecht, Bertolt: *Baal*

Potsdam: Gustav Kiepenheuer, 1922. 91 pp. Several illustrations and title-page.

Nolde, Emil

Painter and graphic artist. 1867–1956.
Nolde provided designs for the covers of various books of art scholarship.

250 Schiefler, Gustav: *Das graphische Werk von Emil Nolde 1910–1925*

Berlin: Euphorion, 1927. 172 pp. Many decorations (original woodcuts) by Nolde.

Nückel, Otto

Painter and graphic artist. 1888–1956.

251 Frey, A. M.: *Solnemann der Unsichtbare*

Munich: Delphin, 1914. 193 pp. Jacket, binding and 13 woodcuts.

252 Frey, A. M.: *Spuk des Alltags*

Munich: Delphin (Verlag Dr. Richard Landauer), 1920. 277 pp. Binding, vignette on title-page, 12 woodcuts.

Odoy, Max

Painter and graphic artist. Born 1886.

253 Herrmann, Max: *Porträte des Provinztheaters*

Berlin: Alfred Richard Meyer, 1913 ('Lyrisches Flugblatt'). Design on title-page.

Oeconomides, Georg

No biographical details ascertainable.

254 Schilling, Heinar: *Die Sklaven*

Dresden: Dresdner Verlag von 1917, 1922 ('Graphische Reihe', Portfolio XIX). 25 copies. 8 woodcuts with the prologue to the poem.

Opermann, Karl

Sculptor and graphic artist. Born 1891. Last known living in Hamburg.

255 Martens, P.: *Die südliche Krone. Gedicht*

Hamburg: Adolf Harms, 1921 ('Die Drucke der Tafelrunde', ed. Karl Lorenz, no. 4). 14 pp. 200 numbered copies. Original woodcut.

Oppenheimer, Max (called Mopp)

Painter and graphic artist. 1885–1954.

256 Benn, Gottfried: *Fleisch. Gesammelte Lyrik*

Berlin-Wilmersdorf: Verlag der Wochenschrift Die Aktion (Franz Pfemfert), 1917 ('Die Aktions-Lyrik', vol. 3). Illustration on title-page and two drawings.

Orlowski, Hans

Painter and graphic artist. 1894–1967.

257 Heine, Heinrich: *Die Cholera in Paris*

Berlin: August Kuhn-Foelix, 1923. 17 pp. 50 copies. Several woodcuts.

258 *Die Seligpreisungen*

Berlin: August Kuhn-Foelix, 1923. 12 copies. Lithographs tinted with watercolour.

259 *Das jüngste Gericht*

Berlin: Wendekreis, 1923 (third book published by the Wendekreis-Verlag). 100 copies. Several woodcuts coloured by hand.

260 *Amiran. Eine georgische Sage*

Berlin: Wendekreis, 1924 (fifth book published by the Wendekreis-Verlag). 50 copies. 4 woodcuts.

Pankok, Otto

Painter, graphic artist, sculptor and writer. 1893–1968.

261 Wilde, Oscar:

Ballade des Zuchthauses zu Reading von C.3.3.

Berlin: Axel Juncker, autumn 1923 (fifth édition de luxe in the series 'Orplidbücher'). 63 pp. 300 numbered copies. Several original etchings.

Pechstein, Max

Painter and graphic artist. 1881–1955. One of the artists of Die Brücke.

Pechstein also did cover designs for a number of books of art scholarship (e.g. Fechter, P., *Der Expressionismus*, Munich, 1919) and almanacs (e.g. *Gurlitt-Almanach* for the year 1920). Portfolios and books of a non-literary character have not been included here.

262 Lautensack, Heinrich: *Die Samländische Ode*

Berlin: Fritz Gurlitt, 1918 ('Die Neuen Bilderbücher', Series 1, Vol. 3). 37 pp. 130 copies. 22 lithographs, some full-page.

263 Sternheim, Carl: *Heidenstam*

In *Marsyas. Eine Zweimonatsschrift*, ed T. Tagger, Vol. 1, No. 4, Berlin: H. Hochstim, n.d. [1918]. 4 original etchings.

264 Stehr, Hermann: *Der Schatten*

In *Marsyas*, Vol. 1, No. 5, Berlin [1918]. 4 original etchings.

265 Pechstein, Max: *An alle Künstler!*

Berlin: [Willi Simon], 1919. Coloured design on jacket.

266 Pechstein, Max: *Aufruf zum Sozialismus*

Berlin: (no publisher), 1919. Introduction by K. E. Meurer.
Design on jacket.

267 *Das Vaterunser*

Berlin: Propyläen-Verlag, 1921. 250 numbered copies. 12 woodcuts in portfolio (nos. 1–50 coloured by hand).

268 *Van Zantens Insel der Verheißung*

Berlin: S. Fischer, 1924. 174 pp. Edited by Laurids Bruun. Coloured design on jacket.

269 Seidel, Willy: *Yali und sein weißes Weib*

Berlin: Fritz Gurlitt, 1924 ('Die Neuen Bilderbücher', Series 5, Vol. 6). 27 pp. 220 copies. 8 original etchings.

270 Hellens, Franz: *Bass – Bassina – Bulu*

Berlin: Axel Juncker, n.d. 327 pp. 1st–3rd thousand. Illustration on cover.

Plünnecke, Wilhelm

Painter and graphic artist. 1894–1954.

271 Büchner, Georg: *Friede den Hütten! Krieg den Palästen!*

Berlin: Ernst Rowohlt, 1919 ('Umsturz und Aufbau'). 39 pp. Edited with introduction by Kurt Pinthus. Design on jacket.

272 Büchner, Georg: *Wozzeck*

Berlin: Axel Juncker, 1919. Several illustrations.

273 Tornius, Valerian: *Abenteurer*

Leipzig: Klinkhardt & Biermann, 1919. Illustrated.

274 Leonhard, Rudolf: *Kampf gegen die Waffe!*

Berlin: Ernst Rowohlt, 1919 ('Umsturz und Aufbau', Flugschrift 3). Design on jacket.

275 Fallada, Hans: *Der junge Geodeschal. Ein Pubertätsroman*

Berlin: Ernst Rowohlt, 1920. Design on jacket.

276 Cervantes Saavedra, M. de: *Die geflickte Tugend oder Die vergebliche Tante*

Munich: Georg Müller, 1921. 50 pp. 500 numbered copies. Wood-engraved illustrations.

277 Leonhard, Rudolf: *Die Prophezeiung*

Berlin: Gesellschaft von Freunden neuer deutscher Kunst, 1922. 30 copies. 5 original lithographs.

278 Wilczynski, Karl: *Choräle zwischen Nacht und Morgen*

Berlin: Gesellschaft von Freunden neuer deutscher Kunst, 1922. 15 copies. 5 original lithographs.

Rabus, Carl

Painter and graphic artist. Born 1900. Was active in Belgium and Germany. Domiciled in U.S.A. since 1934.

279 Goethe, J. W. von: *Die Novelle*

Munich: Hesperos, 1920. 39 pp. 300 copies. 10 lithographs.

280 Wieland, C. M.: *Oberon. Ein romantisches Heldengedicht*

Munich: Hesperos, n.d. [1920]. 241 pp. 350 numbered copies. 18 original etchings.

281 Hoffmann, E. T. A.: *Das öde Haus*

Munich: Hesperos, n.d. [1920]. 500 numbered copies. 11 original etchings. Binding and book designed by Emil Preetorius.

282 Hauff, Wilhelm: *Die Bettlerin von Pont des Arts*

Munich: Hesperos, 1921. 167 pp. 200 copies. A few etchings. The same press issued another edition, numbering 3 copies, privately printed, which contains different, essentially Expressionist, etchings.

283 Paul, Jean (i.e. J.P.F.Richter): *Des Geburtshelfers Walther Viermeissel Nachtgedanken*

Munich: Die Serapionsbrüder, 1921 (second publication). 23 pp. 150 copies. Several etchings.

284 Bud, Elsa Maria: *Kreisende Schatten*

In *EOS. Ein Ausdruckswerk ringender Kunst*, founded and edited by E.Pirchan and P.Baumann, Book 4. Munich: Die Wende, 1921. Several original etchings.

285 Döblin, Alfred: *Blaubart und Miß Ilsebill*

Berlin: Hans Heinrich Tillgner, 1923 ('Prisma', Book 10 of the series). 86 pp. 12 drawings on the stone.

286 Balzac, Honoré de: *El Verdugo*

Munich-Pullach: Paul Stangl, n.d. [1924]. 36 pp. 500 copies. 7 etchings.

Rademacher, Adolf

See Holthoff, Hermann.

Reimer, Emmerich (i.e. Imre Reimer)

Graphic artist and illustrator. Born 1900. Lives in Switzerland.

287 Gorki, Maxim: *Die Geschichte eines Verbrechens*

Stuttgart: Julius Hoffmann, 1922 (fourth book from the Juniperuspresse). 40 pp. 100 copies. Woodcuts.

Richter, Klaus

Painter, graphic artist, illustrator; also made his name as a writer. 1887–1948.

288 Richter, Klaus: *Schrecken.*
Novellen und Federzeichnungen
Berlin: E. Reiss, 1919. 91 pp. 15 illustrations.

Rössing, Karl

Graphic artist (woodcuts and wood-engravings). Born 1897. Lives in Gauting.

289 Gogol, Nikolai: *Taras Bulba*
Vienna/Leipzig/Munich: Rikola, 1922. 148 pp. 150 numbered copies. 30 woodcuts. (Typography by F. H. Ehmcke, who also supervised the printing.)

Rößner, Georg Walter

Painter and graphic artist. Born 1885. Pupil of Lovis Corinth. Rößner's contact with Expressionism was slight; fashionable tendencies apparent as early as 1919.

290 Meyer, Alfred Richard: *Semilasso in Afrika*
Berlin: December 1912 ('Die Bücherei Maiandros. Eine Zeitschrift von 60 zu 60 Tagen', ed. H. Lautensack, A. R. Meyer and A. Ruest, Book 2). 10 drawings.

291 Holz, Arno: *Seltsame und höchst abenteuerliche Historie von der Insul Pimperle daran sich der Dichter offt im Traume ergezzt*
Berlin-Wilmersdorf: A. R. Meyer, n.d. [1919]. 500 copies, of which 60 have original lithographs.

292 Holz, Arno: *Flördeliese*
Berlin-Wilmersdorf: A. R. Meyer, n.d. [1919]. Privately printed edition of 500 copies, of which 60 have original colour lithographs.

Rudolph, Arthur

Painter and graphic artist. Born 1885.

293 Hauptmann, Carl: *Das Kostümgenie*
Berlin: Arthur Collignon, 1920 ('Liliendrucke', Vol. 2). 26 pp. 850 copies. 4 original lithographs, 12 drawings in the text.

Schaefler, Fritz

Painter and graphic artist. 1888–1954.

294 Haringer, Jan Jacob: *Haus des Vergessens*
Dresden: Dresdner Verlag von 1917, 1919 ('Das Neueste Gedicht', no. 24/25). Design on jacket.

Scharff, Edwin

Sculptor and graphic artist. 1887–1955.

295 Tagger, Theodor: *Marsyas und Apoll*
In *Marsyas. Eine Zweimonatsschrift*, ed. T. Tagger, No. 1. Berlin: H. Hochstim, July/August 1917. 235 numbered copies. Original etchings.

296 *Sintflut*
In *Marsyas*, No. 2, September/October 1917. 4 etchings.

297 Wedekind, Frank: *Herakles.*
Dramatisches Gedicht in 3 Akten
Munich: Georg Müller, 1920 ('Welttheater. Meisterdramen mit Originalgraphik', vol. 4). 127 pp. 330 copies. 20 lithographs.

298 Mann, Thomas: *Tristan*
Munich: Drei Masken, 1922 ('Obelisk-Druck', no. 5). 69 pp. 320 copies. 12 etchings.

Schlichter, Rudolf

Painter and graphic artist. 1890–1955.

299 Wieland, C. M.: *Auszug aus Lucians Nachrichten vom Tode des Peregrinus*
Heidelberg: Richard Weissbach, 1920 ('Die Drucke des Argonautenkreises', no. 3). 20 pp. 150 copies. 10 lithographs.

Schmidt-Rottluff, Karl

Painter and graphic artist. Born 1884. One of the founders of Die Brücke. Lives in Berlin. Undertook various jobs connected with book design. Designed the title for the Hamburg periodical *Kündung*, 1921.

300 Brust, Alfred: *Das Spiel Christa vom Schmerz der Schönheit des Weibes*
Berlin: Die Aktion Verlag, 1918 ('Der rote Hahn', ed. Franz Pfemfert). 45 pp. 9 woodcuts.

Schneidler, F. H. Ernst

Book designer and typographer. 1882–1956.

301 Heine, Heinrich: *Atta Troll.*
Ein Sommernachtstraum
Berlin: Morawe & Scheffelt, 1912. 162 pp. Many illustrations, initials and vignettes, also frontispiece and design on cover.

Schramm, Werner

Painter, graphic artist and stage-designer. Born 1898.

302 *Begegnungen. 12 Lithografien mit einem Gedicht von Kurt Heynecke als Vorwort*

Düsseldorf/Berlin/Frankfurt: Verlag der Galerie Alfred Flechtheim, 1921 (18th publication). 70 copies.

Schrimpf, Georg

Painter. 1889–1938.
Schrimpf had no more than a passing contact with Expressionism. Influenced first by Cubism, he soon joined the ranks of Die Neue Sachlichkeit.

303 Verhaeren, Emil: *Die hohen Rhythmen*

Leipzig: Insel, 1912. 85 pp. Coloured pen-and-ink drawing.

304 Werfel, Franz: *Gesänge aus den drei Reichen. Ausgewählte Gedichte*

Leipzig: Kurt Wolff, 1917 ('Der jüngste Tag', no. 29/30). 30 copies, in the collection 'Künstler-Goltz-Bände', were bound by Georg Schrimpf and provided with a cover design.

305 Graf, Oskar Maria: *Die Revolutionäre*

Dresden: Dresdner Verlag von 1917, 1918 ('Das Neueste Gedicht', no. 4). 12 pp. Design on jacket.

306 Graf, Oskar Maria: *Amen und Anfang*

Munich: Bachmair und Co., 1919. 65 pp. 300 copies. Woodcut on title-page.

307 Graf, Oskar Maria: *Ua-Pua! Indianer-Dichtungen*

Regensburg: Habbel, 1921. 59 pp. Cover design and 30 drawings.

Schubert, Otto

Painter and graphic artist. 1892–1972. Lived in Dresden.

308 Günther, Alfred: *Beschwörung und Traum. Gedichte*

Dresden: Emil Richter, 1919 ('Bücher der Neuen Kunst', Vol. 1). 48 pp. 6 original lithographs.

309 Hauptmann, Carl: *Die lilienweiße Stute. Legende*

Dresden: R. Kaemmerer, 1920 (the press's third édition de luxe). 22 pp. 400 copies. 6 original lithographs.

310 *Bilderbuch für Tyll und Nele*

Munich: R. Piper & Co., 1920 ('Drucke der Marées-Gesellschaft', no. 27). 49 leaves. 300 copies. Woodcuts. (A picture-book showing Expressionist influence.)

311 *Die Abenteuer Sindbads des Seefahrers*

Leipzig: Arndt Beyer, 1922 ('Kreis graphischer Künstler und Sammler', no. 1). 117 pp. 600 copies. Lithographs.

Schülein, Julius Wolfgang

Painter and graphic artist. Born 1881.

312 Schiebelhuth, Hans: *Der kleine Kalender*

Darmstadt: Die Dachstube, 1919 ('Die kleine Republik. Eine Flugschriftenreihe', no. 5). 18 pp. A few drawings. (Silhouette on jacket by E. M. Engert.)

Schultz-Walbaum, Theodor

Graphic artist. Born 1892. Lives in Bremen.

313 *Die Offenbarung St. Johannis*

Bremen: Angelsachsen, 1921. 110 copies. 12 illustrative plates, 13 plates of lettering (woodcut).

Schütte, Ernst

Architect, painter, graphic artist and stage designer. 1890–1951. Lived in Berlin from 1945.

314 Mann, Heinrich: *Der Sohn. Novelle*

Hanover: Paul Steegemann, 1919 ('Die Silbergäule', no. 3). 16 pp. Drawing on jacket.

315 Schnack, Anton: *Die tausend Gelächter. Gedichte*

Hanover: Paul Steegemann, 1919 ('Die Silbergäule', no. 16). 16 pp. Design on cover.

316 Moreck, Curt: *Die Hölle. Novelle*

Hanover: Paul Steegemann, 1919 ('Die Silbergäule', no. 18). 16 pp. Design on cover.

317 Hauptmann, Carl: *Des Kaisers Liebkosende. Legende*

Hanover: Paul Steegemann, 1919 ('Die Silbergäule', no. 21/22). 20 pp. Design on cover.

318 Krell, Max: *Das Meer. Erzählung*

Hanover: Paul Steegemann, 1919 ('Die Silbergäule', no. 27/28). 32 pp. Design on cover.

319 Habicht, Victor Curt: *Der Triumph des Todes*

Hanover: Paul Steegemann, 1919 ('Die Silbergäule', no. 29/30). 48 pp. Design on cover.

320 Brendel, Robert: *Die große Hure*

Hanover: Paul Steegemann, 1920 ('Die Silbergäule', no. 57/58). 29 pp. Design on cover.

321 Stinnes, Dési: *Die Söhne. Acht Szenen*

Hanover and Leipzig: Paul Steegemann, 1923. 85 pp. 8 lithographs.

Schwimmer, Max

Painter and illustrator. 1895–1960

322 *Abenteurer*

Leipzig: Friedrich Dehne, n.d. [c. 1918]. Cycle of dry-point etchings. (Prefatory note by Johannes R. Becher.)

Schwitters, Kurt

Schwitters's pictorial work belongs to Dadaism; his contributions to the book have, therefore, been omitted here.

Seewald, Richard

Painter, illustrator and writer. Born 1889. Lives in Ronco. Seewald started out as an Expressionist but many of his illustrations have nothing, or only indirect links, in common with the methods of the movement. See Jentsch, R., *Richard Seewald. Das graphische Werk*, Esslingen, 1973.

323 Kleist, Heinrich von: *Penthesilea. Ein Trauerspiel*

Munich: Goltz, 1917. 200 copies. 24 original lithographs, some coloured.

324 Vergilius Maro, P. (Virgil): *Bucolica. Ecloge I–X*

Munich: Georg Müller, 1919. 300 copies. 30 lithographs.

325 Gellert, Christian Fürchtegott: *Fabeln*

Berlin: Fritz Gurlitt, 1920 ('Die Neuen Bilderbücher', Series 3, Vol. 1). 175 copies. 22 woodcuts, some coloured.

326 Aue, Hartmann von: *Der arme Heinrich*

Dachau: Einhorn, n.d. [1920], ('Einhorn-Drucke', vol. 4). 41 pp. 5 original lithographs, coloured by hand.

327 Stifter, Adalbert: *Abdias*

Munich: Drei Masken, 1921 ('Obelisk-Drucke', no. 3). 154 pp. 320 copies. 12 dry-point etchings.

328 Virgilius Maro, P.: *Bucolica. Hirtengedichte*

Berlin: Euphorion, 1923. 720 copies. 20 woodcuts.

329 *Die Argonauten. Dem Epos des Apollonius nacherzählt von Gustav Schwab*

Berlin: Propyläen-Verlag, 1923. 74 pp. 300 copies. 44 original lithographs.

Segall, Lasar

Painter and graphic artist. 1889–1957. Lived until 1923 in Berlin and Dresden.

330 Dostoyevsky, Feodor: *Die Sanfte*

Dresden: Dresdner Verlag von 1917, February 1922 ('Graphische Reihe', Portfolio XII). 5 lithographs. (Foreword by Will Grohmann.)

Seiwert, Franz Wilhelm

Painter, sculptor and graphic artist. 1894–1933.

331 *Welt zum Staunen. Ein Bilderbuch in vom Stock gedruckten Versen von … mit Versen von Freunden*

Cologne: Kalltal-Gemeinschaft, 1919. The fourth of the group's publication, printed by the Kalltalpresse (taken over in 1922 by the Rheinland-Verlag, Cologne). 16 pp. 100 copies. (An example of an Expressionist picture-book for children.)

332 *Sieben Klänge zum Evangelium Johannis*

Cologne: Kairos Verlag, 1919. 16 pp. Jacket and title designed by Seiwert.

Sintenis, Renée

Sculptress. 1888–1965.

333 Siemsen, Hans: *Das Tigerschiff. Jungensgeschichten*

Frankfurt am Main: Querschnitt, 1923 ('Flechtheim-Druck', no. 26). 33 pp. 250 numbered copies. 10 etchings.

Stegemann, Heinrich

Painter and graphic artist. 1888–1945. Lived mostly in Hamburg.

334 Lorenz, Karl: *Die gelben Blumen*

Hamburg: Adolf Harms, 1921 ('Drucke der Tafelrunde', no. 2). 14 pp. 200 numbered copies. Original woodcut.

335 Ochs, Hans: *Der weiße Baum*

Hamburg: Adolf Harms, 1921 ('Die Drucke der Tafelrunde', no. 5). 14 pp. 200 numbered copies. Original woodcut.

336 Lorenz, Karl: *Die vier Madonnen*

Hamburg: Adolf Harms, 1922 ('Die Drucke der schönen Rarität'). 250 copies. 4 woodcuts.

Steiner, Lilly

Painter and graphic artist. Born 1884 in Vienna.

337 Jacobsen, J.P.: *Gurre-Lieder*

Vienna: Anton Schroll, 1921. 120 numbered copies. 8 original lithographs. Portfolio.

Steinhardt, Jakob

Painter and graphic artist. 1887–1968. Lived latterly in Jerusalem.

338 Nadel, Arno: *Rot und glühend ist das Auge des Juden*

Berlin: Fritz Gurlitt, 1920. Poems to 8 etchings.

339 Perez, Jizchok-Leib: *Gleichnisse*
Berlin: Fritz Gurlitt, 1920. 88 pp. Lithographs.

340 Perez, Jizchok-Leib: *Musikalische Novellen*

Berlin: Verlag für Jüdische Kunst und Kultur Fritz Gurlitt, 1920. 64 pp. 5 original lithographs.

341 Wolfenstein, Alfred: *Der Flügelmann*

Dessau: Karl Rauch, 1924. 2 woodcuts (one on title-page).

342 Goll, Yvan: *Naomi*

Berlin: Soncino, 1924. 2 woodcuts. (Not included in the index. 'Verzeichnis der Drucke der Soncino-Gesellschaft', published in *Imprimatur. Ein Jahrbuch für Bücherfreunde*, New Series, Vol. 5, 1967, pp. 145 ff., by A. Horodisch.)

Stoermer, Curt

Painter and graphic artist. Born 1891.

343 Baudelaire, Charles: *Der Verworfene*

Hanover: Der Zweemann-Verlag, 1920. 79 pp. 1,000 copies. 6 woodcuts and design of binding.

Szalit-Marcus, Rahel

Painter and graphic artist. Born 1896 at Kovno, Lithuania. Formerly lived in Berlin.

344 Dostoyevsky, Feodor: *Das Krokodil*

Potsdam: Gustav Kiepenheuer, 1921 ('Graphische Bücher', no. 7). 54 pp. 21 lithographs.

345 *Fischke der Krumme*

Berlin: Propyläen-Verlag, n. d. [1922]. 100 numbered copies. 16 lithographs in portfolio. (With introduction by Julius Elias.)

Tappert, Georg

Painter and graphic artist. 1880–1957.

346 Dietrich, Rudolf Adrian: *Passion*

Kiel: Die schöne Rarität, 1917. 115 pp. Original woodcut.

347 Ausleger, Gerhard: *Ewig Tempel Mensch. Gedichte*

Dresden: Dresdner Verlag von 1917. 1918 ('Das Neueste Gedicht', no. 9). 15 pp. Design on jacket.

348 Klabund (i. e. Alfred Henschke): *Der Totengräber*

Kiel: Die schöne Rarität, 1919. 22 pp. 500 copies. Design on jacket.

349 *Der Nachtwandler. Acht Holzschnitte zu dem Gedicht von Theodor Däubler*

Düsseldorf: Galerie Flechtheim, 1920 ('Ausgaben der Galerie Flechtheim', Portfolio 4). 10 leaves. 136 copies.

Thalmann, Max

Painter and graphic artist. 1890–1944.

350 *Passion. Dichtung von Albert Talhoff*

Weimar: Bruno Wollbrück, 1921. 330 copies, 8 woodcuts. Portfolio.
Another edition. Jena: Eugen Diederichs, 1923. (Type set in Rudolf Koch's Deutsche Schrift.)

Unold, Max

Painter, graphic artist, illustrator and writer. 1885–1964. Lived latterly in Swabia.
Many of this artist's illustrations are not Expressionist.

351 Flaubert, Gustave: *Die Legende von Sankt Julian dem Gastfreien*

Munich: R. Piper & Co., 1918 (Marées-Gesellschaft, publication no. 7). 37 pp. 150 numbered copies. Woodcuts, borders and initials.

352 Lautensack, Heinrich: *Altbayrischer Bilderbogen. Prosadichtungen*

Berlin: Fritz Gurlitt, 1920 ('Die Neuen Bilderbücher', Series 3, Vol. 7). 155 pp. 10 original woodcuts.

353 *Ghetto. Sieben Erzählungen*

Munich: Georg Müller, 1921. 90 pp. 330 copies. 12 drawings on the stone.

Uphoff, Carl Emil

Painter, graphic artist, sculptor and playwright. Born 1885.

354 *Adam und Eva*

Worpswede: Werkgemeinschaft Das neue Worpswede, 1920. 110 copies. Illustrations and text on 15 leaves. (Poems, drawings and engravings by Uphoff.)

Vogenauer, Ernst Rudolf

Graphic artist. Born 1897. Last known living in Berlin.

355 *Anthologie Die Mutter*

Munich: Drei Masken, 1921 ('Münchener Scriptor-Drucke'). Several illustrations.

356 Moreck, Curt: *Der Flammende*

Stuttgart/Heilbronn: Walter Seifert, 1921 ('Domina-Druck', no. 2). 57 pp. Several illustrations.

Wach, Aloys

Painter and graphic artist. 1892–1940. A member of the *Sturm* circle.

357 Usinger, Fritz: *Große Elegie*

Darmstadt: Die Dachstube, 1920 ('Die kleine Republik. Eine Flugschriftenreihe'). 20 pp. 100 copies, 20 of which are coloured by hand. 4 woodcuts.

Waldthausen, Paul von

Painter, caricaturist and interior designer. Born 1897.

358 Brauchitsch, Eberhard von: *Kumurrus Heimkehr. Aus dem Tagebuch eines Opfers*

Darmstadt: Gesellschaft Hessischer Bücherfreunde, 1923 ('Das Orientalische Cabinett', Book 6). 36 pp. 100 numbered copies. 4 lithographs.

Wanders, Heinz

Graphic artist and industrial artist.

359 Sidow, Max: *Hermaphrodit. Symphonische Dichtung*

Hanover: Paul Steegemann, 1920 ('Die Silbergäule', no. 55/56). 24 pp. Design on jacket.

Wanzer, Will

Painter and graphic artist. 1891–1938. Lived in Bonn.

360 Gourby, Anton: *Welten*

In *EOS. Ein Ausdruckswerk ringender Kunst*, Vol. 2, Book 4. Munich: Verlag Die Wende, 1920. 250 copies. A few shallow lithographs.

Weisskopf, Paul

No biographical details ascertainable.

361 Büchner, Georg: *Wozzeck*

Dresden: Dresdner Verlag von 1917, December 1921 ('Graphische Reihe', Portfolio X). 40 copies. (Foreword by Heinar Schilling.)

Weisz, Josef

Graphic artist and sculptor. Born 1894. Last known living in Munich.

362 Goethe, J. W. von: *Faust (Parts I & II)*

Munich: Hugo Schmidt, 1919/20. 157/236 pp. Many illustrations, vignettes and initials, including reproductions of 33 lithographs.

Werefkin, Marianne von

Painter. 1870–1938.

363 Goll, Yvan: *Requiem für die Gefallenen von Europa*

Zürich: Rascher, 1917. Illustration on jacket.

Wetzel, Ines

Painter and graphic artist. Born 1878 in Berlin.

364 Pulver, Max: *Fünf Sonette auf Puppen*

In *Marsyas. Eine Zweimonatsschrift*, ed. T. Tagger, Vol. 1, No. 1. Berlin: H. Hochstim, n. d. [1917]. 235 numbered copies. 5 woodcuts.

365 Tagger, Theodor: *Biblische Gedichte*
In *Marsyas*, Vol. 1, No. 3 [1917]. 3 lithographs.

Wield, Friedrich

Sculptor and graphic artist. 1883–1940. Lived in Hamburg.

366 Fischer, H.W.: *Nacht des Saturn*
Hamburg: Adolf Harms, 1921 ('Die Drucke der Tafelrunde', no. 1). 13 pp. 200 numbered copies. Illustration for title and 1 woodcut.

Windisch, H.

No biographical details ascertainable.

367 *Palmström. Steinzeichnungen zu Christian Morgenstern*
Leipzig: Johann Lohse, n.d. 100 copies. Portfolio (10 sheets and extra sheet.)

Wörlen, Georg Philipp

Painter and graphic artist. Born 1886. Last known living at Passau.

368 *Narretei*
No place or publisher, 1923. Woodcut block-book. Copy No. 40 is preserved at the Deutsche Bücherei Leipzig.

Worringer, Marta

Painter and graphic artist. Born 1881. Formerly lived at Halle.

369 Dostoyevsky, Feodor: *Die Sanfte*
Cologne: Marcan, 1925. 54 pp. 750 numbered copies. 15 pen-and-ink drawings.

Zangerl, Alfred

Painter and graphic artist. Born 1892. Last known living in New York.

370 Musil, Robert: *Grigia. Novelle*
Potsdam: Müller & Co., 1923 ('Sanssouci-Bücher', ed. F. Blei, no. 8). 47 pp. 2,100 copies. 6 etchings.

Zeller, Magnus

Painter and graphic artist. 1888–1972. Lived near Potsdam.

371 *Entrückung und Aufruhr, mit Gedichten von Arnold Zweig*
No place or publisher, 1920 (printed 1917). 105 copies. Portfolio.

372 Koromandel, Crescentius: *Schuldbrief eines liederlichen Studenten an seinen Vater*
Berlin-Wilmersdorf: Alfred Richard Meyer, 1920 ('Lyrisches Flugblatt'). Design on title-page.

373 Hoffmann, E.T.A.: *Der Sandmann*
Berlin: Nicolaische Verlagsbuchhandlung/R. Strikker, 1921 ('Die Immergrünen Bücher', no. 4). 52 pp. 4 original lithographs.

374 Andreyev, Leonid: *Das rote Lachen. Bruchstücke aus einer aufgefundenen Handschrift*
Berlin: Euphorion, 1922. 111 pp. 320 numbered copies. 7 etchings.

375 Kellermann, Bernhard: *Die Heiligen*
Berlin: S. Fischer, 1922. 66 pp. 12 illustrations.

376 Casanova, Giacomo: *Die Flucht aus den Bleikammern Venedigs*
Berlin: Hans Heinrich Tillgner, 1922 ('Tillgner-Drucke', no. 3). 100 pp. 500 numbered copies. 6 etchings.

377 Holitscher, Arthur: *Ekstatische Geschichten*
Berlin: Hans Heinrich Tillgner, 1923 ('Das Prisma', no. 11). 58 pp. Several lithographs.

Zernack, Heinrich

Painter and graphic artist. 1899–1945.

378 Lauschus, Leo: *Sieben Sagen vom Rhein*
Koblenz: Werkstätten der Rhein-Verlagsgesellschaft, n.d. [1926]. Many woodcuts.

Zierath, Willy

Painter and graphic artist. Born 1890. Last known living in Berlin.

379 *Aus den Liedern der Bilitis. Nach Pierre Louÿs*
Berlin: Leon Hirsch, 1922. Several illustrations.

Zoberbier, Ernst

Painter and graphic artist. Born 1893. Last known living in Wiesbaden.

380 Silbergleit, Arthur: *Die Magd. Eine Legende*
Berlin: Eigenbrödler, 1919. 12 lithographs, coloured by hand.

Works on Expressionism

Listed below is a selection of the most important works. Works on individual artists have not been included; for these the reader is referred to the bibliographies in Hans Vollmer, *Künstler-Lexikon des zwanzigsten Jahrhunderts*.

1. The art of illustration and publishing houses

BÄNFER, CARL: *Bild und Wort im illustrativen Schaffen der letzten 100 Jahre* (doctoral thesis), Münster, 27 February 1952.

BANG, ILSE: *Die Entwicklung der deutschen Märchenillustration*, Munich, 1944.

FRIEDLÄNDER, MAX J.: 'Über das Illustrieren', *Almanach 1920 des Verlages Bruno Cassirer*, Berlin, 1920.

GLASER, CURT: 'Illustrierte Bücher', *Die neue Bücherschau* [Munich], Vol. for 1919, No. 2.

GÜNTHER, HERBERT: 'Alfred Richard Meyer, der Mensch, der Dichter, der Verleger', in *Imprimatur. Jahrbuch für Bücherfreunde*, New Series, Vol. VI, Frankfurt am Main, 1969.

HORODISCH, ABRAHAM: 'Zum Problem expressionistischer Buchillustration', *Antiquariat*, 1968, No. 5.

— 'Der Euphorion Verlag', in *Imprimatur. Jahrbuch für Bücherfreunde*, New Series, Vol. VI, Frankfurt am Main, 1969

KÄSTNER, ERHART: 'Das Malerbuch unserer Zeit', in *Philobiblon*, Vol. VI, No. 1 [1962].

LOUBIER, HANS: *Die neue deutsche Buchkunst*, Stuttgart, 1921.

NIEMEYER, WILHELM: 'Die Hamburger Handdrucke der Werkstatt Lerchenfeld', in *Imprimatur. Jahrbuch für Bücherfreunde*, Hamburg, 1930.

PLÜNNECKE, WILHELM: *Grundformen der Illustration* (doctoral thesis), Leipzig, 1940.

PREETORIUS, EMIL: 'Gedanken zum illustrierten Buch', in *Ganymed. Jahrbuch für die Kunst*, Vol. 5, Munich, 1925.

RÜMANN, ARTHUR: 'Die deutsche Buchillustration. Anmerkungen zu ihrer Geschichte von 1880–1925', in *Imprimatur. Jahrbuch für Bücherfreunde*, Vol. IX. Weimar and Berlin, 1939.

SCHAUER, GEORG KURT: *Deutsche Buchkunst 1890–1960*, Hamburg 1963.

SCHULTE STRATHAUS, ERNST, and W. VON WEBER: 'Hans von Weber und seine Hundertdrucke', in *Imprimatur. Jahrbuch für Bücherfreunde*, New Series, Vol. VI, Frankfurt am Main, 1969.

TIEMANN, WALTER: 'Gedanken zur neuen deutschen Buchkunst', in *Imprimatur. Jahrbuch für Bücherfreunde*, Vol. IX. Weimar and Berlin, 1939.

WEGNER, WOLFGANG: *Die Faustdarstellung vom 16. Jahrhundert bis zur Gegenwart*, Amsterdam, 1962.

ZOBELTITZ, FEDOR VON: 'Das künstlerische Buch der Gegenwart', in *Zeitschrift für Bücherfreunde*, New Series, Vol. 10, No. 7 [1918/19].

2. Expressionism

The artists' programmatic writings, documents and theoretical works have not been listed here; these will be found in the bibliographies of the relevant literature.

General and collected works

RAABE, P. (ed.): *Expressionismus. Aufzeichnungen und Erinnerungen der Zeitgenossen*, Olten and Freiburg im Breisgau, 1965.

— *Expressionismus. Der Kampf um eine literarische Bewegung*, Munich, 1965.

— *Index Expressionismus. Eine Bibliographie der Beiträge in 103 Zeitschriften des literarischen Expressionismus 1910–1925* (16 vols.), Nendeln, Liechtenstein, 1972.

RAABE, P., and H. L. GREVE: *Expressionismus. Literatur und Kunst 1910–1923. Eine Ausstellung des Deutschen Literaturarchivs im Schiller-Nationalmuseum Marbach am Neckar*, 1960 (exhibition catalogue).

ROTHE, W. (ed.): *Expressionismus als Literatur. Gesammelte Studien*, Berne and Munich, 1969.

STEFFEN, H. (ed.): *Der deutsche Expressionismus. Formen und Gestalten*, Göttingen, 1965.
Schöpferische Konfession, Berlin, 1921.
Geschichte der deutschen Literatur von den Anfängen bis zur Gegenwart, Berlin (Vol. 9) 1973, (Vol. 10) 1974.
Stationen. Piper-Almanach 1904–1964, Munich, 1964.

Other works

ALBRECHT, F.: 'Zur Geschichte der sozialistischen Literatur in Deutschland zwischen 1917 und 1933,' in *Weimarer Beiträge*, No. 6, 1960.

APOLLINIO, UMBRIO: '*Die Brücke*' *e la Cultura dell' Espressionismo*, Venice, 1952.

BAHR, HERMANN: *Expressionismus*, Munich, 1916; English edition, London, 1925.

BEHNE, ADOLF: *Zur neuen Kunst*, Berlin, 1915.

BEST, OTMAR: 'Zum Thema Expressionismus', in *Die Sichel*, No. 2, August 1919.

BOLLIGER, HANS: 'Die Publikationen und Dokumente der Künstlergruppe "Brücke"', in *Philobiblon*, Vol. 3, No. 1 [1959].

BUCHHEIM, LOTHAR-GÜNTHER: *Die Künstlergemeinschaft Brücke*, Dresden, 1957.

— *Der Blaue Reiter und die 'Neue Künstlervereinigung München'*, Feldafing, 1959.

— *Graphik des deutschen Expressionismus*, Feldafing, 1959.

BURGER, FRITZ: *Einführung in die moderne Kunst*, Berlin, 1917.

CHASTINET, LUDWIG: 'Zeichnung und Grafik des deutschen Impressionismus und Expressionismus' (doctoral thesis), Munich, 1936.

CRESPELLE, JEAN-PAUL: *The Fauves* (translated by A. Brookner), London, 1962.

DÄUBLER, THEODOR: *Der Neue Standpunkt*, Dresden, 1916.

— *Im Kampf um die moderne Kunst*, Berlin, 1919.

EDSCHMID, KASIMIR: *Über den Expressionismus in der Literatur und die neue Dichtung*, Berlin, 1920.

ERKEN, GÜNTHER: 'Der Expressionismus – Anreger, Herausgeber, Verleger', in *Handbuch der deutschen Gegenwartsliteratur*, ed. H. Kunisch, Munich, 1965.

FECHTER, PAUL: *Der Expressionismus*, Munich, 1914.

FISCHER, OTTO: *Das neue Bild*, Munich, 1912.

GASCH, SEBASTIAN: *El Expressionismo*, Barcelona, 1955.

GLASER, CURT: *Die Graphik der Neuzeit*, Berlin, 1923.

GOEPFERT, HERBERT G.: 'Der expressionistische Verlag. Versuch einer Übersicht', in *Brannenburger Vorträge*, 1962.

GRAUTOFF, OTTO: *Formzertrümmerung und Formaufbau in der bildenden Kunst*, Berlin, 1919.

HAFTMANN, WERNER: *Painting in the 20th century*, 2nd English edition, London and New York, 1965.

HAMANN, RICHARD: *Krieg, Kunst und Gegenwart*, Marburg, 1917.

— *Kunst und Kultur der Gegenwart*, Marburg, 1922.

HAUSENSTEIN, WILHELM: *Die bildende Kunst der Gegenwart*, Stuttgart and Berlin, 1914.

— *Über Expressionismus in der Malerei*, Berlin, 1919.

HEISE, WOLFGANG: *Aufbruch in die Illusion. Zur Kritik der bürgerlichen Philosophie in Deutschland*, Berlin, 1964.

HERZOG, OSWALD: *Der Rhythmus in Kunst und Natur*, Steglitz, 1914.

HILDEBRANDT, HANS: *Expressionismus in der Malerei*, Stuttgart and Berlin, 1919.

HOFFMANN, EDITH: 'Der Sturm, a Document of Expressionism', *Signature*, New Series, 18, London, 1954.

HOFMANN, WERNER: *Zeichen und Gestalt. Die Malerei des 20. Jahrhunderts*, Frankfurt am Main, 1957.

KÄNDLER, KLAUS: *Expressionismus. Dramen*, Vol. 2, Berlin, 1967 (Postscript).

KAUFMANN, HANS: *Krisen und Wandlungen der deutschen Literatur von Wedekind bis Feuchtwanger*, Berlin and Weimar, 1966.

KOLINSKY, EVA: *Engagierter Expressionismus. Politik und Literatur zwischen Weltkrieg und Weimarer Republik*, Stuttgart, 1970.

LANDSBERGER, FRANZ: *Impressionismus und Expressionismus. Eine Einführung in das Wesen der neuen Kunst*, Leipzig, 1919.

LANKHEIT, KLAUS: 'Zur Geschichte des Blauen Reiters', in *Cicerone*, No. 3, [Cologne], 1949.

LÖFFLER, FRITZ: 'Expressionismus in Dresden', in *Imprimatur. Jahrbuch für Bücherfreunde*, New Series, Vol. III, Frankfurt am Main, 1961/62.

LÜDECKE, HEINZ: 'Die Tragödie des Expressionismus. Notizen zu seiner Soziologie', *Bildende Kunst*, No. 4, 1949.

LUKÁCS, GEORG: '"Größe und Verfall" des Expressionismus', in *Probleme des Realismus*, Berlin, 1955.

MEIER-GRAEFE, JULIUS: *Wohin treiben wir?*, Berlin 1915.

MITTENZWEI, WERNER: 'Der Expressionismus, Aufbruch und Zusammenbruch einer Illusion', in *Menschheitsdämmerung*, RUB 404, Leipzig, 1968, pp. 5 ff.

MUCHE, GEORG: *Blickpunkt Sturm, Dada, Bauhaus*, Munich, 1956.

MUSPER, H. TH.: *Der Holzschnitt in fünf Jahrhunderten*, Stuttgart, 1964.

MYERS, BERNARD S.: *Expressionism, a Generation in Revolt*, London 1957; also New York, 1963, as *The German Expressionists, a Generation in Revolt*.

NEDOSCHIWIN, G.A.: 'Das Problem des Expressionismus', in *Kunst und Literatur*, No. 1, 1968.

NEUMAYER, HEINRICH: *Expressionismus*, Vienna, 1956.

PERKINS, G.C.: *Expressionismus. Eine Bibliographie zeitgenössischer Dokumente 1910–1925*, Zürich, 1971.

PINTHUS, KURT: 'Nach 40 Jahren', in *Menschheitsdämmerung. Ein Dokument des Expressionismus*, new edition by Pinthus, Hamburg, 1959.

RAABE, PAUL: *Die Zeitschriften und Sammlungen des literarischen Expressionismus*, Stuttgart, 1964.

— *Der Ausgang des Expressionismus*, Biberach, 1966.

REIDEMEISTER, LEOPOLD: *Künstler der Brücke an den Moritzburger Seen. Ausstellung im Brücke-Museum*, Berlin (West), 1970.

— *Künstler der Brücke in Berlin 1908–1914. Ein Beitrag zur Geschichte der Künstlergruppe 'Brücke'*, Berlin, 1972 (Catalogue of an exhibition in the Brücke-Museum, Berlin (West)).

RITTICH, WERNER: 'Kunsttheorie, Wortkunsttheorie und lyrische Wortkunst im "Sturm"' (doctoral thesis), Greifswald, 1933.

ROTERS, EBERHARD: 'Beiträge zur Geschichte der Künstlergruppe "Brücke" in den Jahren 1905–1907', in *Jahrbuch der Berliner Museen*, 2, 1960.

SAMUEL, RICHARD, and THOMAS HINTON: *Expressionism in German Life, Literature and the Theatre*, Cambridge, 1939.

SAUERLAND, MAX: *Die Kunst der letzten dreißig Jahre*, Berlin, 1935; reprinted with new illustrations, Hamburg, 1948.

SCHLENSTEDT, SILVIA: *Expressionismus. Lyrik*, Berlin, 1969 (Postscript).

SCHMIDT, PAUL FERDINAND: *Die Kunst der Gegenwart*, Berlin 1923.

— 'Blütezeit der Dresdener Brücke', *Aussaat*, Vol. II, No. 1/1 [Stuttgart, 1947].

SCHMIED, WIELAND: *Wegbereiter zur modernen Kunst. 50 Jahre Kestner-Gesellschaft*, Hanover, 1966.

SCHNEIDER, FERDINAND JOSEF: *Der expressive Mensch und die deutsche Lyrik der Gegenwart*, Stuttgart, 1927.

SCHNEIDER, KARL LUDWIG: *Zerbrochene Formen. Wort und Bild im Expressionismus*, Hamburg, 1967.

SEDLMAYER, HANS: *Die Revolution der modernen Kunst*, Hamburg, 1955

SELZ, PETER: *Expressionist Painting*, Berkeley and Los Angeles, Calif., 1957.

SOERGEL, ALBERT: *Dichtung und Dichter der Zeit. Im Banne des Expressionismus*, Leipzig, 1927.

SOKEL, WALTER H.: *Der literarische Expressionismus*, Munich, 1959.

STADELMANN, HEINRICH: *Unsere Zeit und ihre neue Kunst*, Berlin, 1916.

STUBBE, WOLF: *Die Graphik des zwanzigsten Jahrhunderts*, Berlin, 1962.

SYDOW, ECKARDT VON: *Die deutsche expressionistische Kultur und Malerei*, Berlin, 1920.

THWAITES, J.A.: 'The Blue Rider. A Milestone in Europe', *The Art Quarterly*, Detroit, 1950.

UTITZ, EMIL: *Die Grundlagen der jüngsten Kunstbewegung*, Stuttgart, 1915.

— *Überwindung des Expressionismus*, Stuttgart, 1927.

VORDTRIEDE, WERNER: 'Das Verhängnis des deutschen Expressionismus', in *Imprimatur. Jahrbuch für Bücherfreunde*, New Series, Vol. III, Frankfurt am Main, 1962.

WALDEN, HERWARTH: *Expressionismus, die Kunstwende*, Berlin, 1918.

— *Die neue Malerei*, Berlin, 1919.

— *Einblick in Kunst*, Berlin, 1918.

— 'Das Sturm-Archiv Herwarth Waldens', *Jahrbuch der Deutschen Schillergesellschaft*, Vol. II., Stuttgart, 1958.

WALDEN, NELL, and LOTHAR SCHREYER: *Der Sturm, ein Gedenkbuch an Herwarth Walden und die Künstler des Sturmkreises*, Baden-Baden, 1954.

WILLETT, JOHN: *Expressionism*, London, 1970.

WINGLER, HANS MARIA: *Der Blaue Reiter*, Feldafing, 1954.

— *Die Brücke. Kunst im Aufbruch*, Feldafing, 1954.

— *Der Sturm*, Feldafing, 1955.

WOLFF, KURT: *Briefwechsel eines Verlegers 1911–1963*, ed. B. Zeller and E. Otten, Frankfurt am Main, 1966.

WORRINGER, WILHELM: *Abstraktion und Einfühlung: ein Beitrag zur Stilpsychologie*, Berne, 1907; new edition 1948, published in English as *Abstraction and empathy* (translated by M. Bullock), London, 1953.

— *Kritische Gedanken zur neuen Kunst*, 'Genius', Book 2, 1919.

— *Künstlerische Zeitfragen*, Munich, 1921.

ZIEGLER, KLAUS: 'Dichtung und Gesellschaft im deutschen Expressionismus', in *Imprimatur. Jahrbuch für Bücherfreunde*, New Series, Vol. III, Frankfurt am Main, 1962.

Sources of illustrations

The originals of the illustrations to this book have been supplied by: the Deutsches Buch- und Schriftmuseum of the Deutsche Bücherei Leipzig; the Print Room and Collection of Drawings of the Staatliche Museen, Berlin; the Print Room of the Staatliche Kunstsammlungen, Dresden; the Staatliche Galerie Moritzburg, Halle; the Print Room of the Öffentliche Kunstsammlungen, Basle; the Kunsthalle, Bremen; the Kunstmuseen der Stadt Düsseldorf; the Paul-Klee-Stiftung, Berne; Conrad Felixmüller, Berlin (West); Lothar Lang, Freienbrink near Berlin.

The bulk of the photographic work has been done by Christa Christen and Herbert Strobel, Leipzig. Others who have helped are Londa von Berg, Berlin (West); Walter Danz, Halle; Deutsche Fotothek, Dresden; Thea Henkel, Berlin (East); H. Hinz, Basle; Walter Klein, Düsseldorf; Stickelmann, Bremen.

Index

Numbers in italics refer to the illustrations